As It Happened

Edwin Tetlow

As It Happened

A Journalist Looks Back

With a Foreword by
JAN MORRIS

PETER OWEN
LONDON & CHESTER SPRINGS PA

PETER OWEN PUBLISHERS
73 Kenway Road London SW5 ORE
Peter Owen books are distributed in the USA by
Dufour Editions Inc. Chester Springs PA 19425-0449

First published in Great Britain 1990
© Edwin Tetlow 1990

British Library Cataloguing in Publication Data
Tetlow, Edwin
As it happened: a journalist looks back.
1. Great Britain. Journalism – Biographies
I. Title
070.92

ISBN 0–7206–0741–8

Printed in Great Britain by Billings of Worcester

To my wife,
the 'Darling Katy' of so many fervent missives from
the Western Desert and other hazardous places, who
has been – since one golden afternoon in an ancient
Oxfordshire church in September 1932 – the bravest
and most steadfast ally any man could hope to have.

Acknowledgements

A cast of untold thousands played their parts in creating the events described in this narrative. They were mostly soldiers, sailors and airmen between 1939 and 1945, and mostly civilians at other times during the past half-century. They included wartime enemies who did their best to make sure that my story would never be told. I have come round towards forgiving them. I refer those of them who chance to read this book to Sir Thomas More, who told the man who was about to chop off his head: 'You do but fulfil your office.'

A smaller cast of identifiable helpers have made contributions, for which I am deeply grateful. Lords Rothermere, Camrose and Hartwell, principal owners of the newspapers which gave me all my opportunities, were quick to applaud success and slow to mention the opposite. The late Lady Pamela Berry was irresistible in opening political doors in Westminster and Washington. Sir David English, Editor of the *Daily Mail*, generously opened to me the files of the newspaper so that I could check stories I had written up to fifty years earlier, many of which I had never before seen in print. Peregrine Worsthorne equally generously opened the files of the *Daily Telegraph* and *Sunday Telegraph*. The Chief Librarians – Tom Kelly and his successor, George S. Johnson, of the *Daily Mail*, and Joyce Meacham, of the *Daily* and *Sunday Telegraph* – went beyond statutory duty in lavishing time on me and providing photocopies and photographs to confirm and illumine the record.

Others inside and outside journalism helped more than they knew. Jock Ritchie, of Stone Ridge, New York, put me right on many naval technicalities, and his wife, Billie, unerringly clarified passages of Cuban Spanish. Alan Hackland, my kinsman by marriage, performed monumental research in Pietermaritzburg, South Africa, as also did John Chabot Smith, formerly of the *New York Herald Tribune*, in Florida. The late William V. Shannon, before he became United States Ambassador to the Republic of Ireland, shared with me some of the presidential electoral adventures I describe, and later exerted on my behalf his phenomenal memory. Victor Lasky unreservedly shared information with me. Sir Herbert and Lady Merchant guided and nurtured me at tense moments in Castro's Havana and also in London. Herr Willy Brandt, in his early incarnation as Mayor of West Berlin, provided most helpful enlightenment and information. And in London Christopher and Ruth Morris showed over many years that they regard my wife and myself more as members of their illustrious family than as friends.

I thank Peter Owen, my publisher, for inspiring this work, and I apologize to my editor, friend and collaborator, Michael Levien, for provoking him sometimes (I feel sure) further than the normal bounds of tolerance.

Finally, if I have got it wrong anywhere, the fault is mine.

E.T.

Foreword

If, as media people like to say, they don't make foreign correspondents like they used to, Edwin Tetlow is of the mould they broke – the absolutely professional, immensely experienced, thoroughly civilized remembrancer of the world's events. He is certainly not of the trench coat, neo-Hemingway brigade, who except in Hollywood died out before his time, but he is one of that select company of Western newspaper journalists whose task it was to describe humanity emerging from the agonies of the Second World War into the uncertainties of peace. It was one of the most fascinating of times, in which ideologies rose and fell, empires came and went, new nations came into being and old ones faltered. Tetlow saw it all, in peace and in war, and at a time when it was above all the newspaper, rather than the television set, which was mankind's informer. He was notable among his peers for his calm and dispassionate reportage of the passing scene – never sensational, always accurate, and written in a gentlemanly prose that was, even in newsprint, truly representative of the man himself.

Two things say much about Edwin Tetlow, I think. One is that when in the course of this adventurous life he settled permanently in New York State, a place he loves and which has enthusiastically adopted him, he was to remain always and unmistakably the Englishman. The other is that in the middle of it all, in the middle of those confused pageants of the world of which he was the professional chronicler, he found time to write a scholarly study of the Battle of Hastings, 1066. When you read this new book you are seeing the making of history indeed, but history seen through very particular eyes – eyes like no one else's.

JAN MORRIS

Contents

1

Mayhem Memories

A policeman's lot is not a happy one, to echo the song in *The Pirates of Penzance*, but the newspaper foreign correspondent's mostly is. It was even happier in my heyday, before radio and then television robbed us of our primacy and much of our glamour. Even as late as the 1960s (when I was preoccupied in chronicling the bewildering course of Fidel Castro's revolution in Cuba, of which more later) we chosen few foreign correspondents were a cosseted group, very sure of ourselves, never doubting for a moment that we deserved the special treatment we were almost always accorded when on an assignment, and convinced of the importance and power of the words we wrote. I withdrew from the competitive fray before our wings were clipped short by rapidly developing electronic technology.

Yet, if I could have my time over again as from now, I should do it all differently. But I shouldn't fancy adapting to changed circumstances by taking up electronic journalism. The very thought of all those tape-recorders, microphones, lights, cameras and wires appals me after a lifetime spent only with pencil, notebook and sometimes a portable typewriter to worry about. On reflection, I think I should go in for the gathering and writing of material for in-depth reporting, seeking to provide a reader with fuller information than the bare facts so that he or she might be better able to form an opinion about the matter or event under study. Perhaps, as a hobby, I should dabble in historical fiction with the idea of exercising the mind and imagination. In writing historical fiction one may use known facts as bricks and mortar in a process of shaping a literary edifice into whatever design seems most appealing. Contrary to a widespread belief with which I have had to contend for many years, this is not at all what news reporters do. Only very few of the hundreds of men and women fellow-professionals I have encountered were given to exaggeration or deliberate distortion. Those who did so, never lasted very long in a highly competitive field. Word gets around. There are few things more damning than to acquire a reputation among colleagues and competitors of being a faker. Such journalists glitter like shooting stars for a little while. Then they disappear, again like shooting stars.

So I affirm that while it is fashionable, and often useful, to blame the news-gatherer for inaccuracies in newspapers, it is mostly unjust. In my own career of well over half a century as reporter, war correspondent and foreign correspondent I must have written quite a few errors or otherwise

11

got something wrong. Yet, far more often than not, such mistakes have occurred because I have been deliberately lied to or because somebody schemed to use me and my newspaper for some selfish, dishonest or even criminal purpose. Once in Berlin, during the Potsdam Conference and when Winston Churchill was fighting for re-election, I was fed a story that he had been angered by the noise of soldier-sentries patrolling outside his bedroom. Naïvely, I accepted the information and used it in a despatch. Since a postal ballot among troops out of Britain was being conducted at that moment, Mr Churchill's political organizers in London were understandably annoyed and sent an emissary to Berlin to talk to me, presumably to ascertain if I was being vindictively Bolshie in transmitting such an item. I had quite a time proving that I was a fool, not a knave. Similarly, in New York many years later, while I was spending my days reporting the twists and turns of negotiations between a very big business concern based in London and a valuable smaller concern in New York which it was trying to buy, I was told by the spokesman for the small concern that a third company had stepped in and made a bid which could not be spurned. This was totally untrue, but my report caused the original bidder to pay a much higher price for the acquisition than it had bargained for. I had been well and truly used in both these episodes – once for political purposes and once for commercial gain. Without doubt, I was used many, many other times without realizing it.

I have so far been discussing the manipulation of news and newspapermen in peacetime. When we come to talk about the same thing in wartime we must recognize that standards and ethics have to be radically revised. When you are fighting for your own and your country's survival, as so many millions facing German Nazism and Japanese opportunism were doing between 1939 and 1945, to tell the whole truth all the time would be self-destructive. Distortion and the downright lie can be vital defensive weapons, and journalists who become cogs in the military machine have no option but to submit to its demands, even though in the case of Americans and Britons we do retain fundamental independence because we are not conscripted but assimilated.

Censorship was relied upon in the Second World War to ensure that we gave nothing factual away that might benefit the enemy and, very often, also to ensure that something derogatory to or critical of the political and military leadership in the war effort was not published. For the most part I did not quarrel with censors and I soon developed a facility – and a willingness – to tailor my despatches not only to what I estimated might be passed by them but to what I considered might advance the Allied cause. Yet there came a time in early 1944, while I was covering the costly and cumbersome Allied campaign to advance up the jagged, militarily hostile spine of Italy, when I concluded it was my duty to challenge censorship and the tactical leadership of the American Fifth and British Eighth Armies. I had been observing events at close quarters, often dangerously so, for several months, and I had become convinced that the planners and the generals were failing to garner the full fruits of the sacrifices they were asking of their troops. I still believe I was right, even though what I did and wrote brought an unexpected dividend to the enemy, of which I knew nothing until the war was over.

It was in February that I wrote an editorial article in which, after acknowledging the fearful burden of responsibility which lay with the leadership, whose every move spelt life or death to many men, I catalogued the failings that had brought, I felt, an unnecessary delay in knocking out a reeling adversary. 'It is easy to criticise the Allied leaders,' I wrote, 'but I believe they could have done better.' They had failed to capitalize fully on the sacrifice of British lives in forcing a crossing of the Garigliano river and of American lives in making a particularly bloody crossing of the Rapido river. Cassino had been pounded, pulverized and assaulted and still we had not captured it. Allied troops had landed virtually unopposed at Anzio, behind the German lines, but this piece of good fortune had been squandered by a decision to consolidate the beach-head instead of advancing on a clear path to Rome. I was surprised but gratified when my fiery cable was passed for publication by the censors. I could not complain about being smothered. The article was published prominently in the *Daily Mail* under the forthright headline, 'These were the lessons of Cassino', and I learned unofficially that it caused a good deal of comment and discussion journalistically and in the War Office and Whitehall in London.

I charged again almost exactly a month later. In the interval I had noted with increasing concern that Allied units had gained little or nothing after the spectacular and controversial bombing of the monastery at Monte Cassino, which towered atop a massive hill 700 feet above Cassino. This old town had been bombed unmercifully after the mauling of the monastery and several attacks had been made upon it. But all had been turned back, with heart-rending losses. What had gone wrong?

The explanation was not hard to find. Certainly (as I wrote) the bombing had blotted out Cassino as a recognizable town, but the resulting craters and small mountains of rubble had stopped Allied tanks from surging in to support our attacking infantry. Small bridges had had to be flung across some enormous craters for tanks to advance even a few yards. Further, the bombing had been surprisingly inaccurate, even though it had been made against no interference by the Luftwaffe and most of it had been at low levels. I estimated that only about 40 per cent of the bombs had fallen within the target area of one square mile. The rest had dropped harmlessly in fields stretching north from the Rapido river or on the lower slopes of Monastery Hill.

Moreover, I learned, the enemy had known that big attacks were coming and they improvised thoroughly to meet them. They turned wine cellars into deep shelters, set up thickly concreted and metalled pillboxes at commanding points just outside the target area and used bomb craters and caves below the monastery as sites for machine-gun posts and hiding-places for self-propelled anti-tank guns. Naturally, experienced soldiers of General Kesselring's renowned parachute regiments and divisions just raced for shelter once the bombs started falling.

All in all, the facts in my article raised the question of the real value of close-support bombing, a matter of great importance in view of the imminent launching of the Allied invasion of northern France. The air correspondent of the *Daily Mail*, Colin Bednall, flattered me by writing: 'Tetlow's cable, I believe, will be read as one of the most important despatches from the Mediterranean for some time.'

Small wonder that I felt good about my efforts to lift the curtain over operations at Cassino that spring, and continued to feel so until I received some humbling information in 1946, after the war was over. A close friend from pre-war days, Arnold Watts, came home from several years as a prisoner of war in Italian and German camps after having been captured in one of the early battles at Tobruk, in the western desert of North Africa. 'You were a war correspondent, weren't you?' he asked at our first reunion. 'I wondered once in 1944 which side you were on.' He then explained that one of my critical despatches concerning Cassino had been picked up by the German Propaganda Ministry and circulated in the form of a leaflet among Allied prisoners of war to indicate how their side was actually losing the war. Perhaps the censors should have stopped those despatches after all. On balance, I think not. Such adverse criticism may conceivably have influenced planners of the Normandy invasion to avoid errors which so hindered progress in the sacrificial Italian campaign which preceded it.

There have also been times in the last half-century when I have deliberately chosen not to attend happenings, not because I was too lazy or for other personal failings but because I did not believe it would be journalistically worthwhile to do so. Two such instances are especially vivid in my memory because they involved judicial execution of criminals, one by shooting and the other by beheading. They occurred in 1944 and 1945 when a lot of people were losing their lives and the snuffing-out of a murderer's existence was by no means to be looked upon as an earth-shaking event. Yet I realize I was quite wrong to spurn the opportunity in one respect. Availing myself of it would certainly have enlarged my experience of life – and death.

The first missed chance was in Rome in the summer of 1944. I was advised by an officer of the Allied occupying authority that I and any other foreign correspondent who wished could attend the shooting by an Italian firing-squad of Pietro Caruso, chief of police in Rome during the German occupation, who had been tried and sentenced to death by an Italian court for crimes committed against the civilian population. I decided not to go because I could not see much space being spared in a tightly edited newspaper of only four pages for the formal fulfilment of a death sentence by a civilian court. However, several other correspondents and photographers did watch the execution, which was performed on waste ground just outside the city. I satisfied my attention to the event by watching a film of it taken by a newsreel man. It showed the wretched Caruso – who was partly crippled – being driven to within a few yards of a chair placed close to the bare wall of a building adjoining the waste ground. He was helped out of the car and half carried to the chair. He was tied to it, his back facing the riflemen who were to despatch him. When they fired, a piece of his head was sent flying into the air as he collapsed in a pitiful heap on his overturned chair. It was not an edifying spectacle. In fact it was downright crude. But it was nothing like so crude as its bloody prelude a few days earlier which I had had no option but to witness and, I must add, to report fully. This was a lynching, an exhibition of savagery more appropriate to the days of Nero and Tiberius than to twentieth-century Rome.

The Allied occupiers of the conquered city had decided, over-optimistically as it turned out, that the trial of Caruso should be conducted by the newly established civil Italian regime set up after the country's surrender and switch to the Allied side. This, it was hoped, would prove that the new Italy was quite capable of democratic self-rule after she had been rescued from the despotism of the Mussolini era. Alas, unenlightened activists within the Roman populace were resolved to prove the opposite. Evidence of this was forthcoming early on the day when Caruso's trial was to open in a gilded, ornate courtroom of the Palace of Justice on a bank of the Tiber, close to the Umberto bridge. I went there early, prepared to chronicle a heartening advance in Italy's political and social restoration, only to find that crowds of noisy people had flocked to the Palace of Justice and were already overcrowding the courtroom. They were also making an ominous demonstration that the day was not going to work out by any means as the Allies had hoped. Particularly threatening were about ten swaggering young louts openly displaying revolvers. I listened in astonishment as they shouted in varying terms their intention to shoot Caruso once he was brought into the chamber. However, they didn't get a chance to show whether this was an empty theatrical boast or a real threat. Italian guards disarmed them and threw them, not at all gently, out into the street.

This did not, however, do much to restore order. About fifty women dressed in total mourning black now took centre stage in the public section of the courtroom. They told me in dramatic terms and gestures that they represented the widows of fifty inmates of the Regina Coeli prison (the Queen of Heaven prison, of all things!) whom Caruso was charged with having handed over to the Germans as doomed hostages after an episode of resistance in which German soldiers had been killed. The hostages had been duly shot in the San Callistus catacomb on the outskirts of the city.

By this time, long before the trial of Caruso was due to open, the Allied security chiefs had seen enough to convince them that to produce him would assuredly start a riot, or worse. Lt-Colonel Pollock, in peacetime an officer at Scotland Yard, and now chief of Allied police in Rome, ordered a postponement of the trial. 'There would have been bloody blue murder if we had allowed him to be brought into this room,' he remarked to me after an announcement of the postponement had been made in Italian. Neither of us realized that there was soon to be 'bloody blue murder' of an especially disgusting kind.

Rising above the hubbub of anger and discontent being expressed by the frustrated crowd came the piercing voice of one of the women in black. 'There's Caretta!' she screamed, pointing an accusing finger at the shrinking figure of a man seated under guard in the front row of the courtroom. 'There he is!' She had recognized Donato Caretta, the former director of the Regina Coeli prison. He was due to give evidence for the prosecution that Caruso had given him a written order to hand over the fifty hostages. The crowd instantly decided that he would serve as a substitute for Caruso. The chants of 'We want Caruso. Give us Caruso' ceased. Attention turned to the terrified Caretta, at whom the screaming woman, an angel of death as she proved to be, was still pointing. In a matter of seconds I was swept aside as I stood in an aisle and almost thrust underfoot by young Italians making for Caretta. I recovered my balance in time to see them seize their quarry and start punching him as his two guards looked on, powerless. Having pounded him close to unconsciousness, the men began kicking him as if he were a football along the floor of the chamber to the door leading on to the street. As he rolled past me I saw that blood was pouring from one side of his head. They had seemingly torn off part of his scalp. In the street, two or three rival groups fought for possession of Caretta. The winners now dragged him, still struggling but with diminishing strength, across the street to the Umberto bridge and there heaved him over a parapet into the sluggish waters of the Tiber. Caretta was not yet quite done in. He struck out, feebly trying to reach dry land somehow. His tormentors foiled the effort. Three of them dashed off to a point where they had seen a small rowing-boat tied up. They put out towards him, and when they reached their now near-exhausted victim, two of them raised their oars and began pounding him mercilessly, the vast crowd of onlookers in the street shouting and shrieking approval. Within minutes, Caretta was dead. But his murderers had not yet finished with him. Tying his corpse to their boat, they towed him to his former domain, the prison. Mad with blood-lust and fury, they flung his body savagely against the main door. Then they tied him up to hang feet uppermost from a window alongside the door.

The trial of Caruso was held two days later, and it was anti-climactic. Scores of Carabinieri, armed Allied police and Italian soldiers guarded every entrance to the Palace of Justice. Entry was by ticket only. The general public was totally excluded, tickets having been issued solely to prominent members of the many political parties flourishing once again in liberated Italy. They had been ordered beforehand not to disclose to anybody when and where the trial was to be held. Each one of them was searched before being allowed to go inside the courtroom. The proceedings did not last long. Caruso was condemned and, as I have described, shot.

My second refusal to witness an execution came in 1946 when I was serving the *Daily Mail* as its Berlin correspondent. One day, over a drink in the Hotel am Zoo, our press headquarters and indeed our home, on the Kurfurstendamm, the Allied officer administering Spandau gaol (later to be used to house Nazi leaders sentenced at the trials in Nuremberg) invited me to be an official witness to the beheading of a German criminal. Once again I declined, because this was a critical period of the Cold War in which the Western allies and the Soviet Union were battling over Berlin, and I felt I had to devote my whole attention to a situation which might at any moment lead to the outbreak of another war. Also, once again, the execution was a minor news event which might not even be publicized in my newspaper. And, I now confess, I felt I had seen enough of the ugliness of sudden death while recording the Battle of Britain, the war in the desert of North Africa, Italy, southern and northern Europe, and finally in Germany itself. But perhaps I should not have refused the experience.

Ironically, sheer chance decreed that I should not attend the one execution, or series of executions, which I badly wanted to record: the hanging of twelve Nazi leaders condemned at the Nuremberg trials in 1946. I was deprived of this experience because my name was not one of eight drawn out of a hat. It had been decided that each of the four Powers occupying Germany (Britain, France, the Soviet Union and the United States) should be represented at this climactic event by two reporters, one agency writer whose report would be circulated to all newspapers and other organizations subscribing to his employer's service and one 'special' representing an individual newspaper or magazine. These privileged eight would provide a full briefing to their colleagues of the same nationality after they had written their personal accounts of the executions. I was not one of the eight, much to my disappointment.

It was not simply out of a desire to satisfy pure curiosity that I wished so ardently to attend the hanging. No, this was a truly historic happening which needed to be described in the fullest detail for posterity. These twelve men, along with others who had been sentenced to terms of imprisonment or had cheated the hangman by suicide (including Hermann Goering, Heinrich Himmler, Robert Ley, and, of course, Joseph Goebbels and Adolf Hitler), had come closer than almost anybody else in history to conquering most of Europe as well as Russia. They had been guilty of infamous crimes of terror and savagery. Now they were to pay forfeit with their lives. I felt that the bearing and behaviour of each one of them as he stood on a trapdoor and was about to be sent peremptorily into eternity needed to be professionally observed and reported.

I am increasingly sorry that my luck was out because not one of the eight correspondents who did watch the executions produced a report worthy of the event. Maybe I, for all my ardour, might not have done so either, for one reason why the two British and two American participants failed in their task was that they were too drained mentally by the obligation to brief their fellow-correspondents. This was apparently so in the case of at least one of the Britons concerned – Selkirk Panton, of the *Daily Express*. 'I didn't think there was anything more left for me to write,' he told me once in Berlin.

Before we leave this somewhat seamy aspect of news-gathering I have one more story to tell. The episode happened during my early years as a journalist when I was still learning my trade before the war. It is note-worthy because a murderer mistakenly thought I had contrived his doom.

In the mid-1930s I was sent hotfoot to Leighton Buzzard, Bedfordshire, where a local girl had been found strangled after having been raped in what was, inappropriately for her, called Lovers' Lane. It seemed to be a routine sordid crime, but I was soon to discover that, as far as I was concerned, it was to provide much drama, plus a few moments of fear when it looked possible that an arrested murderer might break free of his police guards and strangle me as he had strangled his girl.

This was to be the one and only time during my pre-war career that the keeper of a mortuary insisted on taking me inside his place of business to view the body of a victim. The cold dead body lying there on a slab in the mortuary in the ancient township of Leighton Buzzard made a pitiful sight. It was that of a young woman in her early twenties who, I had been told, was 'pretty, bright, and a good girl'. In assaulting her and violently squeezing the life out of her the murderer had not only defiled her body; he had robbed her of her womanliness. The tragedy that had befallen her was made the worse because police surgeons had necessarily increased the physical debasement in carrying out their duty of scientifically con-firming how she had been ravished and strangled. Their sewn-up in-cisions scarred her neck, her throat and elsewhere. 'They say she put up a good fight for herself,' the mortuary keeper said as he replaced the sheet. 'But he was too strong for her, whoever he was.'

I wondered, after I had thanked him for letting me into his eerie domain, who could have made the dreadful assault upon the girl.

Next day I knew. I was walking along High Street when a youth, a stranger, intercepted me. He seemed excited. 'You're a reporter up from London, aren't you?' he said. I nodded. He drew me aside into the entrance to a shop, held on to my arm, and said rapidly: 'I can tell you

who murdered that girl. Leslie Stone did it. You should find him and talk
to him about it. He knew the girl before he went to India in the Army, and
he's been seeing her again now that he's back.' I asked him how he knew
all this, 'I knew him and the girl, and I've seen them together.' I asked him
where I could find Leslie Stone. 'He works in a quarry, about two miles
outside the town. Down that way.' He pointed in the appropriate direction. We exchanged a few more words and before he scuttled off the youth
told me that he had also given his information to another reporter –
Lindon Laing, of the *Daily Express*.

I sought out Laing and we agreed to try to see Leslie Stone together. It
would be useful, we agreed, for each of us to have a witness to such an
unusual interview as this one promised to be. We drove out to the quarry.
It turned out to be a very large circular excavation with a gallery running
round its circumference. We asked the first man working on the gallery
where we could find Leslie Stone. 'Over there,' he said, pointing directly
across the excavation. 'That's him.' Looking across, I saw a husky-looking
man wheeling a barrow. Lindon and I walked round the gallery towards
him, and when we got to within about ten yards of him he set down
his wheelbarrow and stood, tensely braced, awaiting us. Something
prompted me to blurt out a warning to him: 'We're reporters and we'd like
to talk to you. We're not police.'

Looking back upon this meeting and taking into account all that happened afterwards, I am convinced that when he first saw us Leslie Stone
thought we had come to arrest him. He now relaxed. He seemed to want
to give us his version of the evening he had spent with the girl on the
night she died. He spoke in short sentences. Yes, he had spent a couple of
hours with her. He had met her by chance in the town. They were old
friends. They had had a drink and a chat together in a pub. He had then
walked her some of the way home. They had parted at a point where the
path ahead of them divided. She had taken one way and he the other. It
sounded plausible enough. 'Anyway,' I said when he had told his story,
'the police are said to be connecting you with the murder, but you seem to
be in the clear. We have been told there was a struggle, quite a fierce one,
between her and her attacker. If you'd been involved, you'd have some
scratches to show for it, and I don't see any.'

'Oh no,' came the quick reply. 'She had gloves on.'

The words struck a chill in me. They were by no means conclusive about
anything, but their implication, plus the impulsive way in which Leslie
Stone had blurted them out, was to question his story. I was working
more by instinct than logic. I felt sure then that he had murdered the girl.

Two days later Stone was arrested by Scotland Yard detectives and
formally charged with the murder. I knew nothing about the circumstances of the arrest – whether he had confessed, what conclusive evidence the detectives had gathered – and even if I had known, I should not
have been allowed by law to print much of it. My next connection with the

case came when Stone was brought before a local magistrate who would decide whether there was enough substance to the police charges to justify his committal for trial. This was, of course, a foregone conclusion; but what happened before the decision was made was by no means foregone.

Stone, a dark-complexioned man with the bearing of a professional soldier but not, I had concluded, of too impressive intelligence, looked around him when he was brought into the crowded courtroom. Two policemen guarded him. He soon spotted me. He glared angrily at me and I had a moment of fear when he made a lunge towards me, trying to shake off the restraining hold which his guards placed on him. They held on to him and the magistrate started the proceedings. It was obvious to me why Stone had tried to lay his hands on me. He believed that I – and perhaps Lindon Laing – had somehow brought about his arrest after talking with him at the quarry. This was of course nonsense. We had simply written factual reports of our conversation with him. Scotland Yard had plenty of other and more substantial evidence against him.

He was committed, tried and eventually hanged. He paid the extreme penalty for having so brutally killed the girl when she tried to fight off his lustful attack – with her gloved hands.

2

Inside a Revolution

The luckiest break I ever had came on New Year's Eve, 1958. This was after somebody in the Foreign News Room of the *Daily Telegraph* in London had an idea as he was reading some skimpy new bulletins broadcast by Fidel Castro from somewhere in the wilds of Cuba. Since very different bulletins were emanating from the headquarters of President Fulgencio Batista in the Presidential Palace in Havana, my benefactor made this suggestion: Why don't we get Tetlow to fly down to Havana to do us a feature story on how the city celebrates the coming of the New Year with Castro apparently closing in on it?

The proposal appealed to me as I read the service message outlining it in the New York office of the newspaper, even though its final sentence ran rather forbiddingly: 'Don't write too much as space is tight.' (I was to enjoy rereading that admonition later!) This sounded like a pleasant compact assignment: a two-hour flight into the Caribbean sunshine in the middle of winter, a day and an evening spent roaming the cafés, clubs and casinos of Havana, the next morning spent in writing the story, then back to New York, with everything finished in seventy-two hours at most. There would be novelty, too, for I had never been closer to Havana than its airport. I should enjoy observing the most notorious centre of naughty gaiety in Latin America, even if the wings of the purveyors of gaiety were being clipped closer and closer by a tatterdemalion mob of bearded revolutionaries led by an unpredictable young man who might very well be a troublesome Communist, for all anybody really knew.

Cubana Airlines ran a daily plane to Havana from New York. And when I reached Idlewild Airport, as it was then called, and tried to board the daily plane on 31 December, I had my first indication that everything was not quite normal this day. For one thing, only three passengers were waiting to make the trip. For another, we three had to sit around for some hours while the airline staff, seemingly obeying strict orders from the Presidential Palace, went to lengths to ensure that all three of us were above suspicion. We were rigorously questioned to establish exactly who we were and every piece of our luggage was thoroughly searched before it was taken aboard. But at last everything was cleared, and the plane took off in mid-afternoon. I was happy to note that it was a Britannia. The other two passengers were a young American of playboy aspect going to join friends in Havana for a New Year party, and a taciturn Cuban who may have been a diplomat if not something more mysterious. We had all the in-flight attention we could desire. The attractive stewardess served us delightful rum cocktails and a hearty repast, and she assured us with almost convincing earnestness how much we were going to enjoy being in Havana for the New Year.

The approaches to the city from the airport seemed normal enough as viewed from a big old Buick taxi which I shared with the young American, who confided to me that he expected to find 'a lovely young thing' among those welcoming him to Cuba. The dark-complexioned driver hummed softly to the music from his radio as he piloted us skilfully through the turbulent traffic. The Hotel Nacional, a great oblong block of a place, had a few rooms available, at a hefty rate for those days. I settled in and had a leisurely dinner from an expansive menu in the hotel restaurant, which was filled with well-dressed, and obviously well-heeled, Cubans and a minority of foreigners. Feeling comfortable, I set out to stroll in the warm evening air, dropping in on some of the tourist haunts of suburban Vedado and upper midtown Havana, amassing material for the feature article I should be writing the following morning.

Eventually, around 11 p.m., I strolled into the Casino at the Hotel Nacional to await midnight. I noted that the bar was being heavily patronized. A four-piece band was playing in one corner of the ornate salon, accompanying a lusty and busty Cuban contralto who was singing at full strength to make herself heard above the band and the hubbub from the bar, and the softer, sleeker noises from the casino itself, so different from the rattle, slap and clap made by dice-players as they thumped down their leathern cups on tables in the humbler haunts of the city. As the time passed towards midnight the noise became unbelievably piercing. How Cubans love noise! Eventually neither band nor contralto could be heard as separate entities.

Around the gaming tables, under glittering chandeliers bigger and more fanciful than any I had seen for years, guests both Cuban and foreign gambled with deep concentration. Only occasionally did heads turn and envious smiles appear round tight-lipped mouths when somebody shrieked in ecstasy after hitting the jackpot at one of the fruit machines lining the walls of the casino. Also along the walls were several armed policemen stationed like sentries. I asked once or twice of seemingly knowledgeable guests why they were there. One man just shrugged and said languidly: 'Who knows?' One other man told me they had appeared for the first time only a few evenings earlier.

At midnight there came a token acknowledgement that 1959 had arrived. The intense proceedings at the gaming tables and the fruit machines was halted for but a few moments. A few men and women kissed and some people shook hands and smiled at each other before resuming the serious business of the night. At about 12.30 a.m. the members of the band quietly packed their instruments, the singer folded up her microphone stand, and she and the musicians walked off into the night. Only the bar and the gaming tables continued operations, the former being sustained mainly by a party of American and other foreigners, who, growing more disarrayed almost by the minute, still managed to keep the tiring bartenders busy. At that hour I decided I had seen enough. I wanted to go to bed. Once there, I spent a few minutes jotting down facts and reminders for the writing I expected to be doing next morning. Satisfied that I had my assignment under control, I settled down and went to sleep.

I was awakened before 8 a.m. by an excited phone call from Robert Perez, my local correspondent, an energetic Puerto Rican who had lived for some years in Havana. 'He's gone,' he spluttered into the phone. 'Who's gone?' I asked, still half-asleep. 'Batista! Batista!' came the galvanizing answer from Perez. 'He went in the night.'

So he had. At about the time I was settling down to sleep he and a party of about forty, including many members of his family, had motored over to a military airfield at Camp Columbia, on the fringe of Havana, and – excessively heavily laden with baggage – had boarded an Army plane for a short hop eastwards across the water to the Dominican Republic, then still in the grip of Batista's fellow-dictator, Generalissimo Rafael Trujillo, later assassinated.

Pure luck had landed me in the very centre of a revolution while it was happening and being won. No hasty packing of a suitcase this time, no mad rush to catch the first plane to the scene of action, no hectic chase after news which was already growing old! This was a foreign correspondent's dream come true, and I was determined to make the most of it. First, on the sound recommendation of Robert Perez, I moved out of the lordly but isolated Hotel Nacional and into the Hotel Colina, a small and well-placed observation-post giving a view from my third-floor window of the approaches to the University of Havana, where Fidel Castro had been educated and where he was said to have substantial secret support.

The city was eerily quiet at about 8.45 a.m. as Perez and I made our cautious way to the Colina, not at all sure what might happen as we did so. Weren't revolutions affairs of wild shooting and melodramatic action? Not this one – yet. I felt as if I were in the eye of a hurricane, the centre where everything is still while furious winds whirl all around. Hardly anybody was moving. Perez told me as we inched our way towards the Colina that Cubans in the capital had done exactly what people in most countries of the Caribbean did when, as happens all too often in that steamy region, trouble threatened. They closed and locked their shutters, bolted all their doors, and holed up.

Once installed in my new strategic headquarters I implemented my plan of campaign. I despatched Perez on a mission of news-gathering in the city, asking him to phone me as often as seemed necessary with any information he had. I calculated that because of his intimate knowledge of the city, contacts he had, plus his command of his native Spanish, he would have no trouble about keeping me in touch with what was happening. And he did so with great efficiency. As for myself, I stayed as a willing prisoner in my hotel room. I put in a telephone call to my newspaper after having been told by the local exchange that there was, predictably, 'long delay' in calls to the outside world, including distant London. While I waited I began assembling the story I would telephone as soon as the call came through. I listened to Radio Havana as it broadcast messages from Fidel Castro telling the populace to keep calm while it waited for him to take control of the nation. 'Don't worry, I shall come to you,' he said. I took messages from the assiduous Perez and as best I could I kept an eye on what was happening in the streets leading to the University.

In fact, very little happened all that morning. Only a very few people were to be seen hurrying along in order to carry out missions which presumably could not be put off. I noticed that almost all these scurrying pedestrians kept as close as possible to any nearby wall or other cover they were afforded. However, my heaven-sent story was shaping up well. It was helped greatly by word from Robert Perez that Fidel Castro had sent an amplified message to the people of Havana. Speaking from his field camp near Santa Clara, the last sizeable city between him and the capital, he said he did not accept as a bargaining agent a three-man junta of 'so-called neutrals' whom Batista had left behind to represent him. 'I shall be coming into Havana soon,' Castro promised. 'Keep the peace until then. I am sending a company of Barbudos [bearded ones] to administer Havana until I get there. They will preserve Havana – and you.'

This message galvanized the nervous population of the city. Reassured, thousands of them opened their shutters and doors and got into their cars, to celebrate their unexpected liberation. They staged a fantastic crawl-around of the city streets. They draped their vehicles, almost all of them American-made, with Cuban flags. If the car was a convertible, they wound down the top and then joined the follow-my-leader procession of their neighbourhood. As they did so, more and more people climbed up on and into the cars until, as I counted from my observation-point in the Hotel Colina, there were often as many as ten persons in one car. As each individual procession made its slow progress along the old, narrow streets, the ecstatic celebrants chanted the word *Li-ber-tad* and most of them added emphasis by pounding with their fists their car's side or roof in rhythm with the three syllables of the word for liberty. Very soon the din became hard to stand. I was staggered by the intensity, emotion and, I must add, childlike character of the manifestation of happy relief. Nobody could possibly foresee the tribulations in store for Cuba for the next forty years. . . .

My telephone call to London came through at last in the early afternoon, in time for me to dictate over fifteen hundred words, many of them forming impromptu sentences, as thoughts occurred to me, across the bed of the Atlantic Ocean. Even my vigil the previous evening in the casino of the Hotel Nacional was not wasted; indeed, the languid scene around the gaming tables and the jollity in the bar on the eve of one of the most startling and profound revolutionary upheavals of the century in Latin America added to the impact of the story I was able to tell. This was by far the most vivid first-hand report I had written in fifty years, during war as well as peace; and now that it was safely in the hands of my editors in Fleet Street, I was free to leave my bedroom at the Hotel Colina. I could spend the next couple of hours before my second phone call seeing for myself what was going on in the liberated city.

I permitted myself one substantial tot of Bacardi rum before I set out on the long walk from Vedado to midtown Havana. I had to thrust my way through the thick ranks of people watching, some with tears of joy coursing down their faces, the motorized crawl-around. But just as I was making the last turn into the Prado, which roughly marks the boundary between respectable bourgeois Havana and the livelier but sleazy downtown, I saw that something had happened to cut short the touching celebration. Panic was spreading among both Cubans in their cars and the onlookers who had been cheering them on. Vehicles were peeling off from the processions, screeching away into side-streets, and the crowds were scurrying for cover as quickly as their feet would race. In a matter of minutes I found myself uncomfortably alone in the mid-section of the broad Prado. What had happened?

The answer was forthcoming almost as soon as I asked myself the question. The underworld was taking over. One by one a party of dirty and ruffianly looking young Cubans emerged from Calle Neptuno and other side-streets. Each was carrying a rifle or shotgun across his chest. They walked warily along the street, their gaze darting everywhere as they made sure that nobody was going to challenge them. Nobody did. Batista's hated armed policemen had fled into hiding once they heard that their protector had gone. (It transpired that by no means all of them escaped vengeance. Stories of beatings and murders of these men abounded during the next twenty-four hours.) The small-time gangsters now taking over central Havana were organized and ingenious. Some took up positions as watchdogs at strategic points, ordering away at gunpoint people such as myself, while their comrades went on a rampage of looting. Their first targets were parking-meters. These were smashed apart so that their contents could be rattled out and pocketed. Then came the turn of pinball machines and other gaming devices in arcades and deserted casinos which could easily be entered, including an especially lucrative one close to the Sevilla Biltmore Hotel. Here, from a discreet distance, I watched one gang of looters drag a slot-machine into the street and batter it open with jagged pieces of metal from a destroyed parking-meter. It struck me as a remarkable and possibly unique confirmation of the validity of the old saying that money makes money.

The physical hazards of remaining outdoors grew as the bandits got their hands on rum. They started shooting. Mostly it was the wildest kind of exhibitionism, but even so it claimed victims. Ambulances soon began making screaming runs through the streets on journeys to and from hospitals – and mortuaries. Late in the afternoon I went into one hospital and found it in chaos, overflowing with wounded persons and roughly bandaged out-patients. 'Some have been in street accidents, but mostly they seem to have been hit by flying bullets,' said one nurse to me.

There appeared to be no reason for most of the shooting. Indeed, one series of incidents which I ran into on my way back to the Colina tended to show that Cubans just weren't to be trusted with weapons. A man's rifle would go off either because it was defective or because he had forgotten his finger was on the trigger, or even because of a need – common in Latin America – to show off. The trouble was that very often a haphazard shot would start a chain reaction. Men who heard the shot would start firing their own weapons, with the result that shotgun pellets and bullets began flying around an area, ricocheting off walls, smashing windows and occasionally hitting an unlucky pedestrian. Rarely did there seem to be a justifiable target. Alas, this kind of irresponsibility seemed to be occurring mostly near the University, and I was disturbed to deduce that the perpetrators were not underworld bandits of the kind I had met in the Prado but students who were supporters of Fidel Castro and were apparently obeying his broadcast admonitions to preserve the peace in Havana until he arrived. They were probably earnest enough in their devotion to his cause, but they wouldn't be much use if Batista's police and troops rallied. I reasoned that Fidel Castro would be well advised to get his trained Barbudos into Havana as quickly as he could. If they didn't come soon, there would probably be a confrontation between his amateur followers and the downtown bandits, and if the latter won, which seemed likely, unimaginable bloody chaos would follow.

The most senseless shooting spree of all happened on the afternoon of 2 January, the second day of the revolution. I was standing in the shelter of a shopping arcade near the Parque Centrale, in the centre of Havana, and was looking at the debris of splintered windows and doors and ransacked shelves left by yesterday's looters when I became aware of a noisy commotion on a street corner close to the Sevilla Biltmore. The cracks made by ragged rounds of gunshots were coming from somewhere close at hand. I crept cautiously forward to investigate. A squad of about half a dozen young men wearing armbands to show that they were members of a pro-Castro group which had come out of hiding during the past forty-eight hours were firing rifles and automatic pistols from the west side of the Prado at an upper window of a building on the opposite side of the wide thoroughfare. Their collective aim was atrocious. I could see bullets squelching into stonework far above, below and around the window, and only one or two were flying through it into the room beyond. The attack lasted at least half an hour, without, as I noted most carefully, a single shot coming back in reply. This one-sided 'battle' was happening so close to the Sevilla Biltmore that a party of American tourists, wisely obeying a recommendation from the US Embassy not to venture outdoors, could hear all the shooting but had no more idea of what it all meant than, it emerged, did the men involved.

The facts came to me eventually. Word had reached a volunteer unit of Castro supporters that some fugitives of the Batista regime were hiding in a room on the top floor of the building now being attacked. There were said to be at least a dozen armed followers of Rolando Masferrer, a notorious henchman of Batista, locked inside the room. When the shooting ended, one militiaman said gloatingly to me: 'We got the lot.' In truth, as I was able to confirm for myself a little later, there had been nobody at all in the whole building.

This crazy little episode served as a warning to me for years. On each of the fourteen visits I paid to Havana between 1959 and 1965 I always made a point of looking up at the pockmarked outer wall of that building. Nobody ever did anything to clear away the telltale signs of the 'battle' of 2 January 1959. The same old tattered blind remained flapping forlornly from the top of the unrepaired window every time I went to the spot, and the recurring sight reminded me always to be slow to believe anything told to me by a Cuban (including Fidel Castro) unless it was either obviously true or until it could be confirmed. There is a fey quality in the Cuban temperament, often beguiling but sometimes irritating, which prompts many Cubans to promote drama by exaggerating facts, ignoring inconvenient ones, or simply inventing a few. The delivery is usually accompanied by a wide smile, an expansive sweep of the arm, or an expressive flash of the eye. I learned to beware.

I never got back at night to my cosy bed at the Colina at the end of this eventful day. I hasten to mention that this was not at all because I yielded to the allure of one of the painted ladies who, although very much subdued and clearly worried about their future, still plied their trade in bars and other haunts in downtown Havana; they had heard like everybody else that the bearded revolutionary who now ruled Cuba was something of a social reformer. They had nothing to do with my enforced absence from my bed. It happened because I was taken into what is comfortingly called protective custody by a group of young men, mostly students, trying ever so hard to do what Fidel Castro had asked them.

I had been writing in the evening at the one secure haven I knew in the downtown labyrinth of Havana. This was the office of the *Havana Post*, an English-language newspaper for which Robert Perez worked, near the waterfront at the junction of Animas and Lealtad. Around 9 p.m. I joined a small party of other correspondents, all Americans, for the rather long walk of something like a mile and a half to our hotels in Vedado. There was no alternative to walking on this second day of revolution. Buses and taxis had vanished from the streets. We had covered about half the distance when we ran into trouble. A voice called out suddenly in grating Spanish from somewhere in the darkness a few feet ahead of us: 'Halt. Hands up!' Peering ahead, I could see three men with rifles pointed straight at us. Two of them were kneeling side by side on the pavement while the third, their leader, stood barring the way directly ahead. He had a revolver in his right hand – and an armed Cuban was not a man to be trifled with. His gun might very well go off by chance.

But I have never had much time for amateur warriors anywhere. Tonight, also, I was tired, hungry and consequently bad-tempered and of fallible judgement. I was tempted to bluff my way through and I was slow to comply with the orders of our interceptors. My American companions were perhaps wiser. They all raised their hands and one of them muttered impatiently to me as he did so: 'Come on, man. You'll get us all shot!' Unwillingly, I complied.

Our captors motioned us into the passageway of an apartment house. There, blocking the way, sat an unshaven young fellow at a desk. We were in the unit's rough-and-ready headquarters. The man at the desk started questioning the two Americans nearest to him. I was very hot indeed in that passageway. I sidled back into the street, leaving it to others who spoke far better Spanish than I to argue and protest against this unwarranted interference with the free movement of foreign civilians pursuing their daily task in extremely difficult circumstances, and so on. As I breathed the welcome fresh air I mentally assessed the odds about being able to make a dash for it and go up the hill to my hotel. I decided against trying to do so. Several of these amateur gunmen were still around, for I could hear them talking close to me. Even though there was a good chance that if they fired after me as I ran away they might very well miss me, I considered the risk not worth taking. If I were wounded or killed, my newspaper would be the innocent loser.

Meanwhile our negotiators were making no impression whatever on the man at the desk. He told them he was chief of one of the paramilitary units which had been ordered by Fidel Castro to keep the city peaceful, and he couldn't in good conscience let us go on our way. 'My authority doesn't extend very far,' he confessed. 'There are a lot of bandits still roaming around out there. You might get robbed – or worse – if I let you go off into the night.' It availed nothing that our spokesman told him we were well able to take care of ourselves and anyway intended to hole up in our hotels as soon as we got there. 'Sorry, you'll have to spend tonight under our protection,' the man insisted.

We were bundled into two cars and driven to a dingy-looking house in one of the streets running diagonally off the Malecon boulevard on the sea front. It turned out to have been a 'safe' house used by revolutionary agents and couriers as well as by fugitives from Batista's police. I was shown to a small and none-too-savoury bedroom immediately underneath

a rooftop water cistern. Dumping my typewriter, my only luggage, resignedly in a corner of the room, I obeyed my captors' order to go down to the desk, sign my name in a register and claim a key.

As I did so, the good fortune which had sent me to Havana in the first place and had attended me for forty-eight hours thereafter worked again. I was walking away from the hotel desk when I noticed a big utility truck standing in the street outside the hotel entrance. Half a dozen laughing soldiers – real soldiers this time – were unloading their kit and other baggage from it. I was astonished to observe that two of them standing with their backs facing me had black hair hanging down so long below their shoulders that I should have said they were girls if they obviously had not been blessed with thick black beards. I walked forward and began talking with them. They were, they said, the very first detachment of Barbudos which Castro had promised to send into Havana.

So the seeming ill-luck that had landed me into being arrested had also brought me another lively segment for the morrow's story. This is yet another example of how compensations have so frequently offset what seemed initially to be setbacks in my profession as a journalist. A missed train or plane, failure to establish contact by phone or cable with London, somebody's refusal to tell me something, were irritating when encountered, but so often were followed by a piece of unexpected good fortune. Perhaps this helps to explain my perennial optimism.

The Barbudos were among the fittest and happiest young warriors I have ever seen. They had good reason for being so. They had had very little serious fighting and, as the never-robust morale had seeped away from Batista's conscripts during the past few months in the Sierra Maestra, an astonishingly easy victory had fallen to them. They told me that they had enjoyed a leisurely, unchallenged, advance upon the capital from the eastern province of Oriente, through Camagüey and Las Villas. The peasants in these mostly rural areas had welcomed them with increasing ardour as the reality of Castro's total victory had become manifest. People had been eager to give them anything they wanted. One Barbudo told me he couldn't remember when he had been last paid. 'The one thing we didn't need was money,' he said. 'People couldn't do enough for us. They lavished everything, especially food, on us.'

Proof of this was forthcoming as some of the contents of the truck were arrayed on the counter of the hotel reception desk. There were hams, strings of sausages, cottage-made bread, butter, beer and many other such good provender. We were all invited to tuck into a midnight feast – rebel soldiers, our captors, American reporters, including one lone Englishman, and anybody else who happened to be about. Good fellowship bloomed with every mouthful. There was much hearty back-slapping, joking, talk and toasting of international understanding, and some glowing forecasts from the Barbudos of the future Cuba once Fidel Castro took charge. The devotion of the young warriors, none of whom was much more than eighteen or nineteen years old, for their leader was awesome.

As I talked, watched and listened, my mind went back in memory to another such occasion in 1944. I had flown in as a passenger in a Flying Fortress of the United States Air Force from Foggia, in southern Italy, over German-occupied Yugoslavia to Bucharest, which had just been captured by the Soviet Army. The mission of a squadron of Fortresses was to pick up several hundred American and British airmen who had been shot down over the Ploiesti oilfields and then captured. But the real significance of the occasion for me was that it represented the link-up of Soviet forces surging into Europe from the east and Anglo-American forces advancing at last from the west. The first soldiers in the Soviet Army I met were two young motorcyclists leaning on the handlebars of their machines, each with a light rifle slung across his back, awaiting the landing of my Fortress on the runway of the military airport at Bucharest. We managed to bridge the language gap by using my imperfect German and their even less able command of the same tongue. They told me they were an advance patrol of the main army now taking over the Romanian capital. In Bucharest, as later in Havana, there had been back-slapping, smiles, good fellowship and expressions of faith in international goodwill. Alas, both meetings were to become sterile. As with the Russians, Cubans were to become isolated for decades by political misunderstandings, blunders and prejudices. The Soviet Union was to be betrayed by Joseph Stalin and the Cuban revolution was doomed to lose the happy spontaneity of that first encounter with the Barbudos. Fidel Castro and a succession of American presidents and State Department planners were, between them, to frustrate the impulse of the common man of both nations to offer comradeship and co-operation with his opposite number. National leaders seem determined never to learn.

3

Fidel and Other Phenomena

I had had an unusual and highly satisfactory indirect contact with Fidel Castro before I met him in the flesh on the afternoon of 9 January 1959. By 3 January, the third day of the new era, it had become obvious that he was in no hurry whatever to come to Havana to take over government of the country that had so unexpectedly fallen to him. This might well have been, and indeed I think it was, because he needed time to equip himself psychologically and practically for the immense, delicate task ahead of him. He also needed time for the complicated and unstable political situation in the capital to become sorted out. What better way to gain these ends than by showing himself and talking with as many Cubans as possible? There had already been abounding evidence that he had become almost a godlike figure to a people whom he had rescued from Batista's greedy despotism. He could make his hold upon the country even more permanently secure by close contact, and he did just that.

I decided that however desirable it might be for me to join him on his imperial progress, I could not abandon the turbulent and highly newsworthy situation in Havana. Anything could happen. I solved my problem by asking Robert Perez to go out into the field, locate Fidel Castro, join his expedition and telephone me with accounts of what the Maximum Leader – the title he assumed – was doing as and when he could. I had no high hope that Perez would be able to achieve much and, even if he did, would manage to reach me by telephone or by whatever other channels offered. Internal communications from one region to another had collapsed in the wake of Fidel Castro's tidal wave of victory.

I was in for a surprise. About forty-eight hours after Perez had set out on his assignment I received a scarcely audible telephone message from an officer at the temporary rebel headquarters at Camp Columbia. The officer said he must see me as soon as possible, because he had an important letter for me. Since I was intending to be out for some hours, I suggested that he arrange for the letter to be left for me at the Colina. 'No,' said the officer. 'That won't do. I have orders – from the top – to deliver it personally.'

We set up an appointment. Promptly to the minute the officer arrived at my door. Saluting formally, he identified himself as a lieutenant in the rebel air force. He handed the letter to me and asked for a receipt. I asked diffidently if there had been any expense concerning its delivery which I could repay. The young lieutenant smiled and shook his head. 'I flew it up from Santa Clara, and now that I've delivered it I'm flying back,' he said. After another salute he was gone.

The letter brought me a minor scoop. Castro had talked with Perez during a halt on the ambling journey to Havana. Perez had written out a version in English of the interview and had translated this into Spanish so that Castro should know just what was being attributed to him. He had approved the typescript, endorsing it with what I took to be his signature, and then in one of those grand gestures which were to become familiar had ordered the letter to be flown to me as soon as possible.

The interview was by no means sensational by international or any other standards, but it was the first he had given since his victory to any foreign publication and as a result it did have some historical significance.

It was certainly of great interest to the British Embassy in Havana, when I made my routine telephone call there on the day I received it. (I had been asked to keep in touch with the Embassy so that they should know I was still safe and kicking.) I mentioned that I had an interview with Castro which I was at that moment writing up for transmission to London. A few minutes later I had a return call on behalf of the Ambassador, Mr A.S. Fordham, asking if they could possibly see it. Since the Embassy was not in journalistic competition with the *Daily Telegraph*, and the Foreign Office would be reading it in my newspaper the next morning, I agreed. Some doubt and confusion was spreading about Fidel Castro's future relations with the Western democracies and it struck me even as I was talking with the Embassy that it was already desirable that official and unofficial British and American interests should work together to the maximum permissible extent, and might need to do so even more urgently as time passed. That is, of course, precisely what happened as the revolution swung ever more irrevocably to the Left and truth became steadily more elusive. Even while I was typing my story a senior officer from the Embassy, Mr Parrish, was copying it out as each page emerged from the typewriter.

Next day I had another call saying that Mr Fordham wished to see me so that he could thank me for my co-operation. As I hadn't yet met him, I readily agreed. When I saw him in his office he did more than thank me. 'I think you might like to know that I've just been to see Dr Roa [the Minister of State] to notify him that the United Kingdom has decided to give diplomatic recognition to the new regime,' he said evenly with a bland smile. It was a generous quid pro quo. It was also another little scoop, since it meant that the news of the recognition was being read in the first edition of the *Daily Telegraph* hours before the Foreign Office got around to announcing the news.

Perez had concentrated in the interview on the topic of Anglo-Cuban relations. This had become a matter of immediate importance in the United Kingdom because the British had backed the wrong horse in Cuba. Only weeks before Batista was ousted they had sold him some naval Sea

Fury war-planes and a number of tanks for use against the rebels. Small wonder that the Embassy had been anxious to read what Castro had said to Robert Perez! He had already stated while advancing towards Santa Clara that any British property falling into rebel hands, military or otherwise, would be confiscated. Perez now asked him if that edict was still operative and, if so, whether he intended to take further steps against the British. Castro's answer to this question gave the world a first indication of important facets of his character and his situation at the time of his victory. These included almost total lack of political administration and experience and a tendency to blurt out, under pressure, a statement or decision to which he hadn't given anything like enough thought. Sometimes this impulsive practice got him out of trouble because a snap decision happened to be the right one. But just as often it got him into difficulties because the answer was the wrong one. Time and again, in big and small matters, I was to observe this combination of inadequacies at work in the earlier years of his administration. It helps to explain the extraordinary ups and downs in his fortunes before, and even after, the Soviet Union grabbed him and used him and his island as tools in her long and dangerous duel with the United States, before Mr Gorbachev came along and set about changing everything. 'Our sentiments towards Britain are of sympathy and friendship,' he said expansively to Robert Perez. 'We watched attentively when the British fought in the difficult days of the World War. But our relations with Britain will now have to be carefully reviewed.'

This windy preliminary was followed by an illustration of his administrative inexperience. He had to concede that his hasty announcement about confiscation of British goods had not been implemented. 'It is to be reviewed,' he hedged. 'We are going to ask some straight questions and we shall expect some straight answers – in writing – from Britain. Those Sea Furies were sold to Batista to kill rebels and innocent people. We shall have to study how these shipments came about, who allowed them, why they were made.' He then said that the British tanks, manned by rebel crews, would be included in the victory parade which he intended to hold when he reached Havana. (In a note to me, Perez said he felt quite sure that this decision was made by Fidel Castro at the moment he announced it.)

In the event he never did anything, of course, about reviewing relations with Britain, but the tanks may very well have been among those I saw thumping along the Malecon during the massive emotional parade he held in Havana eight days after his victory. The pattern of relations between the two countries was dictated by hard facts. Castro's need for British exports grew and grew in the first eighteen months of his revolution because the United States, having given up for many reasons trying to reach an understanding with him, stopped supplying him with anything at all. This dependence upon Britain lessened and vanished altogether after the Soviet Union adopted him. By the end of 1962 British diplomats in Havana and British businessmen visiting the city had been frozen out of contact with official Cuba. By this time Castro's revolution had become irreversibly a Communist one.

Fidel Castro strode purposefully, his face alight with a beaming smile, into the Sugar Bar under the roof of the Havana Hilton Hotel on the afternoon of 9 January 1959. Miraculously he was only an hour late, and for him this was equal to being on time. It was certainly nothing compared with the feats of tardiness he was to achieve as time (to which he paid such little regard) went on; he would sometimes appear for an appointment in the early hours of the next day, once awakening a British ambassador at about 2 a.m. and insisting on taking him on a long ride around the city while they chatted.

What an irresistible figure he made this day! I was never again to see him so carefree and so aglow. At thirty-two he still carried the freshness of youth and his athletic body had not yet been mauled by the exactions of a disorganized life which turned night into day, deprived him of good sustaining foods and adequate sleep, and thereby sapped his physique of the reserves which four years as a guerrilla leader in the mountains of Oriente had given him. This afternoon of the first full day after his spectacular emotional entry into the capital he was obviously fired by the knowledge that he had become almost a god in the eyes of most of his 7 million fellow-countrymen. They hadn't given him much solid support while he had seemed to be floundering to no purpose at the head of a small band of bearded followers wandering around the Cuban country-side, but they were now his slaves.

So too, in a way, were the American and other correspondents lolling around the big room set up to accommodate many television crews as well as the forty to fifty reporters. They were psychologically as well as literally at his feet as he stood on a dais, because scarcely a whisper had yet been heard of the weaknesses in his character, the suspicious political ma-noeuvrings swirling uncontrolled around him as the Communists moved in, or the fearful revenge he was taking on those who had served Batista. It was an occasion that offered him favourable world-wide publicity, and he took full advantage of it. Sometimes he clowned, once or twice he lied, and always he evaded committing himself to statements which might later embarrass him. I do not recall his giving a direct answer to anything asked of him. In some instances he probably did not know the answer.

He confessed as much in meeting one question I asked him. I raised the topic of Anglo-Cuban relations which he had discussed with Robert Perez a day or two earlier, asking him if he had yet decided how he was going to deal with the United Kingdom. Fidel Castro looked directly at me with his large dark eyes and thoughtfully stroked his beard while he considered what to say. Apparently a satisfactory answer was still beyond him. 'There are, of course, many things to be considered in connection with. . . .' He stopped abruptly. With a most appealing smile he resumed. 'I just don't know,' he said. He joined happily in the roar of laughter which the unexpected admission provoked. It ended the conference on the happiest of notes. These were still the days of his honeymoon with the world. Almost everybody was still disposed to be happy with Fidel Castro and to laugh at, and with him, when he play-acted.

I stayed in Havana for another three weeks, chronicling the first chaotic phase of Fidel Castro's revolution. Thereafter I kept a professional eye on him and events in the island by constant reading and by making over a dozen visits to Cuba at irregular intervals between 1959 and 1966. It was bureaucratically simple for an Englishman to do so because the United Kingdom and Cuba observed a reciprocal agreement enabling citizens of each country to visit the other without having to get a visa. But it grew increasingly hard and hazardous for a non-Communist journalist to operate in Cuba as the country slid apparently inexorably under Soviet control.

An analysis of Fidel Castro and the revolution is far outside the scope of this book. I feel it might be appropriate, however, to make a few observations based on first-hand knowledge of this phenomenal man and the astonishing transformation of Cuba since 1959. I believe two facts are indisputable. One is that the revolution was never a peasants' revolt. Fidel Castro was brought up in a middle-class environment and had little contact with humble people until his revolution began to succeed. If his crusade had been truly supported by the peasantry, his 'army' would have been far stronger than one of only eighteen at its lowest and a few hundred during the long campaign in the Sierra Maestra. The second point is that the known facts suggest strongly that he intended to achieve one kind of revolution but eventually delivered another. In speeches and other declarations in the years before his triumph in 1959 he promised to replace tyranny and subservience to the United States with democratic rule, complete with free elections and the exercise of free enterprise, no nationalization, and a programme aiming at the emergence of an unfettered Cuba. What happened? There is firm evidence that Moscow-trained Communists whom Castro had earlier ignored or rejected began to join him once he looked like a winner and thereafter cunningly and effectively exploited his political and administrative inexperience, annexing him and his movement. To what extent the United States aided this process by failing to establish contact with him in 1958 and 1959, and just how willingly he accepted conversion to communism, is unclear. As the Cuban revolution pursued its dogged left-wing course into the 1990s, more and more American and other analysts and observers expressed their belief that Fidel Castro must have been a Communist all his adult life. The tidal wave of opinion became so strong that I was sometimes tempted to question my own contrary view. But in 1989 there came powerful support for it from an unexpected source. Margaret Truman, the daughter of President Harry Truman, published some of her father's private papers which showed beyond doubt that he believed Castro was not a confirmed Communist when he came to power in Havana in 1959 and that the United States missed an opportunity to gather him into the American fold at that time. Making a bitter assault on what he believed to be the ineptitude of President Eisenhower, his successor in the White House, he wrote: 'One of the dumbest things that happened during his [Eisenhower's] administration was ignoring Castro when there was a good chance – and I'm certain there was a good chance – to get him on our side rather than Russia's.'

President Truman added that if he had been in office when Castro's revolution succeeded, he would have picked up the telephone and made friends with him, offered him financial aid and other kinds of aid in getting Cuba on her feet again. 'I don't think for a minute that Castro was a locked-in pro-Russian at that point,' Truman wrote. 'I think he turned towards Russia because, when he looked at us, all he could see was a bunch of backs turned away from him. I'd have said: "Listen, Fidel, come on down here to Washington and let's talk." I'd have seen to it that we had a sensible meeting and worked things out, and we wouldn't be worrying ever since about what's being cooked up between the Cubans and Russians on that island just ninety miles away from Florida.'*

As for myself, each visit I paid to Cuba brought its own distinctive experiences and emotions. I can now tell the story coolly and in detail. Fidel Castro's stature as an inspired reformer devoted only to the deliverance of his people from their traditional status, as he saw it, of purveyors of pleasure and economic profit to the Americans, began to diminish very quickly after he had entered Havana. Ugly reports started reaching me of peremptory executions and virtual lynchings, which he did nothing to stop and even justified when questioned. Some of the people killed were undoubtedly murderers and torturers. But could all of the hundreds being summarily put to death throughout the island be guilty of crimes deserving this extreme punishment? I doubted it and believed that old scores were being settled in many instances and also that a fevered population was indulging in a blood-lust which Castro should have subdued. I was given an eye-witness account of one man being hanged without trial from a bridge outside Matanzas after a howling mob had seized him in his home. Another reliable witness told me of a man being hunted like a fox at Varadero and shot to death by his pursuers after he had been cornered. Harrowing photographs, which could not possibly have been faked, were published in the newspapers of Havana. Three of these, printed side by side, showed a burly police chief in a provincial town striding defiantly

---

* *Where the Buck Stops: The Personal and Private Writings of Harry S. Truman*, compiled and edited by Margaret Truman (1989).

from his office, facing a firing-squad without blindfold, and then reeling grotesquely backwards towards the pavement – dead.

I did not believe one story until it was confirmed by an eye witness which indicated that Raul Castro, Fidel's sinister half-brother, was outdoing everybody else. As military commandant of Oriente Province he had organized a round-up of suspects and had then personally supervised the shooting to death of seventy-one of his fellow-Cubans who, after a hurried night trial, had been found guilty of having collaborated with the Batista regime. The condemned men were taken by truck to a military rifle-range and felled in batches as they stood in front of a long trench scoured out to a depth of ten feet by a bulldozer. One newspaper, *El Mundo*, reported that the killings had been interrupted for the light to improve so that operators making a film to be called *Revolutionary Justice* could get better pictures of the ghastly event.

It soon became clear that Fidel Castro intended to take unrelenting reprisals against anybody who had collaborated in the murderous misdeeds of the Batista regime or had actively opposed his revolutionary struggle. He was repaying terror with terror. Reports reaching the United States caused dismay and revulsion. I do not know how strongly this revulsion influenced American official policy towards Castro, but I imagine that it did help to sway the State Department in assessing him and ought therefore to be taken into account when one considers the failure of the United States in these early days to reach an understanding with him.

One day in January I did manage to speak briefly with Castro – he was so elusive at that time that anybody outside his permanent intimate circle had difficulty in getting near enough to discuss affairs with him – as he was being shoved by his bodyguards through the usual crowd of bewitched Cubans who swarmed around him whenever and wherever they saw him. He was on his way to have a late breakfast in the coffee shop of the Havana Hilton Hotel, as had become his custom, after a night spent in making the rounds of political and military sub-stations and offices in the city. (He was by no means alone among Cubans who turned night into day and did not even try to be punctual for appointments. This disregard for the passage of time on the clock led me often to check when making an appointment with anybody in Havana to inquire only half-humorously if they would be observing *ora Cubana* or *ora Inglesa*.) Having got close enough to catch his attention I asked him if it were true, as had been reported, that he had given an order to suspend trials and executions because of the outcry against them in the United States, in several countries in Latin America, and even in distant Europe. 'What order?' he replied angrily. 'There hasn't been any such order. We shall punish every one of these murderers. The time for Americans and any of the others to start worrying was when Batista and his crew were killing innocent people.'

As if to confirm this intransigence, I happened to find later the same day that even schoolchildren were being used to swell the wave of revengeful

hysteria that was enveloping Cuba. I came upon a procession of young-
sters, led by men and women teachers, as they were marching in a street
off La Rampa, in Vedado, carrying banners bearing the slogans *We demand
justice against the assassins* and *Execute the murderers*. The boys and girls
were chanting the same words as they marched on. Presumably they had
been told to do so by their teachers who, I reflected, surely ought to have
known better. But this depressing spectacle did not stir me anything like
so strongly as another which I came upon while I was listening to the first
of those interminable harangues that were to mark Fidel Castro's formal
public appearances during the next thirty years. He had called for a mass
gathering in a park facing the Presidential Palace to join him in demon-
strating against American and other outside criticisms of the executions. I
went to the open-air meeting going on in the January sunshine because I
had heard that Havana Radio had said that a million people had assembled to listen to Castro. Of course I found that there were nothing like
a million Cubans listening to him. The array of faces was, however, most
impressive. I calculated that perhaps some 400,000 people had answered
the call. Whatever the size of the audience, the expression of solidarity
with the Maximum Leader was enthusiastic. People applauded and
shouted vociferously when he said: 'Cuba has no need to apologize to the
United States or anybody else. All that's happening is that justice is being
done to the scoundrels who murdered so many innocent victims.'

I suddenly became aware that in reacting to his words the crowd was
shouting a word of its own – *paredon* – and was emphasizing the three
syllables by appropriately timed shaking of clenched fists. *Paredon* was a
new word to me. I asked a man standing next to me what it meant. 'To the
wall – shoot them. That's what it means,' he answered, his eyes ablaze as
he continued gesticulating with his clenched fist. I experienced feelings of
sadness, revulsion and frustration as I listened to the rhythmic roar of the
crowd pounding out its word of doom. I was sad to think of Fidel Castro
squandering his gift of eloquence on this unworthy, demeaning purpose
of revenge – spurning a heaven-sent opportunity to give uplifting and
profitable leadership to his struggling country. I was revolted by the sight
and sound of grown men and women responding like primitive savages to
his demand for yet more blood-letting; and I was frustrated because there
was nothing I could do to change matters except perhaps to swell the
international protest against the executions by reporting fully all that I was
seeing and hearing in my privileged position as a close observer of the
revolution. Sickened, unable to stand any more of the disheartening
spectacle, I elbowed my way through the packed ranks of inflamed
Cubans and walked dispiritedly to my small bedroom at the Colina to
write my story.

Worse was to come. Fidel Castro's answer to all the criticism being
expressed abroad was not to recognize that by far his most responsible
and advantageous course would be to restrict, at the very least, the

wholesale hasty reprisals being taken by his people. Instead he decided to try to justify them by staging a theatrical show trial which, he foolishly believed, would prove to the world that only justice was being done, with due regard to the rules of law. Because of his poor judgement and, predictably, because thousands of Cubans took full advantage of the opportunity offered them to enjoy a ghastly circus, the trial exposed him and the revolution to increased antagonism and contempt.

He blundered at the start by choosing just about the most inappropriate setting available for the spectacle. This was the Sports City stadium, one of those cavernous, circular monstrosities to be seen in the United States and elsewhere built as concrete imitations of the Colosseum in Rome. The stadium stood just within the city limits and had been constructed on Batista's orders at enormous expense and amid recurring stories of corruption and other scandals. It might have proved useful in the years before Castro for the staging of baseball and other games, but it was no place for a public trial in which a man's life was the stake.

The victim chosen to be thrown to the bloodthirsty crowd was a hapless former officer in Batista's army, Captain Jesus Sosa Blanco, accused of an array of charges including murder, theft, arson and looting, in Oriente Province. The tiers of seats which reached high into the rafters of the stadium were jammed tightly with over eighteen thousand spectators when Sosa Blanco, quaking, was hustled into a roped square about the size of a boxing-ring by half a dozen Barbudos who, none too gently, prodded him on his way. True to Cuban form, the trial was opening three and a half hours after the time announced repeatedly on television and the radio and in the newspapers. The crowd had been getting increasingly restive, showing its annoyance at the delay by rounds of slow hand-clapping and shrill whistling in between gulps of ice-cream and nibbling items such as peanuts, sweetmeats and small squares of fat pork carried around the amphitheatre on wooden skewers by importuning vendors who had paid fees for permission to do so. As the crowd spotted Sosa Blanco shambling into the arena, people began shouting, howling and hooting, and those sitting nearest spat at him as he passed. When he sat down, handcuffed and flanked by guards, he was at first defiant. He glared back at those taunting him, his mouth set firm and his head erect, as if challenging them to do their worst. He made by no means a pretty picture. He was wearing a striped, pyjama-like prison overall like those worn by inmates of Nazi concentration camps whom I had seen in 1945. His swarthy round face, thick black eyebrows and a conspicuously low forehead did not reflect an impressive intelligence. Adding to the image of a caged human animal, every time he moved his hands his handcuffs jangled. He strained to listen as the indictment against him was read out. There was so much noise going on while the crazy trial was opening that it was impossible to tell how he pleaded, though one could hazard a good guess about that.

Once the proceedings got under way his guards relaxed, sensing that he was not going to give them any trouble. One of them leaned back in his chair and brought out a cigar from the breast pocket of his tunic, lit it, and began puffing smoke airily and casually on Blanco's right. American and Cuban photographers lay sprawled on the floor a few feet away from the prisoner. They photographed his every movement and change of expression and often exchanged words with him. They told me later that he had cursed Batista for leaving him in the lurch, as he said, and of course had insisted on his own innocence. 'I never killed in cold blood,' he told one of the photographers. 'I killed only in combat. . . . Batista was a villain, a man without conscience or thought for anybody but himself. I hope he rots in hell.'

The presiding judge, who had two young rebel officers to assist him, was called Dr Humberto Sori Marin. He held two contrasting posts in the Castro government which must have kept him permanently busy, those of Minister of Agriculture and Attorney-General of the Armed Forces. He was a man of about forty, with an air of brisk confidence about him. For the trial he had put on a pair of enormous horn-rimmed spectacles which helped to give him an appropriate judicial gravity. Sori Marin tried hard to keep the proceedings under his control, but never enjoyed complete success during the thirteen hours they lasted. His task of keeping this kind of crowd in order was an impossible one. I heard people crying: 'Get on with it . . . let's kill him off.' And whenever some bewildered peasant brought in specially from the sugar-fields of Oriente failed to locate the prisoner in his cage when asked to identify him, people gave directions with shouts, whistles and pointing fingers.

After about eight hours Sori Marin called a fifteen-minute recess. He used the break to buy an ice-cream from vendors who had now been allowed to roam the official 'court' area. As he began to enjoy his refreshment I strolled over and talked with him. He made one unforgettable remark: 'Yes, my friend, this fellow is the first of many who will be tried and will pay for their crimes.' It was an astonishing thing to hear from a judge half-way through a trial. I glanced over towards Sosa Blanco, who was now being besieged by the photographers, and I was glad that he would never know what his presiding judge had said to me.

Maybe it wouldn't have surprised or shocked him. A Cuban reporter had told me that before the trial started Sosa Blanco had said to him: 'I fully expect to be found guilty, but perhaps I won't be shot.' That hope seemed to desert him as the trial wore on into the night. The early defiance went as one witness after another – many without being directed by the crowd – denounced him. Some accused him directly of killings, but others were allowed to do so by hearsay. Sori Marin had no qualms during this bizarre process about allowing second-hand evidence to be admitted. He allowed one man to say, for example, that he had 'heard that Sosa Blanco had killed forty-seven farmers in one day'. Other evidence was much more damning. There didn't seem to be much room for doubting a witness who graphically described seeing a member of his family killed by Sosa Blanco, or another witness who said he had seen the prisoner commit one of the crimes of which he was accused. Whenever this happened, Sosa Blanco seemed to become deflated. A nervous fixed grin would appear on his face, a reflex of fear, and he would slump in his chair. But whenever his court-appointed lawyer, Lt Aristedes Acosta, scored a point, Sosa Blanco would brighten instantly and automatically, perhaps thinking for a fleeting moment that his obsessive fears would prove groundless after all.

This was not to be, of course. At last, a few minutes after 6 a.m., the trial ended. Only about one-third of the audience had lasted the course, but Sori Marin was undaunted. He used all his Latin gifts of fervour and theatricality as he pronounced the sentence: guilty on all counts. He was almost screaming words as he condemned Sosa Blanco to death by shooting.

The doomed prisoner was hustled away by his half-dozen guards and once again he had to endure the ordeal of harassment by young Cubans among those who had watched the trial through the night. As he was marched along a narrow aisle to an exit they shouted obscenities at him, spat on him, even tried to grab him. Outside the stadium, as he was being half shoved towards a waiting van, a gang of youths made a serious effort to kidnap him, probably with the thought of lynching him. They were roughly handled by the guards after Sosa Blanco had been hoisted hurriedly into the van. They landed with damaging thumps on the stony street.

Before Judge Sori Marin left the stadium for home he came over to me. Smiling behind his big spectacles, he shook hands and said politely that he hoped I had a good story to write. I told him I didn't think what I wrote could possibly do the revolution much good. 'Well, try not to be too hard on us,' he replied. 'We're still trying to catch up. At least Sosa Blanco has had a better deal than those he murdered.'

That was the last I ever saw of the judge. Apparently he became quickly disillusioned with Fidel Castro. Less than a year later I heard that he had started plotting against Castro with other disaffected servants of the revolution. When the Bay of Pigs invasion happened in April 1961, he and his small group of conspirators made a fatal decision that the time had come to move against the Maximum Leader. Cuba had been sealed off from the world outside during this turbulent period and nobody ever really found out exactly what happened to Sori Marin. On one of my later visits to Havana I heard a brief item on Havana Radio that at the time of the invasion he had been wounded 'while trying to avoid being arrested'. Some weeks later there came another announcement. Sori Marin had been executed 'for crimes against the revolution'.

As for Sosa Blanco, he was exploited in the last twenty-four hours of his life to serve the Cuban taste for the melodramatic. A photographer was allowed into the church when he made his last confession. Pictures were published of him lying prostrate before a priest, weeping as he whispered into the cleric's ear, and then embracing his wife before being led back into the condemned cell. He died the following night, far more stoically than one could have foretold from his abject behaviour at his trial. As he stood against a bullet-pitted wall close to a moat in the Citadel, near Morro Castle, as the 103rd announced victim of rebel retribution, he said to the waiting firing-squad, according to a report I heard: 'I forgive you, lads, as I hope also to be forgiven.' He also asked them, according to the same account, to aim at his heart and not at his head. He was also said to have been the first condemned man to ask permission, and be given it, to tell the firing-squad when to fire.

This practice became almost a ritual as executions continued, and I was told by one of the few people who saw them that it often led to sickening scenes. Many half-trained soldiers in firing-squads reacted too quickly to the prisoner's command. They didn't allow enough time to take aim as they obeyed the order. As a result, their aim was bad and the volley was ragged. Often, a man would still be alive when an officer came to give him the *coup de grâce*, and it sometimes happened that he was still sufficiently conscious to make a piteous appeal for mercy: 'Don't shoot. Don't do it!' He would die with the words on his lips as the officer pulled the trigger of a pistol held against the side of his head.

The trial of Sosa Blanco, which was extensively reported outside Cuba, followed by the photographs of his last confession and his last farewell to his wife, did more than bring the revolution into ridicule and abhorrence. The whole episode helped to widen the breach between the United States and Cuba. Many Americans in authority in Washington, as some told me themselves, came to believe that Fidel Castro, the man who showed such appalling judgement in believing that such spectacles would cause the world to accept his claim that justice was being done, simply could not be sufficiently mature politically – and mentally – to be worth courting.

4

Return to Cuba

Laughs were scarce during the seven years I kept my journalistic eye on Cuba, but now and again a day or an evening in Havana would be brightened by an unexpected sardonic sally or comic incident. Usually the irrepressible spark of humour, which is a feature of the quixotic Cuban character, was responsible for an uplift of the spirits. Thus one spring day in 1960 I walked almost two miles from the Hilton Hotel (now renamed on Fidel Castro's orders the Libre) to the Prado. I often did this as a first duty when visiting the island because it provided an opportunity to note any changes which had happened since my last visit, or any new posters and notices which had appeared while I had been absent. By the time I had reached the sea front I was tired and thirsty. My flagging energies improved when I came upon an open-air refreshment stall which had a promising row of bottles arrayed on a shelf behind the counter. 'Rum?' I asked the barman. 'No, señor.' 'Beer?' 'No, señor.' I went along the whole row of empties behind him. It turned out that he had nothing but milkless ersatz coffee to offer. 'What's happened to the rum, the beer and the rest?' I asked him as he prepared my unappetizing drink. Before he could reply, a Cuban sitting hunched on an adjoining stool supplied the answer: 'They're ageing it, mister,' he said, in English.

Again, one evening I went to the Restaurant Miami, one of the few establishments which seemed to have survived the rigours of the revolution, hoping to get something a little more appealing than a skimpy little fish caught by somebody with string and a bent pin in the mucky shallows near Morro Castle. Before looking at the few pencilled items listed on the menu I asked the waiter what speciality he could offer. 'Lots of lovely music, señor,' he answered, without changing his lugubrious expression.

The British Ambassador to Cuba between 1960 and 1963 (Herbert Marchant) provided another chuckle when he told me of one happening in the summer of 1963. He and two or three members of the Embassy staff were offsetting the rigours of official duties in the city by indulging in underwater spear-fishing in a small bay on the coast between Havana and Varadero. As they did so, they saw that a Cuban militiaman bathing nearby was in difficulties. The Ambassador and the British Consul, Joseph Pethybridge, went to his rescue aboard Mr Marchant's home-made raft and managed to bring the half-drowned Cuban soldier ashore. As they lay gasping to recover their breath, they overheard some Cuban civilians

43

telling others who had gathered there: 'Yes, they've saved the life of one of our Barbudos. They're Russians.'

Again in 1963 Fidel Castro himself put on a notable impromptu comic show. Very late one night I chanced upon Commandante Rene Vallejo, a grey-haired doctor who had become Castro's closest friend and adviser, trying to induce his erratic charge to go out through the revolving exit door of the Hotel Libre, where they had been eating supper, for another engagement on the all-night programme. Vallejo told me that, as usual, they were hours behind their schedule. This was not troubling Fidel Castro. He was behaving in fact like a naughty boy. Even when he had been propelled at last by Vallejo and a couple of guards through the crowds of adorers and then through the exit door, he didn't make for his waiting Cadillac limousine. He suddenly swerved left and dived into an outside bookshop, where he scooped up a handful of works by Marx, Lenin and Chairman Mao, and as he emerged thrust them into the hands of members of the crowd still clustered around the hotel exit. 'Read this,' he said to one recipient, and 'Read this' to another, until he had unloaded all the books.

Vallejo now lost patience. He ordered two rebel guards to grab Castro. One on each side of him, they began to drag him towards his car. Fidel Castro, no mean ham actor, took the cue. Putting on a wide-eyed look of helpless innocence, he relaxed all his muscles and allowed himself to be taken like a loosely tied parcel to the waiting Cadillac. As this was happening, he gazed across at me and a couple of friends standing watching the comedy and said something which we couldn't catch but which made Cubans near him burst into roars of laughter. We got an approximate version of what he had said. It ran: 'Why, they don't even do this to American presidents. . . .'

I can think of no obvious reason, except perhaps circumstances governing the zodiacal sign of Taurus, why a Sunday in November 1961 should have been one of the most frightening days of my life in war or peace.

None of it would have happened if I hadn't given way to an impulse, early in the morning of the day before I was due to fly back to New York, to pay a nostalgic visit to the delightful seaside resort of Varadero, where my wife and I had spent a happy holiday soon after Castro had taken over Cuba but before he had had time to cause it to fall into decrepitude. We had loved Varadero for its magnificent beach and its aura of small-town, half-rural quietude.

One reached Varadero from Havana in 1961 by making a bumpy trip of some seventy miles to the coast of Matanzas Province in an American-manufactured bus. The one I chose that Sunday morning left at 9 a.m. and started back at 4 p.m. It was fully loaded with passengers on the outward trip, which passed uneventfully enough. When I got to Varadero I walked round the familiar avenues and lanes, noting the changes that had happened since 1959. The most notable difference in atmosphere was that it was much quieter than of old. Many shops and other small businesses were closed and shuttered. There were less people abroad. Cubans in Varadero had always been active and noisy. Not now. The place was like an English or French village on a wet day. There had also been significant physical changes – none of them, I thought, for the better. Ugly great blocks of apartments and drab office suites had been built in haste and none too thoroughly, judging by the cracks and peeling paint I observed, alongside the ornate Hotel International, a former haunt of the rich but now showing little of its one-time glamour. Some of the new buildings housed branches of the revolutionary administration evacuated from Havana because of the greatly swollen bureaucracy under the new 'Socialist' regime. Others provided weekend shelter for the crowds of workers using Varadero for organized rest and recreation. A small open square in the middle of the town had been renamed the People's Recreation Park, but it had not been modernized.

I went into a modest snack-bar in the People's Park. The only other patrons were four dour Czechs, members of a force of skilled artisans brought over to enhance the revolution's economic performance, and a youngish Cuban couple. The four East Europeans were taking not the slightest notice of anybody else or even of their surroundings as they concentrated with heads down on munching away at their substantial midday sandwich. I felt sorry for them because of the gulf in language, upbringing and tradition between them and the Cubans among whom they had been summarily dumped. They soon left the snack-bar, not having spoken one word of conversation so far as I could hear all the time they had been sitting near me. The two Cubans promptly filled the void. The moment the Czechs had filed through the door, presumably in pursuit of further Sunday recreation, the wife asked me, pointedly speaking English, for the salt on my table. Contact having been thereby adroitly established, the pair asked if they might join me. The husband immediately opened a diatribe of discontent, after having glanced meaningfully at the Cuban serving behind the counter and asking if he might speak in French.

He talked with emphasis and bitterness, leaving no scope for one to doubt his story. He had had a profitable and interesting export business before the revolution, he said, which had taken him into many foreign countries and given him a knowledge of the world not enjoyed by most Cubans. His business had collapsed after 1959 and now he was working as a salesman in a nationalized store. 'Cuba has been turned into a veritable cemetery as far as business is concerned,' he went on. 'The whole island is being handed over to the Soviet Union. If Fidel is doing it, then he must take the blame, but I think it's the Communists around him who are giving our island away. What I don't understand is why Fidel should think he'll get a better deal from the Soviets, with their terrible record since the war, than this country has had from the United States. At least we were prosperous.' The young man went on in this strain for some minutes, until I noticed that the Cuban behind the counter was watching and listening with interest and obvious curiosity. I concluded that it would be as well for all three of us if this session ended. The last thing I wanted was a confrontation with the local rebel authorities; nor did I wish my outspoken new acquaintance to get into trouble. I told the couple that it was time for me to move on. We parted and I sauntered down to a well-remembered part of the fabulous Varadero beach. It was deserted. On an impulse, I stripped down and waded into the sea. The water was just as warm and caressing as I recalled it had been in happier times two years earlier. I swam out enthusiastically until, to my horror, I found when I briefly stopped swimming that my feet no longer touched the soft sandy bottom. I also found that I was being carried further away from the shore every second. Too late I realized I should have remembered that we had always bathed on this stretch of beach on an incoming tide because there was a steep shelf in the sand which added dangerous power to the pull of an outgoing tide. I should also have remembered a sombre remark by George Sumner Albee, the late American writer and a fellow-lover of Varadero: 'I wonder if they've ever figured how many Cubans have swum here on an outgoing tide and never been seen again?' For a few moments I felt sure I was going to add to their number. But some sudden instinct for survival prompted me to strike out with all my strength and start swimming against the tide. I used the breast-stroke, which I always found served me best. At first I made no headway whatever. Then, increasing my effort to my limit of strength, I found myself slowly beating the tide. There came at last a wonderful instant when I knew I was nearer the beach and, lowering one leg cautiously, I felt the tip of a big toe touch sand. I had breasted the shelf. Thrusting my body forward I staggered slowly to safety.

Drained of strength but thankful, I plodded back to where I had stacked my clothes and attaché case at the foot of steps leading down from a house apparently abandoned by some Cuban family which had fled the revolution. I sat down on the bottom step, slowly getting back my wind and drying off in the strong November sunshine. As I did so, I thought of the commotion and mystery that would have been raised had I not survived. My clothes would have been found, minus their owner but plus my attaché case, containing newspaper clippings and notebooks whose pages were filled with memoranda in Pitman's shorthand and home-made hieroglyphics which I used in Cuba to defeat any prying eyes. What would the Barbudos and the Cuban intelligence apparatus have made of it all? Why, they would ask, had this busy foreign journalist seemingly committed suicide? Or had he? Had he left a note somewhere? Or was it all not too obviously contrived to give a wrong impression? Perhaps there was some sinister international spy plot behind his disappearance. He might even have been picked up by some interloping submarine. The possibilities were plentiful and intriguing, in keeping with the aura of melodrama with which the Castro revolution had already surrounded itself. I could picture representatives of the international media, including some of my friends, enjoying this mystery. The sad thing would have been that I shouldn't have been there to savour it.

Feeling restored after a while, I picked up my attaché case and made my way into the town to catch the 4 p.m. bus back to Havana. The sunshine was warm and comforting. I had had a narrow squeak but I had survived. Only a routine bus-ride lay between me and home. That is what I thought. I had no idea that this day had yet another unnerving adventure in store for me. It was one which would make it a day I should never forget.

The bus terminal waiting-room was a long and narrow wooden hut on an avenue leading from the People's Park. I went inside, checked in, and took a seat on one of two hard benches lining its sides. I was the only obvious foreigner among about thirty Cubans waiting for the bus. I leaned back and relaxed. But not for long. Some sixth sense alerted me that I was being watched. Looking around, I found that I was not mistaken. The burly Cuban who, sitting at a desk near the entrance to the waiting-room had checked my ticket a few minutes earlier, was sizing me up intently. I made a show of being unconcerned, but I felt uneasy. As I wondered whether he intended to make some move concerning me, I saw him get up and walk along the hut. He slowed down perceptibly as he passed me. Then he turned back to walk to his desk. But he didn't sit down again at it. He went outside.

There could be only one explanation. He was suspicious of me. Was he going to report me as a foreigner and perhaps an enemy of the revolution? A dark thought passed through my mind. Had that Cuban waiter at the snack-bar reported the conversation in a foreign language? It was not past possibility. I considered whether there was anything I could do. I could think of nothing that might help me. If I got up and went away, however slowly and innocently, that would simply make matters worse. I decided just to wait. If the man came back with a soldier or an official I should probably be arrested. I knew from what had happened in the past year to people, even foreigners, it might take the British Embassy or anybody else several days to extricate me. It might even take some time to find out that I was missing, for I had left Havana without telling anybody where I was going. I had no family or close friends in Cuba who would report my disappearance. In fact, the only people who *might* realize something had happened to me would be two or three members of the Libre hotel staff with whom I had made friends during my periodic trips to the island. My captors would be in no hurry to report that they had arrested me. They would probably say nothing until they had gathered every scrap of information from me, by methods which were unpleasant to contemplate.

These gloomy reflections were passing through my mind when I saw that the man from the desk had come back – alone. My thumping heart slowed down. But only momentarily, for through the waiting-room entrance came a young Cuban soldier armed with a rifle. He walked the length of the hut, there and back, slowing down each time he passed me and giving me a hard scrutiny as he did so. When he returned to the ticket desk he and the ticket-collector talked in low tones for a while. The soldier then repeated his patrol up and down the hut. This was my worst moment of the day. I felt sure that he was coming to get me this time. He again slowed down as he passed me and I noticed that he gave a hard look on his first 'pass' at my lap, on which I was nursing my attaché case. Returning, he didn't even slow down. He just went back for a few more words with the ticket-collector and then strode out of the hut. I had made it, and I believe I know why. My attaché case had saved me. Every East European functionary I had seen in Havana carried a small case like mine. It served as a kind of badge of office. I deduced that my possession of such an item had caused the two Cubans to decide that they would be wise not to risk being reprimanded for arresting an ally of the regime. I presumed they didn't speak any foreign language and, since almost all of the imported Russians, Czechs and others did not speak Spanish – and made no attempt to learn the language – they assumed that I would not know Spanish either, so that any interrogation of me in the hut might be both fruitless and embarrassing. For the first and only time in my life I was only thankful that I had been mistaken for an East European Communist.

The bus came and we all took our seats without further ado. It was still light when I got back to the Hotel Libre. There could have been no more contented man in Havana that evening than I, as I exchanged the usual badinage with the clerks at the reception desk and the operator of the elevator, a particularly humorous character still sporting the resplendent uniform of the bad old days, and eventually slumped down on my bed on the fifteenth floor of the hotel, relishing the evening breeze blowing ever so gently through the open window and massaging my exhausted but now relaxed body.

I suppose I was equally lucky on my next encounter with Cuban spy-chasers in September 1962, although I certainly didn't think so at the time. As so often happens to a soldier, journalist or other person who has necessarily to take risks in the practice of his (or, these days, her) profession in peace and war, I got into trouble when I least expected it. The time I chose for this ninth or tenth visit to Cuba was, I now realize, about the most hazardous of the decade of the sixties for a foreign correspondent to go poking about the contentious island. Few people knew it, but both Nikita Khrushchev and Fidel Castro had something they didn't want the world to know about. And within a month of that fateful September both of them and President Kennedy were to come to the brink of war over the secret installation of Soviet missiles and launching sites in Cuba.

I chose to fly to Havana because obviously something unusual was happening in Cuba. All manner of rumours, reports and fantasies were reaching me in the *Daily Telegraph* office in New York. None of the major participants in the political tussle – Khrushchev, President Kennedy and Fidel Castro – was disclosing anything to clarify the position. The only way to separate fact from legend, it seemed, was to go there, particularly after one informant told me by telephone from Havana that he had learned that several thousand Soviet fighting troops had been landed from four ships which had stolen by night into the harbour at Havana in the late summer.

It did not take long to dispose of that one. Soon after reaching Havana I saw some of these so-called combat troops being driven along the Malecon on the sea front in a convoy of trucks escorted by Cuban police in cars and on motor cycles. These were no warriors. They had none of the stiff bearing and brisk alertness of the professional soldier. There was in fact nothing of the fighting man about them or the manner of their transport. They looked to me to be husky farm-workers, labourers, petty craftsmen – perhaps untrained conscripts starting their military service and detached by Khrushchev to go to Cuba not to fight but to do the physical work made necessary by the Soviet policy of propping up the Cuban economy – and, had I but known it, help to build the sites for the missiles that Khrushchev had sneaked into Pinar del Rio. Nobody said a word to me about that! These workers wore white shirts and nondescript light trousers, and as they passed standing in the trucks travelling at a good clip along the Malecon I observed that many of them were carrying cameras. They were all joking and laughing. They were probably being taken on an outing of some kind.

The next item to be established was, where was Fidel Castro and what was he doing? Diplomats at Western embassies told me they had seen and heard little or nothing of him for some weeks. The concensus among them was that he was nursing a bruised ego. The Soviet Union was up to something, they told me, and Nikita Khrushchev was doing all the deciding. One diplomat said: 'Fidel has been shunted aside. He is being treated like a captured pawn in a chess match.' This sounded more and more true as my stay in Havana lengthened. Indeed, during the whole two weeks I was there I did not sight Castro once. He did not make an appearance in public or deliver one harangue, and experience had shown that if he were not showing himself off to his people or talking interminably at them he was not up to much.

This visit proved to be the most difficult and dangerous of any I made. It became clear from the moment I got to work in Havana that one false step would mean, at worst, arrest, and, at best, expulsion. Raul Lazo, a deceptively easy-going liaison officer at the Ministry of Foreign Relations where I had to go to register and also go through many cumbersome new formalities, made this abundantly obvious at our first encounter. 'Of course, you are not allowed at this time to go beyond the city limits, or into the countryside anywhere,' he said, with a disarming smile. 'And please do not get too close to protected areas, like the docks.' Señor Lazo used other, more subtle methods of limiting my scope. He had numberless pettifogging forms to be filled in so that valueless permits could be issued to me – at his leisure. Whenever I went to his office, quite a way from the centre of the city, he always had unlimited time to spare for pointless chatter and other tools of procrastination.

I do not know to this day how much British diplomats knew about the Soviet installation of missiles capable of reaching the United States only upwards of ninety miles away, but I feel sure it was far more than they were telling people like me. They went as far as they dared in keeping me advised of the hazards of my situation. Michael Brown, who in addition to his principal duties at the Embassy served as information officer when required, was blunt in his warnings. 'You're going to be watched and shadowed wherever you go,' he said. 'Don't venture far off main streets and avenues. Be most careful in talking to anybody you don't really know. The've got informants all over the place.'

I learned that foreign diplomats in Havana were being extremely careful not to let Cuban officials know how much they knew. They exchanged information with each other by writing pencilled notes, and I noticed that whenever I called on the British Ambassador and we came round to talking about anything of substance, he moved close to an open window on the eighth floor of the Edifico Bolivar, in Capdevila, overlooking the harbour mouth and the Presidential Palace. Presumably he did so to avoid any microphones which the Cubans might have installed in the old building.

Michael Brown was only too right about the shadowing. It was amateurish, but it was dogged. I perceived that whenever I walked out of the Hotel Libre by day a plain clothes agent or detective trailed me. These men were always identifiable, not only because of their persistence but because they invariably kept about ten yards behind me and tried to mask their presence by making sure that other pedestrians were between them and me. Whenever I went from the hotel by taxi in the evening I was shadowed by one particular vehicle, an old green and white Chevrolet carrying three men. It was instantly recognizable because it had only one headlight that functioned. They seemed unable to fix the other lights, chiefly because spare parts for American vehicles were becoming very scarce owing to the blockade of Cuba imposed by Washington early on in the impasse with Fidel Castro.

I gradually lost my awe of the shadowing once it became clear that the Cubans did not intend to molest me in any way, provided I behaved myself according to the directives given me by Señor Lazo. The shadowing and surveillance did have one drawback, however, for I always felt somehow that when I was speaking to somebody an invisible third presence was there. It wasn't, of course, but perhaps the uncomfortable feeling I experienced was one of the inhibitions the Cuban intelligence services intended to achieve.

Of course I took every care not to invite trouble. But I was destined not to escape unscathed from the Havana hot-house. A most unnerving exit was in store for me when eventually I planned to fly off to Jamaica and the United States, even though in my reckoning I had done nothing whatever to arouse suspicion or antagonism, and certainly I had not tried to telephone London or New York or cable any material to either of these capitals. Not that it would have been very satisfactory to do so. There was a good chance that any cable would either have been censored, heavily delayed or just 'lost', and any telephone call I made would certainly have been cut if I had tried to communicate anything of my suspicions about the machinations of the Soviets in this menacing phase of the revolution. As for any references to what I felt sure was a sulk by Fidel Castro, that would have also been enough to end a telephone call. I stifled any urges I had to unload myself of all I had learned and decided to wait before writing until after I had reached Kingston, Jamaica. One further argument against trying to write a story was that, thanks to the uninterrupted surveillance I had had and the cramping restrictions on my activities, I was not in a mental state to write coolly and objectively, as duty demanded. So I had carefully jotted down notes and reminders in a small brown notebook which I could stow away easily in my side-pocket. I never thought that this little notebook would cause me intense uneasiness and put me in some danger before I got away.

After several trying sessions with Señor Lazo and one final trip on foot to the remotely sited Ministry of Immigration, I eventually acquired an exit permit and a booking on a KLM plane to Kingston. I got up long before dawn to be ready to leave the Hilton in time to be at the airport by 6 a.m., although the plane was not due to leave Havana until midday and, if the Cubans ran true to form in coping with arranging its departure, it wouldn't leave until hours later.

With a travelling companion, Robert Betts, a journalist from San Diego, California, who had shared some of my ordeals of the past fortnight and was to share the last one of all, I went to the lobby, only to find immediately that this was to be no ordinary exit. After saying goodbye to members of the hotel staff, as always, because they had all been so friendly and helpful, again as usual, I was walking with Betts towards the first of a line of taxis waiting beyond the revolving door of the hotel entrance when the bell captain, another old friend, intercepted me in some embarrassment. 'No, Mr Tel-low, not that one,' he said. 'I'll get you one.' He hurried out and, turning left, disappeared down a side-street. Several minutes passed before he came back, riding alongside the driver of the taxi he had obtained. He was so flustered that he waved away the sizeable tip I offered him.

Nothing had yet happened to cause anxiety, but I was puzzled by both the action and demeanour of the bell captain, usually so easy and light-hearted a man. I was yet more puzzled to note after we took off in the taxi that the driver was keeping a close watch in his mirror. I turned and looked through the rear window. Yes, there it was – the one-eyed green and white Chevrolet which had tailed me the previous evening to and from a farewell dinner at the home of Michael Brown and his wife. My taxi-driver gave me a meaningful look when he saw that I had spotted the familiar Chevrolet. He had no need to say anything, and didn't. That look told me that he had been unwillingly conscripted to the task of co-operating with the three government agents inside it on the trip to the airport. I handed him one of the few remaining American cigarettes in the last packet of a dozen I had brought with me from New York for use as gifts and tips to appreciative Cubans.

The Chevrolet abandoned us only after its occupants had satisfied themselves that Betts and I had in fact entered the departure building of the airport. They had handed us over to other agents. These were unmistakable: two young Cubans wearing most casual clothing, cigarettes dangling from their lips, and projecting an air of indifference as they lounged around, awaiting us.

My early puzzlement now turned to alarm as they followed us to the KLM ticket-counter and stood watching us from a range of a few yards. Once again they followed us as we went to the airport cafeteria and bought almost undrinkable cups of coffee, made from acorns, I suspected. One agent stationed himself at the entrance to the cafeteria and the other at the exit. A third who had appeared from somewhere sauntered with calculated nonchalance past our table and back again.

What on earth did all this mean? The only explanation I could muster was that the Cubans had somehow got the idea that I might be a spy – *espia* to them – and, lacking proof of this and having no evidence so far that I had done anything improper or harmful to the regime, were making sure that I did leave Cuba and didn't try to make a bolt for cover instead. The one thing they didn't know presumably was how much information I had gathered during my stay in Havana. They were to make one last unsuccessful effort to fill that blank, as I was to find out soon enough.

Betts had told me that his father had been an inspector at Scotland Yard, and I should now have been grateful that some of the self-control which Betts senior had needed professionally had been transmitted to the son, who – also perhaps because he was not so closely involved as I – was taking the morning's trying nonsense much more calmly. My instinct, knowing as I did that I was not an *espia* and had nothing else on my conscience, was to try to make a fuss about the harassment. Instead, Betts suggested that I carry out an arrangement I had made with Michael Brown to ring the British Embassy to advise them that it looked as if we were both to get away safely rather than be arrested and flung into some awful Cuban gaol. I got up and went to a pay-phone (local calls were still only five cents on Castro's orders), and one of the agents promptly followed to watch and listen. I telephoned without incident, and very soon afterwards wished I hadn't.

Midway through the morning a grating voice on a loudspeaker interrupted a monotonous chant of exhortations like 'Yanqui no – Cuba si – Vinceramos!' to say that passengers to Jamaica should report to the processing hall. This was a large oblong salon which had long ago been given the scathing nickname of 'The Cage' because, once everybody with a ticket was inside it, its glass doors were locked, effectively separating departing Cubans, contemptuously called *gusanos* (worms) by Fidel Castro, from their friends and relatives. It was impossible for a person to leave The Cage once the door was locked, unless, as I had seen happen, he or she was disqualified from leaving Cuba on some pretext or other and was thrown out. Somebody had evidently tried either to escape from or get into The Cage illegally by butting the glass partition separating it from the public area of the terminal. The shattered glass on one side of the partition had been covered roughly with plywood; the outline of a human figure could be discerned on the other.

Passengers were called one by one to face examination at one end of the salon by three uniformed soldiers sitting side by side at a long table. As I awaited my turn I observed the time-consuming and demeaning ordeal that intending emigrants had to endure. Fidel Castro was not letting his people go very willingly. There were no less than eleven checks of documents, followed by lengthy questioning. Every item in the one piece of baggage that a Cuban passenger was allowed to take away had to be examined and verified against a list which the passenger had previously made out; every little trinket or piece of jewellery carried on the person was pored over by one member of the grotesque Star Chamber, and the precious piece of paper authorizing departure was slowly read through and scrutinized in case any alteration had been made in it. The process of examination varied from fifteen to thirty minutes per passenger or family of passengers. No wonder we had been told to be at the airport six hours before our plane was due to leave for Kingston.

This day the only passengers who ran into trouble were Betts and myself. We survived the main interrogation comparatively quickly because we were obviously neither Cubans nor emigrants. I was even beginning to feel that we were on our way when I was told to join preceding passengers at an open-air bench running along the runway side of The Cage upon which luggage was laid out. I saw my one suitcase and, obeying a peremptory gesture from a watching soldier, placed my battered old Underwood typewriter (vintage 1921) and my attaché case alongside it. The soldier expertly checked my one piece of luggage, probing every corner as well as its base, and made sure that an electric razor, toothpaste and various other toilet articles were still there, by checking them against a list on an official slip of paper which had been inserted in my passport when I landed two weeks earlier. Grabbing my arm, he roughly confirmed the presence of a wrist-watch which had also been listed on the slip of paper. He was going to extremes in making sure that I hadn't been dabbling on the Havana black market.

Next he took out every piece of paper, including clippings from newspapers, an assortment of letters, and two or three telegrams from my newspaper in London, and, alas, a mimeographed copy of a despatch written weeks earlier by an American reporter and published in a newspaper in California. The soldier had obviously been looking for something incriminating, and I could tell by the grim expression on his face that he believed he had found it. I had brought the despatch merely for reference and I had never dreamed that it could be used against me, since it had been written so long ago and been published in the United States. But it did contain a reference to an anti-Castro organization of exiles in Florida, and that was enough for the soldier. He slowly read the despatch and then showed it to a woman dressed in rebel uniform who had been watching him deal with my belongings. They whispered together and then she took the clipping away to some office in the hinterland. The soldier waved me on to the next ritual of departure – changing remaining Cuban pesos into US dollars. I thought this would be the last act of a rather trying drama. I was wrong. Several snares, some crudely contrived, still lay in my path towards the waiting KLM airliner and freedom.

The first trap emerged while I was changing my money at a tiny kiosk in The Cage run by the National Bank of Cuba. The man ahead of me was one who had attracted my attention because he was obviously a North American and had been ostentatiously showing off a much-used travelling-bag of the kind issued free of charge by the bigger airlines. He had seemed to be intent on making sure that I knew he was not only a North American but a travelled one as well. He now appeared to be in some kind of difficulty. He was arguing in English and in loud tones with the clerk behind the grille. 'I'm a Canadian, and I've only spent seven pesos because I've been the guest of Cuban friends for a few days,' he said. This sounded a little odd. The clerk explained in a halting blend of Spanish and English that there was a regulation that every visitor must spend at least ten dollars a day while in Cuba. The Canadian professed not to comprehend and turned to look at me with a show of helplessness. I was about to obey an impulse to try to help him when I felt a strong nudge delivered by Betts into the small of my back. The message was plain: Don't.

I obeyed, and I believe it was just as well that I did so, for everything that happened afterwards indicated that the Canadian, if indeed he was one, was a *provocateur*. He was trying to get me involved in his dealings with the bank clerk, Betts suggested later, so that possibly I might be lured into revealing how I had spent my own money and, it could be, provide some evidence of having profited in currency dealings, a tempting field of activity, since the Cuban peso was selling at about one sixth of its artificial parity with the dollar. Charges of illegal dealing in currency had been used, of course, in the Soviet Union and elsewhere behind the Iron Curtain since 1945 to destroy the credibility of Western foreign correspondents, and in some instances to justify arrest and expulsion. Perhaps the Cubans, inexperienced amateurs as yet in such international manoeuvres, were trying to improve their skills through me.

This did not look at all far-fetched after we eventually joined the other passengers who had long ago completed all the formalities. I noticed that the Canadian was the only non-official person in The Cage allowed to go freely in and out of doors leading to rooms and small offices used by the military and civilian functionaries of the airport. Even more suspicious was the fact that he was also allowed to use an unusual camera he was carrying. This was a rare privilege in the Cuba of those days, and I had seen foreigners stopped and arrested for taking the most harmless of photographs. But the Canadian now overplayed his hand. He walked to a window of The Cage giving a view upon the airfield and he made as if to take a picture. I looked out in the direction in which the camera was supposed to be pointing and saw that there was just nothing to take there. I looked a little closer at the camera and, to my astonishment, saw that its shutter and lens were actually built into its side, not its front. The man was in fact taking photographs of Betts and me as we sat a few feet behind him. We pretended not to notice.

The Canadian's puerile antics were, however, followed a quarter of an hour later by something much more menacing. Two Cuban soldiers with rifles unslung clanked into The Cage and made for Betts and me. Tapping each of us on the shoulder, they motioned us to stand, pick up our brief-cases and packet of travel documents and go with them alongside the tarmac to a small cluster of buildings standing isolated a short distance from the main terminal block. I knew these buildings. I had been in them twice before, once to clarify a wrong entry made by a Cuban official on my passport and secondly to inquire what had happened to a British colleague who had not turned up when expected at the Hotel Libre. I had been told that he had landed but had been sent right back to Mexico City because his papers weren't in order. Maybe the Cubans knew something.

The buildings were the headquarters of the G2 Intelligence Unit at the airport, and being now taken under armed guard into them intensified my lurking fear that Betts and I simply were not going to be allowed to leave Cuba this evil day. As I marched along with my guard a pace behind me I reflected that I should have much preferred being thrown out of Cuba without further delay to what looked like being detained, and worse.

Betts was taken off into one small room and, apparently not being suspect, soon reappeared. We were not allowed to speak to each other before I was taken into the same small room. A Barbudo officer standing there told me to empty my attaché case. Out came letters, cables, keys, pencil, leaflets carrying proclamations by Fidel Castro – everything. The officer then went away, leaving me to watch a young militiawoman begin to separate the contents of the attaché case into two piles. She said not a word and never changed the blank expression on her unprepossessing face as she did so. I was interested while watching her to be able to overhear the news despatch previously taken from me being translated, slowly, into Spanish over a telephone in the next room. And I was equally interested to recognize the voice of the translator as being that of an official of KLM who had been most helpful to me when I checked in at the airport what now seemed days ago. The Intelligence Unit had apparently been forced to use him as a translator because it had nobody sufficiently fluent in English to do the job. This was evidence of the declining use of English in Cuba. Now that American and other holidaymakers were no longer coming into the country, there was only a straggle of professional visitors such as myself on whom to practise. Further, it was perhaps now considered that anybody using English was being untrue to the Castro revolution. Those élite Cubans to whom English had been a second language had long ago fled to Miami and beyond.

At last the translation was finished. A short conversation followed between the Dutchman and the officer who had taken away my papers. Moments later both came into the room where I was being held. The KLM man addressed me most formally in English. 'I am very sorry to tell you. . . .' I heard the words and leaped disconsolately to the worst conclusion – this was it, I was going to be arrested, and heaven knew when I would emerge again.

I was wrong.

' . . . that none of your documents will be allowed to leave Cuba.'

What nonsense was all this? I could scarcely believe my good fortune. None of the material mattered any more to me. There was surely nothing of any value in them either. They could keep them all, and good luck to them. I tried not to let my elation give me away. I had the wit to put on a show of annoyance and defeat. I pleaded with all the false earnestness I could muster, as an actor *manqué*, to be allowed some of the papers which the militiawoman had stacked up in two piles. 'No, not one,' said the rebel officer, severely, in Spanish. With what I hoped was a convincing shrug of frustration I picked up my little brief-case, now containing only my passport and travel documents. Inwardly, I glowed with a renewed hope that at last I should probably be allowed to depart.

I did have one worry. Inside the right-hand pocket of the light jacket I was wearing was the small notebook in which I had jotted down all the notes and reminders I needed for use when I came to write my story. Within its pages, in shorthand or in my own specialized abbreviations, were my notes of the facts about Soviet penetration of Cuba, and other significant items of information I had gathered in the last two weeks. Worse, it also contained some telephone numbers which might be incriminating to informants in Havana. My one hope was that this day's inquisition was over and that nobody would now want to examine that notebook. The hope was fortified when, to my astonishment, the Cuban officer held out his hand for me to shake. So Cuban politeness was surviving, after all. I took his hand, shook it, and gave him a smile. I thought he had earned one if he was preparing to release me.

As I was walking back to The Cage escorted by the KLM officer he began talking to me in low tones from one side of his mouth, without turning his head even slightly. 'British Embassy been on phone,' I heard him say. 'Worried about you. I'll phone them soon and tell them it looks now as if you're going to get away.' I nodded.

Alas, we were reassuring ourselves too soon.

Names were being called for waiting passengers to leave The Cage for the KLM plane when a militiaman strode up to Betts and me as we waited in line and motioned to us to follow him, back to the G2 complex. We did so under the burning sun, and the splendid KLM officer fell in step beside me. What a magnificent friend in need he was proving! Again he spoke words of hope: 'They say it will be only for a few minutes. . . . We're holding the plane for you.'

Betts was taken off once again into a small room and I was left in the custody of a black militiaman who lounged back in a tilted chair, at his ease and with his gaze fixed on me, watching my every movement. Obviously this was not a moment for me to put a hand into my jacket pocket and take out the precious notebook; he would almost certainly relieve me of it and attention would have been unnecessarily directed towards it. What could I do to ease the tension that enveloped me? I observed a telephone on a table beside the black soldier, and the sight gave me an idea. Perhaps I could telephone the British Embassy. I pointed to the instrument and asked the man if I could use it. Without opening his mouth or changing his comfortable posture on the tilted chair he shook his head. So I had to wait, defeated, until Betts came back into the room. He looked somewhat shaken. 'They searched me from tip to toe,' he said. It was now my turn. I had no doubt that the searcher would find the notebook, and my fate thereafter would certainly be detention. I looked hopelessly at Betts and went on command into the room he had just left. A waiting militiaman motioned to me to take off my jacket. Once again it was a wordless order. I had to presume that these low-ranking soldiers were under orders not to say anything to us in case a conversation was started in which they might give something away. The militiaman took the jacket and methodically emptied its pockets. Out came the notebook. He laid it on the table with everything else and held the jacket up to the light. Finding no secret seams, he felt the lining. Again finding nothing, he moved towards me and proceeded to search me, running his hands lightly but efficiently down my sides, across my chest, down to my shoes. I sensed, however, that he was in a hurry, probably on account of the waiting aircraft, because I had heard from Cubans and Americans who had been similarly searched that the routine had included the removal of their shoes, which were then searched.

He now stuffed everything back into the pockets of my jacket – everything, that is to say, except the notebook. This he picked up and began flipping the pages, and then an unbelievable fluke happened. He was holding it, by chance, from back to front. I had filled only about three-quarters of one side of its pages. The result was that when he flipped the pages rapidly he exposed only the blank sides! I could scarcely believe my good fortune. My hands trembled as he gave it back to me, still saying not a word. I stuffed the notebook back into my jacket pocket. It was then that I saw he was holding out his hand to me. Again that unexpected politeness. A vision flashed into my mind of a drawing I had once seen in a book of English history showing an executioner kneeling humbly before his victim (Sir Thomas More, I was to be reminded, years later), begging forgiveness for having to chop off his head. The legend under the drawing ran roughly like this: *I forgive you with all my heart. You do but fulfil your office.* So it was with me and the militiaman. He had but fulfilled his office, after all. I grasped his outstretched hand and shook it warmly. I was really thanking him, wordlessly, for the almost incredible escape he had unwittingly allowed me.

Now, at last, they had finished with me. Whatever they had hoped to achieve, they had failed in their objective. The KLM officer, watchful to the end, was waiting to escort Betts and me to the aircraft waiting on the tarmac. It was my turn to talk through the side of the mouth. 'Please tell the British Embassy we were searched and all my papers were confiscated, but we weren't arrested,' I muttered. 'Damned scary. . . . Don't phone until we've taken off. Thanks for all you've done. Deeply grateful.' He nodded in acknowledgement, and we both smiled for the first time since we had met hours earlier.

Robert Betts and I boarded the aircraft. It was full except for the two seats which had been kept for us at the front. The Canadian pseudo-tourist was sitting one row behind us, tailing us to the bitter end. I didn't care about that. But I did feel an urge to vent my contempt for him, incompetent sneak that he was. 'I'd just like to punch him in the face,' I said to Betts. Once again he was the sensible counsellor. 'It wouldn't help,' he said. Simmering, I sank back into my comfortable seat.

We took off and I watched the hot little island passing below. A steward came along holding a tray. I stretched out my hand for the most delectable rum and tonic I have ever enjoyed. As I sipped it I felt that I never wanted to see Cuba again until her damned revolution had run its course. But I knew I should be back before that happened.

Meanwhile, there was my story to write. I laid across my knees my little old typewriter, which KLM had been guarding for me, and began to tap away.

I did enjoy some unexpected professional recompense for the rigours I had had to endure. On reaching Jamaica and telephoning my office in New York I was told that Emmanuel Freedman, Foreign Editor of *The New York Times*, was asking if I would write them a comprehensive story of what I had learned and found during the past fortnight. So, after writing and cabling a long despatch for my own newspaper, I settled down and produced another one of some fifteen hundred words for *The New York Times*. That admirable, and insatiable, newspaper flattered me by asking for more. I spent a morning in my apartment in East 79th Street producing several hundred more words. The entire piece was given an impressive display on the front page next day and was then distributed across the United States and in several other countries via *The New York Times* News Service.

I was mystified for some time after I had returned to New York, trying to account for the unwelcome attentions which Cuban intelligence had lavished on me during my hectic visit to Havana. Eventually I worked out the outlines of a possible explanation. I could prove nothing, of course, because basic essentials to successful intelligence operations are: (1) never give anything away, and (2) cover your tracks so that nobody can know that you have been anywhere, done anything or said anything. I was forced to consider several variants of a theme.

It would appear that by some means or from some source G2 in Havana learned that I might be 'an enemy of the revolution', a British spy or a journalist who hadn't swallowed Fidel Castro and his revolution whole. Various channels existed for the transmission of information about me to Havana. A Castro agent operating in either New York or Cuba herself was one obvious channel. Another was the Cuban Mission to the United States and Prensa Latina, the official Cuban news agency, which worked within the Mission. Somebody connected with either could have read articles I wrote for my own newspaper or *The New Republic*, *The New York Times*, *The Economist*, or other publications in the United States and Britain. Or he might have heard some of the lectures I gave in the United States or broadcasts I made for the American Broadcasting Company, the Columbia Broadcasting System, and the national public broadcasting system (Channel 13) in New York, Boston and elsewhere. Whatever the source, I must assume that my name was added to the list of foreigners who had to be watched. When I went to Cuba during the delicate period in which Khrushchev was putting his missiles in place in Cuba, the intelligence machine would naturally do everything it could to obstruct me and, if possible, obtain some evidence to justify arresting me. Perhaps Michael

Brown, of the British Embassy, knew more about this than he could indicate when he warned me to be careful while in Havana and to realize that I was going to be watched and shadowed wherever I went.

The actual operations of G2 were, as I have related, amateurish and inefficient – these characteristics were, of course, applicable in the early 1960s both to Fidel Castro and his whole apparatus – but it must be conceded that they were a worry and a hindrance to me, and they probably stopped me from finding out anything about the Soviet missiles. To that extent, they succeeded.

Finally, I now realize that several times I came perilously close to falling into the revolution's clutches during that September visit. One error, a false or foolish move, or an illegal act, could have done me in. I also understand now why, as I learned much later, my wife persuaded my newspaper to take out a special insurance policy covering me and my life while I was in Havana on this particular assignment.

I was by no means alone in failing to uncover the stratagem of Nikita Khrushchev in arranging to aim missiles, at extremely short range, at the United States mainland. Years later it became known that nobody in the Western world was aware of the installation of missiles in a comparatively remote part of Cuba until Oleg Penkovsky, one of the most celebrated of pro-Western 'moles', alerted Washington to the fact. Penkovsky was a scientist and technical expert working for Soviet intelligence in Moscow, and his feat in getting out the information was outstanding. He had not been wholly trusted in the past by American and British counter-intelligence offices, but his accurate tip on the missiles established his credibility beyond any doubt. It also cost him his life. Some months after the so-called 'Missile Crisis' had passed, he was arrested and shot.

5

Ernesto Guevara, Transient Star

Ernesto Guevara (better known as 'Che', meaning 'buddy' or 'mate'), the Argentinian crusader who in the 1960s was an inspiration to Cuban revolutionaries and other left-wingers across the world, was in many aspects of temperament, behaviour and beliefs the very opposite of the man he served, Fidel Castro. He was a shy man who never enjoyed, much less sought, the limelight. He was a dedicated Communist with a deep hatred of what he believed the United States to be – a heartless, all-devouring, capitalistic monster. Whereas Fidel Castro was, in the early days of the Cuban revolution at any rate, like a modern Robin Hood devoted to delivering his country from her bondage, as he saw it, as the exploited handmaiden of the United States, Che Guevara had the much wider goal of ultimately imposing communism on the whole world. This difference leads me to conclude that in any moderated political climate an accommodation between Castro and the United States was and still is possible. Not so with Guevara. The only circumstance in which he would ever have co-operated in such an accommodation would have been in the scarcely believable event of the United States becoming a Communist, or a near-Communist, country. To him, until that happened, the United States was to be opposed and cut down in stature by any and every means because it was the one big obstacle to the expansion of communism. He attached himself to Fidel Castro's political movement from its very early days in Mexico and the mountains of Cuba because he saw it as a timely instrument to be used in the effort to achieve the fulfilment of a universal purpose. So far as anybody can possibly know, for Fidel Castro has given only teasing and evasive answers when pressed about it, this difference between the political aims of the two men was eventually to lead to Guevara's severance from the Cuban revolution and to his early death.

I first set eyes on him in Havana early in January 1959, when he arrived there a day or two before Fidel Castro, charged with the task of controlling a chaotic situation which had developed in the wake of Batista's hasty and unexpected flight from the city. He quickly succeeded. He looked very much the romantic adventurer that day, with his long black locks streaming around his shoulders, a mocking smile on his small handsome face, and one arm in a black silken scarf because of an injury sustained a week or two earlier in the Sierra Maestra, as he clutched the side of a Jeep weaving a fast passage along the Malecon. A vast crowd of noisy, excited

Cubans lined the thoroughfare. I could well understand as I watched his progress why they should howl their delight at the sight of this handsome young warrior come to prepare a smooth entry into the capital for their ultimate idol, Fidel Castro.

Guevara's path and mine had actually converged four years earlier. Guevara was in the entourage of Jacob Arbentz, the near-Communist President of Guatemala. Guevara, though scarcely out of his teens or perhaps because of that, was already a burning revolutionary and Arbentz, as a beleaguered left-winger in the American backyard, was an irresistible magnet to the young Argentine medical student. The United States was boldly and flagrantly fomenting and paying for an 'insurrection' prepared in neighbouring Honduras and mounted for the precise purpose of ridding Central America of its sole revolutionary threat. The man on the spot for the United States was her flamboyant Ambassador to Guatemala, John Puerifoy, who went about his business with a pearl-handled revolver strapped round his middle.

I was on the opposite side to Che Guevara. Sensing that the most promising story lay with the invading forces under Colonel Castillo Armas, I joined his ragged host, advancing upon Guatemala City from the north-east, by riding a mule all one night over the mountains separating Guatemala from Honduras. This was an experience not to be forgotten or to be recommended except to the most hardy globe-trotter. Ending my trip to the front in a more orthodox but still uncomfortable fashion, I travelled in a military truck standing jammed in among about a score of Castillo's conscripts. I'm afraid I developed a poor opinion of their potential fighting qualities, for many of them were vomiting and wailing as we swayed along. It might have been travel sickness, but I doubt it.

As events developed, there was no fighting worth the name. Arbentz's troops melted away before battle was joined and Guevara had to flee. He made his way to Mexico, where as it happened Fidel Castro was planning the expedition which took him and a handful of supporters (including Guevara) by sea to Cuba – and eventual triumph. So I never met Guevara at that time.

Soon after I saw him riding along the Malecon in 1959, he pitched into his task of restoring order in Havana and then, after Castro's Caesar-like entry, of consolidating the revolution, which was badly in need of pulling together. He did all this without fuss and with conspicuous effectiveness. He also gave every evidence of enjoying himself. He was ever cheerful and smiling in between puffs at a cigar whenever I saw him. I never heard him utter one word of criticism of his boss, who was paying no attention whatever to his responsibilities but was having a marvellous time roaming Havana by day and night, making extravagant promises to his people which could not possibly be fulfilled, and every few days finding a convenient platform to harangue hundreds of thousands of doting Cubans (and a few sceptical foreign reporters). I still do not understand how

Cubans swallowed it all. I became sick of listening to his ranting and eventually gave up paying him any heed. But I was not Cuban and I suppose I was consequently immune to his Hitler-like spellbinding.

Guevara imposed his fey individuality on every job he undertook in the months after the capture of Havana. In so doing, he advanced easily and unchallenged into the *de facto* position of deputy to Fidel Castro as he accomplished one feat after another and moved from post to post to fill a gap caused by an impulsive Castro dismissal, a defection, or even an execution for alleged treachery. He had no competition from the one who ought to have become Fidel Castro's right-hand man (or, perhaps one should say in all the circumstances, left-hand man) – Raul Castro. Few had any liking for this sneering, uncouth young man. I met him only once and was immediately repelled by him.

The most important official post occupied by Guevara was that of President of the National Bank of Cuba. He took on the job when Dr Felipo Pazos, a banking administrator highly respected internationally, resigned after having had enough of the irresponsible antics of the Maximum Leader. Guevara had had no training as a banker, but, as he showed, he certainly had a head for figures. I talked with him one day in his office at the imposing headquarters of the National Bank and was amused to see him sitting comfortably with his feet crossed on top of his big desk. Sporting his usual well-trimmed beard, he was smoking a cigar and wearing his equally usual loose-fitting and crumpled green Army fatigues. He hardly looked the part of a banker controlling a country's finances, I thought. Probably he adopted both garb and attitude to show his communistic contempt for orthodox, proper bankers of the Western world. He certainly treated the Cuban currency flippantly. When he signed the prototype for an issue of pesos under his authority he simply scribbled down his nickname, 'Che'. Several of these unique banknotes passed through my hands, but short-sightedly I did not keep one as a souvenir. They are scarce now and, presumably, valuable.

Guevara's loyalty to his chief was obvious, and I always felt there was complete trust between them until their sudden and mysterious parting in 1965. I recall one hilarious example of their close relationship. In the early 1960s I attended a mass meeting at which Fidel Castro was supposed to outline in a speech, which was being televised, the economic goals of the revolution during the coming twelve months. He made an appalling botch of the task. He was holding a sheet of paper on which were written all the facts and figures he would need. Either he had not read them beforehand or they just hadn't registered on his unmathematical brain. As he floundered on, misquoting and stumbling over the data on the sheet of paper, I saw Guevara, who was sitting immediately behind him, holding his head in his hands and gesticulating in mock horror. Castro soon surrendered. With a theatrical flourish he turned towards Guevara and, amid a gust of laughter from the people sitting with them on the platform, thrust the paper at Guevara and said: 'Hey, Che. You do it.' Laughingly, Guevara took the paper and went across to the microphone. He explained the figures and calculations succinctly and understandably, and when he finished to affectionate applause he handed the microphone back to his chief and quietly went back to his seat in the second row.

Many observers of the Latin-American scene, myself included, feel that if Guevara had survived he might very well have become a much more effective figure in the affairs of that region than Fidel Castro. Latin America as a whole is one of the most turbulent areas of the world. Its political and social aspects are constantly changing, at a much faster pace and in more volatile fashion than is happening elsewhere, but this fact is obscured for long periods because terrorism, strife between its component republics, and bloodshed as a whole, are not so rampant or spectacular as in, say, the Middle East. During the 1980s there was, however, a steady shift leftwards in such countries as El Salvador and Nicaragua, and the domination of dictators and established right-wing elements in Mexico, Chile, Uruguay and Argentina weakened perceptibly. There would have been many fields of activity from which Guevara would have been able to choose. He would have had ample scope to prosecute his mission of promoting communism and anti-Americanism.

I first felt the full impact of his charisma, his self-control and his understanding of international affairs on the memorable afternoon of 11 December 1964, at a session of the General Assembly of the United Nations in New York. The contrast between the Guevara of that afternoon and the Guevara whom I had last seen less than two years earlier was astonishing. In early 1963 he attended a garden party in the grounds of the still elegant Zarragozana Restaurant in a suburb of Havana a day or two after he had returned from a visit to Moscow to see Nikita Khrushchev. That day he had shocked me by the deterioration in his physical (and sartorial) appearance since his entry into Havana in 1959 and during his service as head of the National Bank of Cuba. He was overweight, his natural gaiety had deserted him, his beard and hair were untrimmed and he was wearing dirty, creased and ill-fitting tunic and trousers. He reminded me more of a reincarnation of Rasputin than the Lochinvar who had so impressed me earlier. In New York in December 1964 he showed that in the interval he had developed into a poised world statesman. He had lost his excess weight of 1963, and he was well laundered and well dressed. To be sure, the earlier youthful ebullience had gone and had been replaced by a more sober mein, which was of course appropriate for the occasion, since he was deputizing for Fidel Castro and presenting the revolutionary regime's statement of policy for the coming year. He looked most convincing as he stood on the speakers' rostrum beneath a marbled dais where sat that year's president of the Assembly. Appropriately for the speech of crusading Ernesto Guevara the president was Alex Quaison-Sackey of Ghana, the first black ever to hold that post.

In polished phrases, the Spanish-speaking delegates listening directly to his voice while the rest of the Assembly heard him in one of three simultaneous translations, Guevara recited a series of complaints about the evil acts he claimed the United States was committing against Cuba, Latin America and elsewhere. I wondered if when compiling the speech Guevara might have sat with a map of the world at his elbow and picked out all the countries and regions which could conceivably be considered vulnerable to American machinations. It must be clearly understood (he said) that in the Caribbean preparations for aggression against Cuba were happening, above all off the coast of Nicaragua. In South-East Asia millions of human beings were threatened and subject to the whim of the United States. Cambodia was suffering brutal attacks from Yankee bases in South Vietnam. Laos was another target of imperialists. American warmongers were out to extend the war in Vietnam by attacking North Vietnam. He extended greetings to suffering non-whites of Rhodesia and South Africa and to the Arabs of Palestine. The Puerto Rican people, seeking independence, had been used by the United States as cannon-fodder in imperialist wars such as Korea.

So it went on for almost two hours. Although the accusations were harsh, the manner in which they were spoken was mild and mocking, as if Guevara knew he was playing the diplomatic game – something which wasn't altogether real but was to be enjoyed while it lasted. Perhaps he found solace in it, for he well knew already, young though he still was at thirty-six, that life had its pains; he had been plagued since boyhood by chronic asthma, which often laid him low for days on end. Considering him now at a range of a quarter-century, I wonder if maybe he also sensed then that life was not going to last as long for him as it did for most people.

He was about half-way through his speech when there came an un-canny interruption. A loud thump sounded from somewhere very close, perhaps just outside the building. The Assembly chamber shook. Delegates exchanged startled glances, and some rose from their seats, looking inquiringly about them. Guevara, the experienced guerrilla warrior, hardly paused in his delivery. He had heard thumps like this before, and he had caused quite a few of his own. Since this one had not created visible damage or hurt, it could be ignored, even though it was almost certainly hostile to him.

After he had finished, to vociferous applause from the delegates representing Cuba's friends and allies, including all the captive sheep in the Soviet fold, and to the polite plaudits of the rest, he shook hands with Quaison-Sackey and strode out of the Chamber. I followed suit, to try to identify the source of the thump. United Nations officers had found some surprising facts. Persons unknown had fired a bazooka, or mortar, shell at the UN building from a spot on the opposite bank of the East River 2,700 feet away. It had fallen several yards short of its target, but near enough to shake the building and do some trifling damage. A small Cuban flag had been found tied to the barrel of the mortar gun to provide a pointed clue to the identity of the perpetrators.

I then found out that, confirming the origins of the unusual 'attack', there had been a melodramatic demonstration on the Manhattan side of the UN building. As the bazooka shell exploded, scores of anti-Castro Cubans, who had been penned behind police barriers across the street outside the main entrance to the UN, began shouting anti-revolutionary slogans and hoisting placards bearing such words as *Quevara – carnichero* (Guevara – butcher). This was simple libel. Unlike the unpleasant Raul Castro and, to lesser degree, Fidel Castro, Guevara had never demonstrated any taste for blood-letting. He had killed in the heat of combat, without a doubt, but in all the years I watched him and in the revolution I never heard one word to suggest that he had killed in cold blood or ordered any killing.

As the demonstration began, a young woman wearing tight-fitting coloured trousers and brandishing a nasty-looking knife with a blade more than six inches long detached herself from a crocodile of fellow-demonstrators and made a dash for the UN entrance. She never got there, being brought down none too gently by UN guards, who descended upon her as she ran. She was still shrieking 'I want to kill Che Guevara' as she was handed over to New York City policemen and escorted away, the excited demonstrators shouting insults and epithets after them. It was all very Cuban, I thought – spectacular, ill-planned and a profitless failure. The would-be Charlotte Corday was identified as Molly Gonzales, who had fled Cuba and resettled in New Jersey. She had this one glorious moment in the limelight and thereafter was never heard of again.

Guevara reacted suavely when told of the background to the thump. As he stood relaxing in the Delegates Lounge with some friends I heard him say, approximately: 'Maybe it would be better to be killed by a woman with a knife than a man with a gun.' It was a characteristic wry remark, and it was an eerie one in view of what was to befall him less than two years hence. After his break with Fidel Castro he went on a badly organized, hopeless revolutionary crusade in Bolivia. It never got anywhere. Half crippled by wounds and worn down by untreated asthma, he was captured by soldiers of the Bolivian Army who had routed the remnants of his tiny revolutionary company and he was summarily executed by a soldier with a tommy-gun.

On 8 October 1967 his body was tied to the undercarriage of a helicopter and carried off into oblivion. It was a pitiful end for a man who, if he had had better luck, could have become a powerful reformist leader in Latin America. As he had said at the UN, the butcher's knife of Molly Gonzales might have been preferable to a tommy-gun.

6

Monty: Outfoxing the Fox

On 23 October 1942, at 9 a.m. precisely, Lt-General Bernard Montgomery, only three months into his pivotal new job as Commander of the British Eighth Army, strode into a large marquee near the battered old railway station of El Alamein. Watched by many curious eyes, he sat down behind a long low table to face an audience of some sixty officers and war correspondents whom he had summoned 'to put you into the picture', as his spokesman had said, about the all-out attack he had prepared on the German Afrika Korps and its supporting German and Italian units, under the command of the redoubtable and so far victorious General Erwin Rommel, the Desert Fox.

This was the first time I had ever seen Montgomery, having reached El Alamein only the night before. There he sat a yard or two in front of me, a black beret covering his small head, a grey pullover over an obviously trim figure, the slender hands clasped as they rested on the table. He looks like a cross between a hawk and a cock sparrow, I remember thinking. The beaky nose, the narrow, tightly drawn mouth, and the cold blue eyes, were suggestively hawklike. The likeness to a predator was softened by the jaunty set of the head – sparrowlike. I now realize that an equally appropriate assessment of him would have been to liken him to his adversary – Rommel, the Fox.

Beside him sat Air Marshal Sir Arthur Coningham, commanding officer of the Desert Air Force, younger, conventionally handsome, whom one had hardly noticed, so compelling was Montgomery's presence. Coningham was theoretically Montgomery's equal partner, but he was eclipsed from the start of their association in the desert. There was no doubt about who was the lead player – also the comedian, perhaps – and who was the straight man. But there were sceptics in the audience who had yet to be convinced of Montgomery's abilities – desert-hardened officers and correspondents like Christopher Buckley, of the *Daily Telegraph*, and Ronald Monson, a brave and talented Australian correspondent who had been mentioned in despatches for gallantry under fire. These two had been reporting from the desert for the past eighteen months and to them Montgomery was as yet just another of those British generals who had come to North Africa to lead the Eighth Army (often helter-skelter backwards) and had stayed awhile until humbled by Rommel, and had then gone away.

Very soon after taking command of the Eighth Army in August 1942, Montgomery had gathered a highly controversial reputation in Cairo. He had used unexpected methods in his first task of reorganizing the Army and restoring its sagging morale. With Rommel little more than a hundred miles north-east of Cairo and clearly getting ready to make a final decisive push, there were not many optimists in all three British services in the Middle East. Montgomery was not daunted. He lectured officers and men about their need to be physically fit, their duty to obey orders strictly, and he decreed that in future there must be 'no bellyaching' (his favourite term for complaining). He decreed that nobody should smoke while with him, and he let it be known that, as a teetotaller, he frowned upon anything more than a minimal consumption of alcohol by anybody else. Some officers scoffed at him in private to me and others as a 'crackpot'.

Within little more than a month, however, he began to gain respect. Early in September Rommel made a speculative attack, showing his usual boldness, with the idea of finding a hole in the British defences through which he could thrust tanks and motorized infantry, which would drive on to Suez and thereby destroy the entire British position in North Africa. The resulting battle had lasted only four days and ended with Rommel having to turn tail and go back whence he had come, minus substantial losses in men and material. The encounter, known as the Battle of Alam Halfa, had aroused cautious admiration for the new 'crackpot' British general and had worked wonders for Eighth Army morale. It showed that Rommel *could* be beaten.

So it was not surprising that people who had not yet got to know Montgomery should be curious about him when he made his first public appearance of any importance on 23 October. His opening words, spoken briskly but with a suspicion of a lisp, as his keen gaze roved round his audience, confirmed that here was somebody very different from those who had come and gone before him. They were the words of an individualist who would not easily be diverted from his purpose. 'Gentlemen,' he said, looking at the correspondents seated in front of him, 'the battle starts tonight.' He paused. Then, through a tight mouth: 'During the moonlight a big battle will be fought. You may go where you want. See all you want. Talk to anybody you want.' Then he went back to Alam Halfa like, I thought, a schoolmaster summarizing history. 'When Rommel came into the Eighth Army area he had to be pushed back. He *was* pushed back.' He now became even more schoolmasterish in briefly surveying the whole campaign. 'It has been very discouraging to the troops, you know – this succession of advances and retreats. All they want now is success.' Another pause. Then: 'They are quite first class. Properly led, the soldiery will never let you down.'

I was too surprised to smile at this odd use of an old-fashioned term I hadn't heard spoken for years. I recall thinking as I took down those last nine words in shorthand: Where on earth did they get this chap from?

Soldiery! My mind flitted back to my schooldays. Memory stirred. Hadn't somebody in British history said or written something about the 'brutal and licentious soldiery'? It was Edmund Burke, a fiery Irish politician. He was describing the behaviour of British troops almost two hundred years ago in his native country. Montgomery obviously had a far higher opinion of the British Tommy than had Mr Burke.

Montgomery finished his racy discourse by forecasting in cricketing jargon the end of the battle not yet started. 'We're going to knock Rommel right out of the ground,' he said. 'We're going to knock him for six. Right out of North Africa he's going.'

We were still digesting those tough, cocky words as he turned to Air Marshal Coningham, sitting on his right, and invited him to say something for the Air Force. Coningham wisely didn't try to match Montgomery's performance. He confined himself to very few words. 'I've visited every unit in my command and explained to them what is expected of them,' he said. 'They're all ready.' He and Montgomery got up and walked out of the tent as we in the audience stood respectfully and waited until they were gone.

I joined the file following Montgomery and Coningham out of the tent and as I did so was handed a copy of Montgomery's personal message to his officers and men. It was in the same pungent, staccato style he had just been using. It began:

'1. When I assumed command of the Eighth Army I said that the mandate was to destroy ROMMEL and his Army, and that it would be done as soon as we were ready.

2. We are ready NOW.

The battle which is now about to begin will be one of the decisive battles of history. It will be the turning point of the war. The eyes of the whole world will be on us, watching anxiously which way the battle will swing.

We can give them their answer at once. "It will swing our way."'

What was one to make of this emphatic man? I pondered the question as I walked back to my typewriter to write an account of what I had just seen and heard. Of one thing I was immediately sure. The Eighth Army – the Desert Rats – had at last found a real leader. Crackpot he might well be in some respects, but he was clearly a dedicated and wholly professional soldier as well. He had been able to talk freely at all the briefings he had conducted because he had turned all the territory under his control into a sealed prison. For forty-eight hours before the start of the battle, at 9.30 p.m., nobody was allowed to leave it. And I learned as I was writing my despatch that he had given orders that soldiers due to go on patrol in no man's land separating the two armies on the eve of battle were not to be told that it was to start on 23 October because they might be captured and under questioning give away the fact to the enemy.

I had a firm conviction after I had watched and listened to him that he would succeed in 'knocking Rommel for six' out of the ground. It was the same unusual conviction I had had ever since September 1939 that, no matter what happened during the war, we were certain to win it. This was a conviction shared, I found, by almost all the British people I met between 1939 and 1945. I do not know whether these feelings of certainty about victory were just blind foolhardiness or whether they were based on something much more mysterious, perhaps a deep feeling within the British character that right *must* always prevail eventually.

Montgomery did fulfil his boast about knocking out Rommel, as I was to learn at first hand in the desert during the next gruelling, dangerous but exhilarating nine days. Years later, when everybody closely concerned was publishing his memories of the battle, it emerged that at least twice while it was being fought Montgomery's subordinates almost lost it for him, and it was due solely to his firmness in imposing his will upon them that he gained the victory.

He knew he had won when next I saw him. On the morning of 5 November, a day after Rommel's army had begun to disintegrate and was scurrying westwards to save the pieces, Montgomery sent a message to the few correspondents within close range of what he called 'my office', in reality a roomy caravan pitched close to the sea behind the northern sector of the line manned by the 9th Australian Division, that he would like to see us because he had 'something interesting' to tell us.

We made a ragged group as, dressed in crumpled khaki shirts and shorts and most of us needing a haircut and a bath, we awaited him. Despite our unkempt appearance we were all glowing within because, after three years of having to record one setback and loss after another, we had at last a sensational victory to describe. We were in receptive mood when we saw him emerge from his caravan and walk towards us, looking as relaxed as if he were merely taking a post-breakfast stroll in the sunshine. He was about as casually dressed as we were, but, as I noted enviously, his clothes were clean and well laundered. He wore a light, loose-fitting pullover over his shirt, but he was without a cap on his head.

After greeting us, he tucked his thumbs into trouser pockets and stood facing us with his craggy face tilted cockily upwards. He wasted no time in pitching in, dramatically, with his promised news. 'Well, gentlemen,' he said breezily, 'I captured von Thoma a couple of days ago.' The startling words momentarily evoked a farcical picture of him, advancing with pistol upon a cowering General von Thoma and grabbing this illustrious victim – Commander of the Afrika Korps and outranked only by Rommel – by the scruff of the neck and yanking him off to the nearest prisoner cage to join the other Germans incarcerated there. The facts were that von Thoma had been captured when British troops came upon him as he stood helpless alongside a truck which had been hit and stopped during a short but violent encounter less than an hour earlier.

This was vintage Montgomery. He displayed arrogant bombast backed by enough logic to give it something like credence. Since he was ultimately responsible for everything, for good or ill, that happened on his territory in the desert, he could argue that he should assuredly take credit for the nabbing of the highest ranking officer opposing him in the field, even though his soldiery had done the job for him.

'I've just come from having breakfast with him,' he went on. 'We went through the battle again. We traced the action on the table-cloth. It very rarely happens for a general to capture an opponent like this.' He halted, to let the magnitude of the rare feat sink in. 'I told him a few things he didn't know.'

One fact he did not tell us that morning was that he had tried without success to hoodwink von Thoma into giving him a hint about Rommel's likely moves in his retreat.

My account of this session with Montgomery which appeared in the *Daily Mail* was illustrated by a photograph of General von Thoma walking away from his talk with Montgomery. He looked very much the professional soldier, a tall, slender figure striding out purposefully and with his dignity unimpaired by defeat. His features were deeply seamed by long exposure to sun and sand, and by obvious fatigue. The eyes were sunken. He was a German one could respect. He was a man of few words but cool judgement. Years after the war he was quoted in an Australian book (*Tobruk and El Alamein* by Barton Maughan) as having said of Montgomery: 'I thought he was very cautious considering his immensely superior strength. But he was the only Field-Marshal in that war who won all his battles.'

Before he left us that November morning in 1942 Montgomery gave us his own version of how he had won the victory. It showed that he had decided – for the rest of his life, as it turned out – that he was not going to admit that any hitch of any kind had marred the smooth fulfilment of his 'Master Plan', as he called it. 'The night before last we finally drove two hard wedges into the enemy line,' he said. 'I passed three armoured divisions right through this place and they are operating in the enemy's rear area.' There it was – a nice clean incision which had split Rommel's army into two and had led to the headlong retreat which was now going on.

Not for many years did Montgomery say anything about his troubles with rebellious or reluctant field commanders who wouldn't do as they had been ordered or about appalling confusion for a while at the point of breakthrough. Only when his memoirs were published in 1958 did he disclose that he had had to be awakened at 2.30 a.m. on Sunday, 25 October to deal with a crisis caused when some of his senior field commanders wanted to call off the whole assault, and his account of this episode was so self-inflating that one of the officers concerned, Major-General Gatehouse, threatened to take legal action against him. Montgomery could afford to have been more expansive about his troubles because, as most military analysts concede, his determination and speed in meeting such crises and the alacrity with which he changed the point of attack just before the breakthrough were the stuff of victory. After studying him and his career closely, I suggest that an extraordinary streak of petty meanness and a permanent excess of vanity were the most damaging flaws in Montgomery's make-up. Yet I, for one, never lost my faith in him. How could I possibly do so? As von Thoma observed, he never lost a battle over which he had personal control; and he took me on a trail in which I never had to retreat – in the desert, to Naples, Cassino, Rome, Brussels, Amsterdam, and the ultimate goal of Berlin.

Montgomery was never allowed, even if he had wished, to disclose that while fighting Rommel he had the use of one fantastic, decisive weapon. This was the code-breaker later named 'Ultra', a process whereby every signal which passed between Rommel and Hitler was intercepted by British cryptologists and, many times, was being read by Montgomery before it reached its destination. He died in 1975, some years before the ban on any mention of Ultra was lifted. From what I knew of him, I think it safe to say that he did not lose any sleep on the enforced secrecy about Ultra while he was fighting the Germans. Or when he was writing his memoirs. But for the secrecy ban, these would have been rather different from those published in 1958. They would have been far less impressive from his point of view. Further, the lustre of his reputation might have been dulled, which I am sure would have troubled him considerably.

The existence of the code-breaker was known in the desert only to him and two high-ranking officers on his staff, the minimum necessary to ensure continuity in its use. It was not revealed even to the Americans until May 1943, and it was never made known officially to the Soviets. They had to wait until its existence was universally disclosed. When talking or writing to Franklin D. Roosevelt and giving him the benefit of Ultra intelligence Winston Churchill referred to it as 'my secret source'. Even with its priceless help the Allies took five years to destroy Hitler. Suppose they had not had it? How long would victory then have eluded them? Ten years? For ever?

Ultra was the fruit of an amazing feat of code-breaking by a group of mathematicians working at Bletchley Park, Buckinghamshire, and headed by an eccentric homosexual named Alan Turing. It became available to the British military services as from 1941 and was in full use by mid-1942, just in time to help Montgomery at the Battles of Alam Halfa and Alamein. The Germans never guessed that their 'unbreakable' code machine, Enigma, had been penetrated. This was the most astonishing fact I ever learned concerning the Second World War.

I have always counted myself lucky that I could not be assigned to cover an operation which, because of its costly total failure, created the only blot on Montgomery's military record. It was not an operation which he personally commanded but it was one which he devised and superintended from afar. This was the disaster at Arnhem, Holland, in 1944, which took place at a time when I was in Italy, plodding a wet and weary way north of Rome with the American Fifth Army under General Mark Clark, a controversial soldier who was later to be absolved after an inquiry into his direction of an abortive assault over the Rapido river, south of Cassino, which cost the lives of many members of the Texas Rangers division of the Fifth Army. But I was peripherally concerned because it emerged that the carnage and failure at Arnhem would not have happened if Montgomery and his field commander, Lt-General F.A.M. ('Boy') Browning, had heeded the anguished warnings of my friend Brian Urquhart, then serving as Chief Intelligence Officer of the British Airborne Corps based on the well-known golf course at Moor Park, outside London, and later to give long, devoted and brilliant service to the United Nations in New York.

Montgomery had been stung by criticism of his slowness in capturing Caen and breaking out of the Cherbourg bridgehead while American generals such as Patton (who loathed Montgomery) were surging eastwards towards Paris and the German frontier. Wounded pride played its part in Montgomery's acceptance of an ill-conceived plan to land British paratroopers behind the retreating Germans and thereby shorten the war by a masterly stroke. The operation, called Market Garden, failed dismally, with the loss of over 17,000 British troops in killed, wounded and missing, and over 3,000 German casualties.

Urquhart related that he became so disturbed during the planning at the big odds against Market Garden succeeding that he arranged for reconnaissance photographs to be taken to confirm or disprove his fears. The reconnaissance photographs were taken at a low angle over the proposed landing zone by a plane 'smuggled', for security reasons, into a formation of Allied bombers making a raid on the Ruhr from Benson aerodrome, Oxfordshire. When developed and minutely scrutinized, the photographs revealed the horrifying fact that two German Panzer divisions, the 9th and 10th, were refitting at Arnhem after having been mauled in recent fighting. Their tanks were identified sitting parked beneath trees close to the main dropping zone chosen for Market Garden paratroopers. Urquhart rushed with five of the most revealing photographs to General Browning, only, as he wrote 'to be treated once again as a nervous child suffering from a nightmare'. Worse, Montgomery at his headquarters in Brussels uncharacteristically pooh-poohed the idea of postponing the operation, saying that he wasn't at all worried about the mauled German armour. Urquhart was told that he was suffering from acute nervous strain and exhaustion and he was ordered to go on sick-leave. On being told that if he refused he would be arrested and court-martialled for disobeying orders he went to Amberley, Sussex, where his wife was expecting their first child.

When I discussed the episode with Brian Urquhart in 1987 at the Foreign Press Center in New York he told me he was still affected by memories of it. 'And by the way, those five photographs are now nowhere to be found,' he added. 'I suppose that kind of thing does happen.'

I last saw Montgomery at close range, and talked with him, in the summer of 1953, when he crossed the Atlantic to New York and went on to see his old chief, the former President Eisenhower, at Gettysburg. I was then stationed in New York as a correspondent for the *Daily Telegraph*, and when he reached New York I could not resist the temptation to see him again after almost a decade. I took advantage of the fact that in those days it was possible for a newspaperman to board a US Customs cutter to be taken beyond the entrance to the harbour, climb aboard a stationary transatlantic liner which had come from Europe and talk to arriving notabilities while the Customs officers performed their duties and the liner finished the last few miles of her trip.

Montgomery arrived in the *Queen Mary*. He received a small company of American reporters in the Garden Lounge. I stood inconspicuously at the back of this fragrant corner of the splendid ship while the interview went on. I rejoiced to see how trim and fit he looked and how little he seemed to have changed since I heard him recount his capture of General von Thoma. When the interview ended I went up to him and reintroduced myself. 'We last met at El Alamein,' I said as we shook hands. He made just about the last response I could have expected. 'Ah, yes,' he said. 'So you were there too.' I was completely disarmed. We talked amiably for a few minutes and then he was gone on his way to see Dwight D. Eisenhower and, as he told me, to retrace the course of the Battle of Gettysburg – in much the same fashion, I imagine, as he had re-enacted the Battle of Alamein with von Thoma nine years earlier.

7

Charnel House

Patrols of the British Second Army advancing westwards across north-central Germany, against no opposition, stumbled without warning upon Bergen-Belsen Concentration Camp on 18 April 1945. I followed them after the terrible place had been inspected and medical officers had sanctioned entry. Like everybody else who went there and saw it in its raw state, I feel I shall never fully recover from the shock, but from time to time as the years pass I have to look at photographs taken then to assure myself that I really did see the scenes they depict. Those photographs show human degradation and suffering of an appalling and sickening kind.

As I rode in a Jeep along a straight country road twenty miles north-east of Hanover I could easily understand how our patrolling troops could not guess what lay ahead. We who followed them were upon the hideous camp long before we expected as we bowled along on this beguiling morning when the Hanoverian countryside was looking its springtime best. Heinrich Himmler and the others in charge of 'the Final Solution' had been most careful to make camps like Bergen-Belsen as inconspicuous and hard to find as possible.

The first clue came when I chanced to notice that behind the tall pines lining the left-hand side of the avenue there could be vaguely discerned the roofs of a row of long and low wooden buildings with tubby chimneys at one end. Moments later we swung sharp left at a point where stood a pair of high gates, wide open and unguarded. Beyond them to the left stood the line of huts I had just seen. To the right was a track leading to other buildings and an open square which presumably marked the centre of the camp. I had to go through one significant ritual before being allowed to set foot in the tainted prison. I was taken into a small guardhouse near the entrance gates and dusted thoroughly from head to foot with a white disinfectant powder. This was a precaution insisted upon by the Principal Medical Officer of the Second Army, a brigadier who had earlier given us an understandably disjointed and emotional account of what he had seen and heard when he had been called to the camp after the forward troops had reported their entry into the dirty, smelly, dusty, diseased confines of Bergen-Belsen. 'It's the most frightful and horrible place I have ever imagined,' he said. 'There were people dying in the compounds, dying in the mass before our eyes. There was one crematorium, but the Germans did not use it simply because it could not cope with the number of deaths occurring all the time.' Starvation, he believed, was actually causing more deaths than rampant typhus. 'And a large number of prisoners must die before we can prevent it. There had been no drinking-water for days. I saw men and women standing naked in the open, trying to get themselves clean with cupfuls of water from small ponds and ditches. We saw some enormous death-pits into which bodies had been flung. One had not yet been covered over. It contained a great pile of blackened naked bodies. There was typhus in every compound, and in one compound typhus cases were not separated from other prisoners not yet infected.

I could hardly credit what I was hearing. Never a whisper about the existence of such a charnel house, of such awful treatment by one class of human beings of another, had reached me in all the years of war. Now I was within a few miles of the horror and would be seeing it for myself.

'People were lying dead in gutters dug outside the huts,' the brigadier went on. 'They had gone outside to rest more comfortably and had died as they lay down. In one women's compound – in full view of a children's compound only fifty yards away – was an enormous pile of naked dead women. It stretched about sixty yards by thirty.' I quickly estimated that there must have been at least a hundred dead women lying there. Among them must have been the mothers of the children who could see the ghastly medley.

The Principal Medical Officer ended this unprecedented briefing with a statement which, he said, he hesitated to mention because he could not vouch for it, although it rang true. 'The German prison doctors whom I interviewed told me there had been cannibalism,' he said. 'Prisoners took out and ate the hearts and livers of people who had died, they stated.'

It was infinitely more heart-rending to see such sights than to hear about them. The worst experience of all was to see people who had been literally starved to death collapse and die before my eyes, knowing there was absolutely nothing I could do to save them. In particular, I came upon one young man, who must have been a physically impressive person before Belsen claimed him, sitting on one edge of the dusty track which bisected the camp. His mouth was wide open and he was slowly swaying from side to side. He looked the more like some grotesque doll or puppet because he was wearing a long coat which was now far too big for his pitifully shrunken frame. His feet were lost inside heavy old boots with their laces all broken. In his lap he loosely clasped something wrapped in a dirty cloth.

As I approached him, frustrated because I knew there was nothing I could do for him except perhaps say something to comfort him, he suddenly swayed heavily to his left. His mouth remained open, still seeking air, but his eyes in their sunken sockets slowly narrowed and closed. As he keeled over and lay still, the cloth reposing in his lap rolled away from him and what it contained could be seen. A sizeable bone lay there in the dust. It had been picked clean. Was it human? I shall never know.

This young man had died in front of me. His pitiful remains would be lifted up and taken away to enlarge one of the piles of other victims of starvation or disease who had gone before him.

Next, I came upon tall wooden gallows standing bare and stark in the square at the centre of the camp. The forbidding structure had been so placed as to be visible from most of the areas used by inmates. It was empty. But as I walked towards it I discerned an emaciated girl, probably ten to twelve years old, standing in front of it and looking up. She was wearing rags and she was dirty. She was sobbing uncontrollably. What dreadful happening was she reliving? Once again I felt impotent to help, as I had felt a few minutes earlier in the case of the young man who died. I simply walked up to her and laid my hand upon her straggly, unkempt hair and gently patted her head in what I hoped would be accepted as a comforting gesture. She responded by turning her thin, tear-streaked and contorted face towards me. I stifled a professional urge to ask questions and, so wrung was I by pity for this child, that I did not even intrude by offering her banal words of consolation. I swung away and left her with her private grief. She was so young.

There were more horrors to come. Walking on, I reached a long hut with its door wide open. Peering into the interior gloom, I made out two untidy rows composed of about fifty women, one row on each side of the wooden building. Some of the women were managing to prop themselves up on skinny arms and elbows. They looked at me apathetically – too weak, I surmised, to say anything. Others lay supine, unable to move, much less hold themselves up. All seemed to be alive, but some only barely. Yet, as I walked between the two rows, a couple of them did summon up a faint smile of greeting and perhaps joy at the sight of a friendly face at last. Mostly, however, there was neither response nor reaction. This hut radiated doom. It was a compound, I learned later, which had been thoroughly inspected by British Army doctors who had determined that at least one half of the women could not survive.

By this time, I have to confess, I was beginning to feel repugnance. Pity had been replaced by a fear that I might become contaminated, I am ashamed to recall. I found myself treading a way round the rest of the camp with heightening nervousness and unwillingness, not even wanting my boots to touch more heavily or more often than absolutely necessary the diseased soil of Belsen. The apprehension and distaste reached a maximum pitch at the last sight of all on this bad day. In my defence I shall plead that I might have seen more than a man should be expected to withstand in the space of a few hours. The last ghastly spectacle was a great heap of naked bodies piled up at the eastern end of the camp. Men, women and children had all been dumped together in ultimate indignity. Some of the bodies were upside-down, some lay awkwardly stiff on their sides, and a few were spreadeagled gauntly with arms outstretched wide, reminding me of my last glimpse of the young man after he had collapsed, dead. One or two of these corpses seemed even to be embracing each other in a clumsy parody of living love. Had these half-skeletal cadavers ever been living humans? I found it hard to believe. They had lost recognizable resemblance to the upright, dignified and in some cases probably graceful and even beautiful people they had once been. Imprisonment, cruelty, debasement, starvation and disease had reduced them to the bundles of skin and bone that lay in this hideous untidiness before me. The culminating sight was so unreal and unbelievable that for a few moments even my feelings of repugnance were dulled. Only when I found myself looking at one woman tightly cradling a blackened baby in her spindly arms, mothering it in death, did pangs of compassion and anger surge again within me. The sight restored me to something approaching normality. At that instant I hated everybody and everything German far more fiercely than ever before during the war.

I hurried as quickly as I could out of Belsen to my Jeep for the journey back to base, to write everything I had seen that terible day while it was all fresh in my mind.

I felt better after that duty had been accomplished. Writing my story emptied me of emotion, restoring me to a realization that I was not a participant in the horror but a professional observer with the duty of telling others what Belsen was like. I felt even better the next morning. I knew I must go again to the camp, not because, heaven forbid, I wished to do so but because this was obviously no routine assignment to be covered briefly and then forgotten. Discovery and appraisal of Bergen-Belsen was obviously something which would take its place in the history books. It must be dealt journalistically with as much thoroughness as possible, so that there would be a full contemporary record which historians would later use as foundation for their ultimate assessment of all that it signified.

I set out early that morning to go again into Bergen-Belsen, and as soon as I had been redusted and was able to set about taking a second look at the camp, I found that something quite unexpected had indeed happened to me overnight. I realized that I wasn't treading anything like so nervously – fearfully might be a better word – as on the day before. The scenes which had affected me yesterday were not now having anything like such a strong impact. At one point I found myself talking to a prisoner, ambulatory and still looking like a human being despite the drabness of the striped pyjama uniform he was wearing, with my right foot actually touching a dead body lying on the outer edge of corpses which had been collected overnight from the compounds. I was momentarily shocked. Had a process of brutalization started already on me? They did say, didn't they, that one could quickly get used to almost anything? Or, I tried to reassure myself, pure professionalism had reasserted itself now that the first shock had been absorbed. My mission was rather like that of a lawyer, doctor or other professional. I was here to record the scene, not to become part of it.

Whatever the explanation, I was quite cool and detached when at last I found Josef Kramer, the commandant of the camp and now a prisoner. He was standing in an open-air cage, isolated from his staff, who were being kept in two groups, one male and the other female, in a compound on the perimeter of the camp, away from those used for inmates. Perhaps they were being kept at a considerable distance from their victims because of the danger that they might be murdered if any liberated inmates got close to them. Kramer's face was bruised and swollen. He had been pretty roughly treated, I deduced, by those members of Montgomery's soldiery who had found him and kept him under guard all night. I suspected that his injuries (some of which had been roughly doctored with purple medication) had been caused by the fists of men who had been stung into excesses from fury at what they had seen and found in the camp and for which they held him responsible.

Kramer was short and heavily built, dark of visage and dull-eyed. I formed an opinion as I viewed him and talked with him that he was not very bright, well below average intelligence. As he now stood, looking sheepish and uncomfortable, in front of me, I tried to get an explanation from him of the appalling state of affairs we had found at his camp. He said that everything had been 'satisfactory' until a few weeks earlier. Then, as more and more German territory was overrun in all directions, the flood of prisoners from other camps who were dumped on him became so great that he and his staff were not able to cope with it. 'Things got out of hand,' Kramer said. It sounded plausible enough until one examined the facts a little more closely, and I found it significant that he did not look me squarely in the face as he gave his 'explanation'. He knew as well as anybody that there had to be more to it than he was saying. There had had to be many months of deprivation and cruelty to reduce the population of the camp to the state in which we had found it. I asked him if there had not been a deliberate policy of ill-treatment of Jews and others in Belsen and the other camps which, we had heard overnight, had been found by other units of the advancing Anglo-American armies? (It must be remembered that until April 1945 not a word about the Nazi pogrom in Germany had reached the Allied armies in the field.) Kramer did not answer. When I told him that I simply couldn't believe his 'explanation' he shrugged and, with a resigned expression on his face, looked down at the dirt floor of his prison-cage. Maybe he knew what his fate was to be. (He was duly tried, convicted and hanged.)

Leaving him, I spent several hours watching events at the camp. They all seem so unreal to me now that I feel I can best serve the purpose of recording them by repeating what I wrote for my newspaper as soon as I got back to base that afternoon. I kept the recital as factual and un-emotional as possible:

We found today that several hundred more inmates had died during the night. Their emaciated fellow-sufferers, many of whom are themselves doomed, dragged the naked bodies from the huts and laid them in great piles at the entrances to the compounds. We decided to give the awful task of burial to some of the men and women guards who have been responsible for much of the horror of Belsen. When our troops went into the cells in which these ghouls are being kept they found that one S.S. man had hanged himself. Two others have now committed suicide by trying to run away. They must have known they would be shot if they did this; they did, and they were. They ran deliberately, the others said, because they could face no more of the work they had been doing for the past two days.

Nine of the young S.S. women were ordered to haul scores of naked corpses from lorries and fling them into a mass burial pit in which hundreds of sprawling bodies were already lying. Groups of prisoners watched them do so. The S.S. women, the eldest of whom was only 27, were unmoved by the grisliness of their task. One even smiled contemptuously as she helped bundle the corpses into the pit.

Meanwhile, the male S.S. guards were piling still more bodies into lorries elsewhere in the camp. They withstood the ordeal worse than the women. They cringed and shrank, and a dreadful fear was in their eyes. Some worked feverishly, as if expecting that at any moment if they did not do so they might be shot by their British guards or lynched by the crowds of prisoners looking on. When they had filled a lorry they climbed up themselves and were driven, along with their terrible cargo, to the burial pits.

Such was part of the report of my second visit to Belsen as it appeared in the *Daily Mail* of 21 April 1945. It was reprinted in a book called *Lest We Forget* which the newspaper published later that year. In this book the story – illustrated with grim and shocking photographs – was told of what irrefutably had been found in all the concentration camps liberated by American and British forces as they advanced eastwards.

There was to be an odd sequel to publication of my first report from Belsen. It happened thirty-six years later. On 10 August 1981 *The New York Times* printed an interview with Frau Wendelgard von Staden, a member of a German aristocratic family, who had recently written and published a moving book about the horrors she had seen at a concentration camp built by the Nazis on her family's sequestered estate near Stuttgart. The book had, somewhat surprisingly, been read avidly in Germany, going into seven printings in less than two years. The *Times* interview ended thus:

Some years after the war someone told Frau von Staden about a despatch sent from Bergen-Belsen in 1945 by a British reporter who saw the liberation of the camp. It was said to begin: 'I have the duty now to report something beyond the scope of human understanding.'

Frau von Staden's voice began to tremble. 'And that,' she said, 'is what it was.'

The quoted words formed the opening sentence of the cable I sent to the *Daily Mail* from Bergen-Belsen on 19 April 1945.

8

Getting Out the News

Pedantic news editor on telephone: Are there any news, Joe?
Reporter on assignment: Not a new, chief.

Old Fleet Street joke

When, if ever, is it permissible for anybody to stop or delay disclosure of news? Superficially the answer would appear to be, never. The very word, news, would seem to deny any such permission. But one has to concede that such considerations in times of war as security and morale do justify some constraints and that, in peace as well as in war, in the case of international items of news it is desirable to recognize that daytime in one country can be dead of night in another. However, people do tamper with news. I doubt if there is one foreign correspondent hailing from any of the major Western democracies who has not been frustrated many times by somebody or something – a government, a bureaucrat, a vested interest, or even a public relations schemer – decreeing that a piece of news may not be broadcast or published before a certain hour for reasons which do not appear to be valid.

Conversely, many of us have applauded sources who have taken extreme measures to ensure that news is made public at the earliest possible moment. The simplest and most dramatic instance of efficiency in this respect within my experience happened when King George V died during the night of 19/20 January 1936, some hours after his doctor, Lord Dawson of Penn, had issued his famous bulletin: 'The King's life is drawing peacefully to its close.' The royal establishment has been a model of promptness and veracity for at least the past half-century and on this sad occasion it surpassed its reputation. It made an arrangement that, when the much-loved monarch breathed his last, somebody in the death chamber would raise and lower a blind covering a large window so that the hordes of reporters waiting outside and below would know that the inevitable had happened. One of them, F.G. Prince-White, who was representing the *Daily Mail*, told me: 'That silent symbol was followed by a stampede, the like of which I had never seen.'

During the forty years in which I was concerned with international affairs – during the war, immediately thereafter in tormented Berlin, at the United Nations in New York, and in the whole of the Americas – the paramount suppressor and obfuscator was the Soviet Union. Nobody applauded the advent of Mikail Gorbachev more ardently than I.

I had to take the wartime transgressions of the Soviet Union at second hand because I was otherwise occupied, but correspondents who were stationed there at that time have told lurid stories of their tribulations at the hands of Stalin's so-called spokesmen and his censors. 'My most difficult job after hearing something in Moscow was to try to tell whether it was a red or other herring,' one of them said to me. Personally, one occasion which has become unforgettable happened in Berlin in the late 1940s when a Soviet fighter pilot, harassing a British aircraft flying in the aerial corridor linking West Germany with Berlin, clumsily – and fatally for himself and many others – rammed the plane and caused it to crash, in the full view of people on the ground. Incredibly, the Soviet element in the Allied Control Commission claimed at first that no fighter aircraft had been involved and then, abandoning that flagrant lie, said that the British passenger aircraft was to blame for the accident. I do not recall how the affair ended, but I expect that as in so many instances before and after the 1940s the Soviets eventually climbed right down the pole of denial.

Similarly, at the United Nations, I have heard one Soviet delegate after another brazenly deny, lie and suppress. The most offensive performer was Andrei Vyshinsky, who led the Soviet delegation in the early days of the United Nations. He usually put on an exaggerated and unconvincing display of histrionics in a mistaken belief that this would shroud his wrecking tactics and mask his distortions. For example, I could scarcely believe my eyes when I read, in Berlin, that he had declared in the Security Council in New York that the blockade of Berlin (which I was reporting as well as enduring) was neither threatening world peace nor causing any hardship to the population of the Western sectors of the hapless city. When I read that item I was sitting alone in my home in the Grünewald without electric light and only the most primitive rations for my supper; and I, as an Allied occupier, was much better off than the Germans living around me.

The most skilful, and likable, of the Soviet representatives in New York was Jakob Malik, who served two terms, in the 1950s and 1970s. Although he had the same unworthy responsibilities as Vyshinsky in violating truth and suppressing facts, he managed to do so quietly, without histrionics, and without arousing the antagonism and anger of those who had to listen to him and then to negotiate with him. 'You could always do business with him, whenever necessary,' Lord Gladwyn observed to me during an interview in London in 1970. 'He was always tough – but reliable – a most sensible man.' Lord Gladwyn was in an excellent position to appraise Jakob Malik, for, as Sir Gladwyn Jebb and leader of the British delegation to the UN, he was Malik's adversary in many sparring matches there. In so doing he became a star on American television, for he was personable, persuasive – and no mean actor.

Malik's finesse as a negotiator was amusingly illustrated when in 1948 he was told by Stalin to arrange, without the Soviets losing face, for the Western Powers to be told that the Soviet Union wanted to call off the blockade of Berlin. The reason for this radical move was, as always with the Soviet Union in those days of the Cold War, realism in recognizing defeat. The blockade had been frustrated by the brilliantly conceived and executed Anglo-American airlift and Stalin saw that there was no chance whatever of its achieving its goal of forcing the Western allies to abandon Berlin and leave the city unchallenged in the hands of the Soviet Union. So, reasoned Stalin, end it.

Malik hit upon the bizarre scheme of fulfilling his orders by using the privacy of the delegates' lavatories to intercept Dr Philip Jessup, the American representative, and start the parley there. He told Dr Jessup, in English and in total privacy, that the Soviet Union would end the blockade if 'suitable arrangements' between the two warring sides could be made. Malik was negotiating, of course, for an accommodation in accordance with usual diplomatic practice. The victor in an international dispute does not go too far in humiliating his beaten adversary if there still remains another area of disagreement in which the vanquished has an advantage and might use it profitably. And there were several places elsewhere in a turbulent world where the Soviet Union could make trouble for the West. Malik's use of the delegates' lavatories was typical of him. It appealed to his sense of humour and, practically, it ensured that the ever-vigilant eyes of the international press would not see him negotiating with the other side.

By far the most famous – or perhaps the most infamous – instance of the use of an embargo on important news occurred in May 1945, when the victorious Allied powers decreed that the news of Germany's uncon-ditional surrender would be delayed for twenty-four hours. This frustrat-ing and, in the opinion of many people, unjustified embargo cheated the expectant world, and it wrecked the career of my friend, Edward Kennedy, of the Associated Press, who defied it.

I first met Kennedy in Cairo in 1942, where he was working as bureau chief of a branch of his agency. He was an endearing individualist. He was almost always accompanied in public by a perky little puppy-dog and this unprofessional idiosyncracy, coupled with a suggestion of feebleness conveyed by tired eyes blinking behind spectacles, often led to his fierce rivals, working for other highly competitive news agencies, to underrate him. Kennedy was in fact a brilliantly efficient operator, and a dedicated and tireless one. He even chose to live in a tiny and uncomfortable apartment within a few yards of the Immobilia Building, the news centre of Cairo, because this ensured that he would almost always be the first to reach the cablehead in the Immobilia Building with his copy. I suppose I should have guessed that this singular man would one day make news on his own account.

He certainly did. When the war ended in May 1945, Kennedy was one of seventeen Allied correspondents nominated by the Public Relations section of Supreme Headquarters in Paris to witness, on behalf of the world's press, Germany's formal surrender at Rheims. Each of these seventeen reporters was required in advance to pledge on his or her honour 'as a correspondent and an assimilated officer of the armed forces' not to transmit the news until it was officially announced. When the surrender was completed, in extremely tense circumstances, in the early hours of 7 May, the correspondents were told that the formal news of it would not be released until 8 p.m. on 8 May, when there would be simultaneous announcements in Paris, London, Moscow and Washington. They would then be permitted to file their messages reporting the announcement and describing the scene when the surrender was made.

Kennedy told me he brooded for hours about 'the autocratic and unjustified decision' to deprive the world for more than a day of the great news it had been aching to hear. In the early afternoon of 7 May he resolved that he would be justified in breaking the oath he had taken – 'a mass one taken under duress', as he put it. He always maintained that he broke it because he felt strongly that it was a serious injustice. Knowing him as I did, I can't help feeling that this was only his public excuse. I deduce that he had more compelling private reasons as well. He wanted to get even with military officialdom, which he felt had treated him unfairly several times during the war, usually in stopping him writing something or censoring it when he had done so. He also saw a chance to repay his rivals of the United Press and the International News Service for what he considered some unfair tricks during the permanent competitive war of their own making. Finally, and this might have been the paramount reason, he must have been influenced by the thought that in breaking the embargo he would be scoring the biggest scoop of the war by announcing its end before anybody else.

There had been one tussle between Kennedy and the US command, including General Eisenhower, in which his arguments had been turned down, only to be proven right soon afterwards. The clash concerned treatment of the episode in which General Patton, a gifted but unbalanced warrior if ever there was one, had slapped and kicked a soldier in a hospital tent in Sicily. Patton believed, wrongly as it emerged, that the man had shown himself to be a coward. In August 1943 Kennedy was one of about twenty correspondents who agreed not to file stories about the incident. Several of the signatories decided instead to take what now seems to be the arrogant course of writing to Eisenhower asking that he order Patton to apologize to the soldier. The inference was that if Patton did not apologize, they would write the story.

Kennedy was much more shrewd and professional. He asked to see Eisenhower and, when he did so, he pointed out that since the embarrassing item about Patton's indiscretion was sure to get into print eventually, it would be better to let the correspondents in the field write it because they would present it much more sympathetically than somebody outside the control of the military who would probably hear about it at second or third hand. Eisenhower saw Kennedy's point but still didn't want the story published. He contended that publication would deeply embarrass the American command in the eyes of its own troops and those of America's allies and would also provide the enemy with some highly useful propaganda. So the story was quashed – and three months later Kennedy's argument was confirmed. Drew Pearson, the muck-raking columnist working from Washington, heard about the incident and printed a lurid version. He was able to do so because he wasn't subject to censorship or other restraints.

Whatever his motives, Kennedy decided to warn the military authorities about what he was doing. He went to the censor's office in the aptly named Scribe Hotel in Paris and announced: 'I want to give you full and fair warning here and now. I'm going to file my story about the surrender.' And he did, using a subsidiary telephone circuit to the office of the Associated Press in London. He was cut off by censors after he had dictated about two hundred words of his historic message, more than enough to cause joyous pandemonium in most parts of the world.

But Kennedy's own world collapsed about him. He was disaccredited and ordered out of the European theatre by the incensed Supreme Headquarters. Over fifty of his outraged (and scooped) colleagues wrote to General Eisenhower describing his deed as 'the most disgraceful, deliberate, and unethical double-cross in the history of journalism'. These fevered words reflect one psychical fact which has become forgotten as the decades after the war have rolled by and blurred men's memories. Correspondents were simply unbalanced in 1945. Most of them had endured almost five years of highly debilitating nervous strain, and some of us British correspondents had gone through almost six years of war. We had spent ourselves physically and mentally in an artificial situation in which we had not been fighting a tangible enemy, as were the soldiers (indeed, we were forbidden to carry arms and engage in combat), but were enmeshed in a constricting web of frustrations. We had to contend with censorship, military officialdom which held all the trump cards, fierce competition from our journalistic rivals, nagging anxiety about uncertain means of communicating our precious despatches which had cost us so much in physical effort and strain, rarely getting adequate nourishment and rest, and, for those of us in the field, continuing risk of injury or death as we tried to get as close as we could to the scenes of action. If anybody was war-weary it was the correspondent. I have always been pleased that I was not among that squabbling and overwrought group in Paris in May 1945. I had been in enough lesser goldfish bowls to give me my fill of them in Cairo, Algiers, Naples, Bari, Rome and elsewhere, as well as in dozens of temporary press camps in fighting areas (I remember with especial affection one near Sessa Aurunca, Italy, pitched on the grave of a dead horse). I do not find it hard to picture the neurotic bedlam in Paris. One fact I observed during the war was that internal upheavals worthy of the name almost always happened whenever there was a lull on the field of battle and nobody had much to write about. Now the greatest slow-down of all – peace – had come. There would be plenty of time to concentrate on the malefactor, Ed Kennedy.

I had a most agreeable armistice. I was in Holland and watched Col. General Johannes Blaskowitz and some of his subordinates surrender German forces between the Weser and western Holland to the First Canadian Army under General H.D.G. Crerar. While awaiting the arrival of the defeated Blaskowitz and his colleagues I found myself chatting pleasantly that May morning with Prince Bernhard of the Netherlands, who was serving as a liaison officer between his people and General Crerar. 'This is a sweet moment for you and for us Dutch,' I recall Prince Bernhard saying. 'We've all suffered too much from these Germans.' Prince Bernhard and I watched Blaskowitz, a short, tubby man wearing a shiny black greatcoat, which I thought seemed too long for him, go stiffly through the humiliating formalities of acknowledging defeat and making unconditional surrender to a sober-looking Crerar and then listening to an interpreting officer giving him Crerar's precise orders about how he should dispose his troops. The brief proceedings ended as he brought his heels together, saluted and strode off to do as he had been told.

I last saw Edward Kennedy in New York in 1962. He had been dismissed by the Associated Press in 1945 and he had never again figured on the international scene. He went into comparative obscurity by serving as managing editor of the Santa Barbara Press, a small newspaper in California, later becoming editor of the *Monterey Peninsular Herald*, also in California. He used to come to New York from time to time, and in 1962 he telephoned me in my office in the Associated Press building in Rockefeller Plaza. We met for a chat, as we had done before, in one of the cafés below street level in the building. He was understandably even more subdued than when we were together in Cairo. But he claimed he was now happy. 'I was treated very badly by everybody in 1945, but it's all over and done with,' he said, blinking as of old. 'I don't feel any anger any more. I'm enjoying myself in California.'

Alas, he wasn't to enjoy this professed happiness much longer. He was knocked down in a street in Monterey on 24 November 1963, and he died five days later.

9

Farm-boy from Kansas

Dwight D. Eisenhower was but a name to me – a distinguished and respected name, of course – until one day in the early spring of 1945, when I drove from British headquarters inside north Germany at Süchteln to Allied Headquarters in Brussels. Soon after I got there I was told by an American colleague (whom I had last seen in far more primitive conditions south of Cassino, in Italy): 'Ike is here and he's giving a briefing this afternoon. You should come to it.'

The conference was an eye-opener. Its informality was in startling contrast to the brusque stiffness of so many similar sessions with General Montgomery and other high-ranking British commanders in the thirty months since the Battle of Alamein, the trek westwards across North Africa, the trudge up Italy, and now the culminating advance in north-west Germany. Those conferences had been for the most part strictly business affairs, with only formal contact between military brief-giver and the war correspondent. Now came the breeziness of the New World.

General Eisenhower sat perched on a corner of a deal table, one leg dangling free and his left hand in his trouser pocket. Lolling in chairs in front of him sat the correspondents, almost all American. They were as free and easy as he was. Some of them addressed him as 'Ike' when they posed their questions or made confident comments and, in return, he often used their given names as he answered: 'Well, Hank, you know as well as I do . . .' and 'Joe, let's put it this way. . . .' It very soon struck me that this conference was like a friendly chat between men who had become good friends while fighting a war which was now virtually won. I noted the charm displayed so unaffectedly by General Eisenhower. The warm gaze of the blue eyes and the broad grin which so readily illumined his face were evidence of an innately friendly and comparatively uncomplicated man. I had heard that he liked sometimes to describe himself as 'a farm-boy from Kansas' and maybe the characterization was apt, for here at the age of fifty-two was a man who had never lost an aura of youthful simplicity. Yet for a farm-boy he had come marvellously far in his profession, having risen to become Supreme Commander of Allied Forces in Europe, with a shining record of courageous decisions and well-planned achievements before and after the Normandy invasion and enjoying a reputation as a masterly manipulator of a parcel of ambitious, meddlesome, temperamental and quarrelsome generals of widely different backgrounds and nationalities. His record as a military administrator could not be faulted.

But, alas, it was to be shown before the war ended that his political education had not kept up with the military one. Even as he sat there in this room in Brussels he had already decided that when the time came he would not order his armies to capture Berlin, the nerve centre of Nazidom and the symbolic and political prize for which the Allies had been striving for years, but would leave it to the Soviets to take. It emerged much later that he had exchanged telegrams to this effect with Stalin and, incredibly, had accepted without question an assertion by the double-faced despot that 'Berlin has lost its strategic significance'. Equally incredibly, he had believed Stalin's assurance that he would allocate only a small force of second-class troops to take Berlin. In fact, he reserved well over a million of his higher-grade soldiers under General Zhukov, one of his most forceful commanders, for the task. Eisenhower concedes in his own book, *Crusade in Europe*, published in 1948, that Winston Churchill seriously objected to his action in negotiating directly with Stalin and also 'was greatly disappointed and disturbed because my plan did not first throw Montgomery forward with all the strength I could give him from the American forces, in the desperate attempt to capture Berlin before the Russians could do so'. Eisenhower discloses further that in a message to General Marshall, his superior in Washington, on 30 March 1945, he wrote: 'May I point out that Berlin is no longer a particularly important objective. Its usefulness to the German has been largely destroyed and even his government is preparing to move to another area.'

This naïve and narrow military conception of the value of Berlin was to cost the Western Allies dearly. As I saw for myself in Berlin between 1945 and 1950, the vengeful troops who captured and looted the city and terrorized its women were backed by a fanatically stubborn Soviet bureaucracy within the Allied Control Commission which, on Stalin's orders, sabotaged all efforts at co-operation and in 1948 even risked a third world war by seeking, and eventually failing, to oust the Western occupiers from their sectors of the city.

When I next saw Eisenhower in the autumn of 1952 he had exchanged his Army uniform for a smartly cut business suit and was seeking the presidency. Outwardly he was the same smiling, approachable man of the war years, but there was a significant difference in his attitude when he was not on display to the people who were being encouraged to vote for him. He was not the same old free-and-easy Ike with the reporters, and the reason was that he was being managed – 'merchandized' was the word used by those managing him – because he had become a standard-bearer for the Republican Party, a candidate with such overwhelming credentials that it was believed he could not possibly lose except as a result of some such misadventure as an ill-advised remark or admission blurted out to somebody who could publicize the indiscretion and ruin the whole show. So Ike was no longer readily available to the reporters covering him; they had to be satisfied with what they saw of him whenever he emerged to make a semi-royal progress in an open car through the streets of a town or city or mounted on a platform or at the rear end of a train to make a speech couched for the most part in words and sentences carefully prepared for him by his writers.

For the first time in history an American presidential candidate's campaign was being stage-managed by an advertising and public relations agency, a top-ranking one with the impressive shingle of Batten, Barton, Durstine and Osborn (known across America as BBD and O, a contraction that slipped over the tongue just as smoothly as the effective slogans and one-liners produced by the agency to promote the Eisenhower cause). The professionals of BBD and O were so slick, thorough and successful in their assignment that they started a development which achieved a radical – and, it has to be faced, regrettable – transformation of not only the character of presidential elections but of presidential press conferences, presidential election 'debates' between the two candidates, and the relationship between the presidency and the press and ultimately the American people.

Other professionals in Madison Avenue (heart of the advertising and PR industry of the United States), as well as planners in the White House and the headquarters of the Republican and Democratic parties, were quick to appreciate in 1952 what 'merchandizing' could do. They saw how every detail of Eisenhower's public appearances was being stage-managed. Advance men were sent out to work with local organizers and politicians to whip up enthusiasm for the candidate's coming appearance. Tons of confetti were bought to be showered by cheer-leaders upon Eisenhower, to add lustre and propagandist appeal to pictures of his triumphal progress through a town or city shown on the evening television news and published in next morning's newspapers. A booklet of thirty-nine pages was produced to confirm every fact and arrangement for a one-day visit by Ike to Philadelphia. BBD and O summed up its task in one telling sentence. Reduced to its essentials, declared a presentation, it was a matter of 'merchandizing Eisenhower's frankness, honesty, and integrity, his sincere and wholesome approach'. Eisenhower himself was privately upset at one point by this strategy of selling him. During one briefing by the professionals he seemed to Sherman Adams, his close confidant, to be perturbed about something. Adams asked him afterwards what had bothered him. 'All they talked about was how they could win on my popularity,' Eisenhower replied. 'Nobody said I had a brain in my head.'

What was not talked about was the tactic of keeping the reporters at a safe distance from Eisenhower. I do not recall having one opportunity during the days I was travelling with him by train through several states to share with him a relaxing moment or two, much less an interview. This segregation of the candidate from the reporters and correspondents, who were after all the eyes and ears of the people in this era before many of them became presidential inquisitors as well in the 1970s and 1980s, seemed to me to be the most harmful aspect of the new 'merchandizing'. Coupled with the cut-and-dried blandness of the speeches written for Ike, it made his campaign about as interesting to me as a bazaar opening. I could leave it, of course, as and when I chose, for I was under no obligation to give equal attention to him and to Adlai Stevenson, his Democratic opponent, because not a single vote would be influenced by anything I wrote. American reporters assigned to the campaign were not so lucky. They had to stay with it until relieved, to withstand the boredom and drudgery as best they could. One story which went the rounds of the press accompanying Ike was probably apocryphal but it was highly illustrative. During a whistle-stop trip one reporter was said to have asked another as he looked out of a compartment window: 'Where are we now?' The second journalist, equally weary, replied: 'Probably crossing the 38th platitude.'

For all the restrictive and manipulative nature of the campaign, the BBD and O planners were wholly correct in concentrating on exploiting their candidate's personality. When he spoke, his earnest and simple delivery and his reassuring demeanour made the vaguest generality and the most crass platitude sound important and valid. I noted the extraordinary rapport between him and his audiences. It scarcely mattered what he said: *how* he said it was what counted. They were proud of him for his military record during the war and afterwards, and most of them wanted him as their president. I had not been observing him for very long before perceiving that he was a certain winner, barring some unpredictable disaster. But his campaign just didn't make news.

A progressive decline in public respect for, and interest in, the American political apparatus and the administration of national affairs, and the presidency itself, began very soon after the introduction of Madison Avenue methods into the election of 1952. I suspect that the systematic stifling of informal contact between President and press, parcelling out of scanty items of managed 'news', artificial enhancements to public appearances by the President and his chief lieutenants, and timing of events and announcements to catch the evening news programmes on television, were significant factors in developing the adversarial relationship between the Government and the media. Presidential press conferences in the White House degenerated into gaudy theatrical performances watched by diminishing television audiences who came to expect not important news but laughs and gaffes and undignified exchanges between inquisitorial and sharp-witted questioners and their presidential target. Eisenhower himself felt the pressures and discomfitures once he took office; he often became disjointed and grammatically obscure in his reactions to off-beat, needling questions by such as Sarah McClendon, a veteran from Texas, by whom he seemed hypnotized when it came to selecting the next questioner. Richard Nixon, tottering towards resignation because of his bungling of the Watergate crisis, got into unseemly arguments with Dan Rather, who – partly because of his well-publicized performance at the press conferences – later became a national star as anchor-man on CBS news programmes. Similarly, President Carter was often unsettled by the persistent assertiveness of Sam Donaldson, of the American Broadcasting Company, who also became a star on television thanks to his activity at White House press conferences. One president who managed in the earlier and less dangerous days to steer a deft, humorous way through the thickets was John Kennedy.

Not only press conferences at the White House suffered from the deteriorations in relations and standards after 1952. So-called debates on television by presidential and vice-presidential candidates every four years became travesties of what they once were, notably in the days in 1960 of hard-hitting and newsworthy exchanges between Richard Nixon and John Kennedy. Rules governing these 'debates' were the subject of keen bargaining between the advisers to both political parties, and by the 1980s they had become so controlled and stage-managed that they were worthless as a medium for enlightenment on the policies of the rivals. One between Ronald Reagan and Jimmy Carter became memorable only for a classic response by Mr Reagan – 'There you go again!' – to an unfounded accusation from his adversary. Again, in 1988, an encounter between Lloyd Bentsen and Dan Quayle, who were fighting for the vice-presidency, will be recalled perhaps for ever by Bentsen's cutting insult – 'You are no Jack Kennedy!' – and Dan Quayle's simple rejoinder: 'That was really uncalled for, Senator.' Not one of the 'debates' between 1960 and 1988 is remembered for any substantial revelation of differences in approach and policy between the candidates on serious economic and social problems facing the country.

Eventually, discontent and disillusionment, provoked by the straitjacket into which not only the candidates but the format of the so-called debates were being contained, erupted. The League of Women Voters, which had provided the auspices under which debates in past elections had been presented, announced that it was withdrawing its sponsorship of a second televised encounter between George Bush and Michael Dukakis. 'We have no intention of becoming an accessory to the hoodwinking of the American public,' said the president of the League, Mrs Nancy Neuman. She elaborated by explaining that her organization would not participate in a debate in which the campaign managers had set the ground rules, selected the moderator and the panel of questioners, and even arranged the seating of the various sections of the studio audience and the positions of the cameras filming the debate. 'We have been presented with a done deal,' she protested. 'It is clear that the campaigns wanted the League's stamp of approval on a shoddy product.' The format drawn up by the Republican and the Democrat organizers provided for only brief answers to questions and equally brief rebuttals, all controlled by the moderator's clock, before the debate shifted to another topic. In other words, there would be no deep discussion of anything.

The party managers filled in the void created by the League's withdrawal by announcing that a commission created by themselves would stage the debate. At the same time as this upheaval was happening the two candidates held news conferences, their first for a fortnight, and they did so on a day when the anxious attention of the nation was riveted by the launch of the Discovery space shuttle, the first since the disaster to the Challenger shuttle in January 1987 had temporarily paralysed the whole American space programme. The party managers obviously knew that there would be little time on television and space in newspapers for their press interviews. When reporters questioned Mr Dukakis about the rarity of contact between them and the candidates he answered, with some flippancy: 'Take advantage of this opportunity. You never know when it will happen again.' There was naturally a good deal of comment about the tactics being employed by both parties. Tom Goldstein, Dean of the School of Journalism at the University of California at Berkeley, pointed out that both sides had adopted the principle of selecting a theme and hammering it home without letting anything else interfere. 'The intermediary of the press is an inconvenience,' he told *The New York Times*. 'You can't script reporters.' Put another way, reporters would ask unexpected questions and bring up difficult topics. They might even provoke a serious discussion.

Only once during the ten years in which from time to time I was assigned to report the activities of Eisenhower as political candidate and American president did I have evidence of the latent fire behind the round, appealing visage of the grown-up farm-boy from Kansas. The revelation came in a brief episode in Santiago de Chile towards the end of a so-called 'Goodwill Tour' of Central and South America which he made as President between 22 February and 7 March 1960.

By the time we reached Santiago after half a dozen stops at capital cities (and a delightful off-duty one at Bariloche, a jewel of a place among the lakes far south of Buenos Aires, where James Hagerty, the presidential press secretary, danced an Irish jig alongside an Argentine sheep roasting on a revolving spit), I had had to report that the 'Goodwill' trip had not gone by any means as smoothly as the White House had hoped and planned. Demonstrations of anti-American sentiment had marred the venture at intervals after a first one met Eisenhower unexpectedly when he made his first short stopover after leaving Washington at the airport at San Juan, Puerto Rico. A crowd of young people, penned behind barriers out of the President's sight but not his hearing, were shouting slogans demanding independence from the United States for their island as the

President and his party left their aircraft to stretch their legs while it was being refuelled. The demonstration was by no means sizeable or noisy as these things go, but it was a first reminder of the widespread feelings of hostility towards the United States which had spread significantly after the advent of Fidel Castro as a Cuban liberator in 1959. It also gave a hollow sound to words that Eisenhower had used in an address to his nation on television a few hours before leaving Washington. 'Impassioned language has been used to assert that the United States has held Latin America in a colonial relationship,' he had said. 'That is a blatant false-hood.' The words were to haunt him during the following ten days.

When I wandered over to see the Puerto Rican demonstrators at close quarters as they stood behind barriers out of sight of the President but not beyond his hearing, I found that some of them were holding aloft signs carrying slogans such as *The United States is trying to destroy Puerto Rican nationhood* and *Independence is our legitimate right*. I also saw one woman, heavily pregnant, holding a sign inscribed with a crude caricature of Eisenhower enveloped in dollar signs. Probably more significantly, men near her were flourishing small Cuban flags and they were chanting 'Viva Fidel'. One member of the presidential party muttered 'I'd never have believed it unless I'd seen it' as we walked away from the demonstration.

The atmosphere was much more agreeable to the visitors at the next stop at Brasilia, the newly created capital of Brazil. Eisenhower was effusively acclaimed wherever he went after surviving a comic-opera interlude as he arrived. The President of Brazil, Juscelino Kubitschek, was not at the airport to greet his famous visitor because he had been advised that his aircraft would be arriving half an hour late. In fact it was early. The President duly disembarked, though had to go back into the aircraft when told that Kubitschek had not yet appeared but was on his way. He waited eight minutes and then, with Kubitschek in position, he disembarked again. Even then there came another hitch. It was found that the red carpet to be laid down for him was about twelve feet too long. Amid good-natured laughter on all sides, Eisenhower grinning even more broadly than most people, a soldier armed with an enormous pair of scissors snipped off the superfluity of carpet, and all was well again.

The happy day at Brasilia was offset, however, by a particularly ugly one at Montevideo. Police had to put on anti-riot equipment and use water-hoses, tear-gas canisters, clubs, sabres and even one or two pistols to subdue young Uruguayans who were determined to demonstrate that, in spite of the massive welcome put on by the majority of the capital's population, Eisenhower and all that he represented was not welcome to them. Tear-gas fumes halted Eisenhower and his host, President Nar-done, as they were driving past university buildings standing up in an open car. They had to sit down to wipe their eyes, and Eisenhower was still red-eyed some time later when he spoke to a joint session of the National Congress.

Although drenched by hoses cascading water on them at full nozzle, the demonstrators stubbornly held their ground as the procession passed, and when I was driven past them in a car a little way behind Eisenhower's I saw that, here again, Fidel Castro was the inspiration. The demonstrators were holding aloft a large banner carrying these words in Spanish: 'Out with Yankee American imperialism. Viva Fidel Castro.' The demonstration was not bloodless. One young man was taken to hospital with a bullet wound in a leg, and another was carried off on a stretcher. He had suffered a nasty wound from a police sabre.

It was at Santiago, Chile, that other Latin-American students produced the least offensive, best-planned and most effective of all the anti-American outbursts that marred this so-called Goodwill visit, and it was here that Eisenhower responded with a flash of fighting spirit that impressed everybody who saw it. He had been fatigued by the flying he had had to do and deeply upset by the unevenness of the reception he had been given and the evidence of more widespread anti-Americanism than he had been led to expect. Yet he gathered all his reserves to meet the challenge of accusations made by the Federation of Students of Chile in a letter of around fifteen hundred words which was delivered to him by hand soon after he had been driven into Santiago from the airport. Copies of it were distributed courteously and efficiently among the American and foreign correspondents accompanying him. My copy was handed to me as I sat at my typewriter composing my story for the day. The young student who gave it me smiled and bowed as he handed it over.

The letter itself was restrained and respectful, qualities that added immensely to its impact. It contained a list of the alleged mistakes and acts of exploitation perpetrated, said the students, by the United States in South America, and it carried a blunt warning that, if these continued much longer, all the countries in the southern subcontinent would one by one abandon democracy and turn in desperation to communism. The letter had been drafted in English with great care by the leaders of the 25,000 students attending seven universities in Chile. This remarkable document contained irrefutable facts about the American attitude to and treatment of Latin America. There were sharp criticisms in it which could not be rejected or ignored. It evidently stung Eisenhower so sharply that it roused him temporarily from the fatigue that one knew had enveloped him. He reacted to it with an impassioned outburst which lasted only a few minutes but which demonstrated that, for all his limitations as politician and statesman, he did have the instincts of a champion – one who can summon up, however briefly, the reserves needed to meet a sudden challenge.

This revelation came at the first public opportunity that offered. It was a routine engagement at which he met and saluted members of the permanent American community in Santiago. The setting was the small Windsor Theatre in the centre of the city. As I watched him walk along a middle aisle of the auditorium towards a platform from which he was to speak, I was much disturbed by his appearance. Although his face bore a deep tan acquired from exposure to a fierce sun while he had been fishing and golfing at Bariloche two days earlier, its lines were deeply etched. His eyes lacked lustre. His mouth sagged. He looked to me very much like a man of whom too much was being asked.

Concern about him deepened as he read his set address. His voice was weak and he slurred words like 'exist' and 'interest', as if finding it hard to pronounce some consonants. Worse, he referred to 'North America' instead of 'South America' and said 'production' for 'protection'. At one point I wondered whether he would be able to get through this small ceremony, much less the rest of the day, without some form of breakdown.

Then he suddenly delivered a surprise. He laid down his written speech on his lectern and, standing there erect, began a fiery, unexpected reaction to the accusations in the students' long letter. He shed his fatigue as if it were an uncomfortable outer garment and, gazing intently at the audience in front of him, spoke some glowing sentences. They were generalities but so striking that I took them down in shorthand and have kept them on record ever since. Reading them again after a quarter-century I sense that he had been mulling them over and probably had talked over the wording with one of his close assistants; but when he spoke them they were his own, delivered from the heart with a vigour which he had summoned from heaven knew where. 'Surely no nation loves liberty more, or more sincerely prays that its benefits and deep human satisfactions may come to all peoples, than does the United States,' he said. 'We *do* adhere to a policy of self-determination of peoples. We subscribe to and observe with constancy the cardinal principles of inter-American life – the policy of nonintervention. We repudiate dictatorship in any form, right or left. Our role in the United Nations and in the Organization of American States . . . in two world wars and in Korea . . . stands as a beacon to all who love freedom.'

He stopped after only a few minutes by saying he realized he had not given anything approaching a full and formal answer to the students. 'I shall do that in a letter to them,' he said. He then gathered up his discarded text and, once again a tired traveller, finished it mechanically. I sensed that even this brief outburst had sapped him. But Eisenhower had shown his mettle, and I admired him for that.

The report I cabled that day to my newspaper in London was one of the most fervent I ever wrote, in war or peace. I had been greatly disturbed by the President's appearance and demeanour during most of the time he was in the Windsor Theatre. I believed that too great a demand was being made on him during this exacting and unhappy tour and I felt it my duty to say so. 'Today's official programme was hardly an hour old before Mr Eisenhower showed beyond all further doubt that he is a very tired man and, the more so because of his fatigue, an angry one as well,' the cable ran. 'He looked a tired man as he climbed on to the platform in the Windsor Theatre. His face was superficially ruddy from the sun that burnt him while he was golfing and trout fishing in southern Argentina but there was an underlying greyness to his features, his jowls were sagging and there was a faraway look in his blue eyes. Here was a devoted, perhaps nearly spent old man, still intent upon his duties.'

I went on to say that the tour, almost three parts over, had drained him physically and had had, disappointingly, many more jarring notes than optimistic American planners had hoped. 'It showed too that they will be well advised to nurse their President's resources during the rest of the trip and, in the opinion of many people here, the rest of his fortunately short remaining period of office.'

Did I go too far? Probably so, because of my concern. The United States Embassy in London certainly thought so, for I was advised from the Foreign News Room of the *Daily Telegraph* that they had telephoned, because of their sensitivity to any report reflecting on the ability of the President to function in his office, to suggest that he was probably no more tired than anybody else (including myself, I suppose) enduring the rigours of the Goodwill mission. But I stood by my story, and I was rewarded a day later when James Hagerty announced that when the President reached Puerto Rico he would have only one engagement at a luncheon and would spend an extra day relaxing and playing golf before flying back to Washington.

Eisenhower's performance during the Goodwill Tour, and notably his rally in the Windsor Theatre in Santiago, served to explain why he never lost popularity or respect during his tenure as president, no matter what blows and setbacks came his way, whatever exorbitant demands were made upon him, whatever defects of judgement he showed, or whatever blunders were committed in his name. Everybody knew that he could be trusted to give of his best. Many of his international troubles arose from his stubborn – and admirable, if mistaken – faith in John Foster Dulles, his Secretary of State. Dulles was disliked and mistrusted by most of the world leaders who had to deal with him, but Eisenhower stood steadfastly by him, right up to his death on 24 May 1959. In a biography of the President, Professor Stephen E. Ambrose writes: 'In Eisenhower's judgment, Dulles was one of the greatest of Secretaries of State.' By way of contrast I recall Lord Hartwell, Editor-in-Chief of the *Daily Telegraph* at the time, saying to me in the late 1950s: 'Dulles is a blunderer – a total disaster. But Eisenhower is a treasure.'

10

The Reluctant Candidate

No such depressing controversies marred the progress of the Adlai Stevenson Bandwagon, which I boarded in 1952 as soon as it became apparent that the Eisenhower production was a bust as far as news was concerned. The Stevenson campaign deserved the evocative title of Bandwagon for, even though he was (in my opinion) pursuing a hopeless struggle, Adlai Stevenson was fighting a stimulating, enjoyable and high-minded one. There was no hint here of 'merchandizing' or organizing the candidate to the best advantage. Indeed, haphazard planning and last-minute improvisation marked most days as we all sallied out from the candidate's headquarters in Springfield, Illinois (the state of which he was Governor), by plane or train. Not for this singular intellectual-turned-politician such inferior products as machine-tooled speeches and manu-factured occasions. He would minutely scrutinize the orations produced in draft for him by his speech-writers and edit them line by line, adding here and taking away there. When he came to deliver a speech he usually added a leavening joke or uplifting observation entirely his own. Some of the jokes lost part of their sharpness when read coldly later, but I found them captivating as I listened a few feet away from his platform. One I remember with particular pleasure was his response to a criticism made somewhere in print that he was talking above the heads of the voters and was really an intellectual egghead. 'All I want to say in answer to that is – eggheads of the world unite. You've nothing to lose but your yolks,' he said with a disarming grin.

Such quips, coming unexpectedly in the course of a serious speech couched in elegant and telling language, endeared him to his audiences in much the same way as Eisenhower's uncomplicated presence endeared him to his. The difference, I felt as I listened and observed, was that too many of Stevenson's listeners came to his meetings because they wanted to hear what he had to say – and enjoy his jokes – but were not going to vote for him when the moment of decision came in the polling booth. Most of Eisenhower's listeners, on the other hand, had already made up their minds to vote for their hero before they even saw him in the flesh.

Members of Stevenson's staff were totally devoted to him and would do anything for him, day or night, and I noted that most of the American reporters assigned to him had also come under his spell. The very op-posite, it seemed, had happened in the case of Adlai Stevenson to what happened to Richard Nixon throughout his career.

This fact inspires a tantalizing speculation. If the presidential candidates in 1952 had been Richard Nixon and Adlai Stevenson, which of the pair would have won? It would have been a contest between a scholarly, liberal Democrat and a determined, hard-slogging, right-of-centre Republican. I think Nixon would have won, albeit narrowly, in spite of a predictably hostile press and some of the failings which I shall discuss later in this book. In the 1960s and 1970s he proved to be a surprisingly effective campaigner when he was running for election himself as president instead of as second fiddle to Eisenhower. His pragmatism and shrewdness evidently appealed to the inherent combative trait which I have observed in the past thirty-five years to be conspicuous in the American character. Stevenson on the other hand was always suspect as one who might not be firm in coping with the immense international pressure exerted on the man in charge of America's fortunes, and the world's, to an increasing extent. After Stevenson lost to Eisenhower in 1952 and again, even more heavily, in 1956, he never again had a chance to show his mettle, and he might very well have proved to have had much more of that quality than many of us thought in the fifties. Nevertheless, I still feel he had frailty as a political leader. He exerted a magical influence upon millions of Americans, but he could not persuade them to vote for him in anything like sufficient numbers for him to win.

One who never shared this doubt about Adlai Stevenson was William V. Shannon, my companion of the 1950s, later to become one of the most perceptive political analysts in the United States as well as a power on the editorial board of *The New York Times*, and eventually to serve President Carter as his Ambassador to Ireland. 'We underestimated Stevenson,' he said to me a month before his untimely death in 1988. 'The presidential ability was there. We simply forgot what winning does for a man like him. It develops him wonderfully. I think Stevenson would have been an outstanding president.'

One unique fact about the first election in which he figured was that both he and his opponent, Dwight D. Eisenhower, were very reluctant candidates before the campaign started. Ike had taken scant interest in politics during his career as a soldier and nobody knew until late in 1951 whether he was a Republican or Democrat because he had never registered as either, presumably because his military preoccupations had given him neither time nor inclination for political diversions. He had in fact been approached for nomination as the Democratic candidate in the previous election in 1948 and he had then said curtly: 'I would not accept a nomination even under the remote circumstance that it were tendered me.' He repeated his unwillingness to run four years later. After it had become known that he was a Republican (much to the chagrin of the incumbent President Truman), he insisted that he did not want a shot at the presidency, and it was only after Senator Cabot Lodge, the party's most persuasive emissary, had flown to Paris, where Eisenhower was serving as chief of NATO, and made a fervent appeal, that Eisenhower relented. Lodge apparently used the only argument which would influence so devoted a soldier: that it was his supreme duty to his country to volunteer to lead it through the dangerous period of the post-war years 'after twenty years of Democratic misrule'. This was all very persuasive, but the reality was that the fortunes of the Republican Party were at a low ebb and Eisenhower, with his reputation as a war hero and almost an idol as he was to most Americans, looked like an unbeatable candidate. Once persuaded to run, Eisenhower did so with surprising willingness.

Adlai Stevenson had shown himself to be even more unwilling, at the outset, to become a candidate. He kept on rejecting overtures long after the preliminary primary elections were over, and even as late as two days before he was nominated at the Democratic convention in July he was making this remarkable statement to a gathering of his party's regional leaders: 'I have no fitness – temperamentally, mentally, or physically – for the job. I just don't want to be nominated.' Yet he was.

Often as I sat in the press plane and watched a stretch of America roll by thousands of feet below I pondered this phenomenon of the two baulking conscripts of 1952 and wondered if it could happen in any other country. I doubted it. I also reviewed with bewilderment and some concern the artificial and antiquated oddities of the electoral process under which Stevenson and Eisenhower were now battling against each other with belated ferocity. The sad fact is that a presidential election drags on for so long that Americans (who are by no means noted for their patience) get bored with it weeks before polling day in early November, with the result that only about 50 per cent of those eligible to vote do so – the lowest electoral percentage of any of the major developed nations of the world. The only way to end this lamentable situation in a country which is supposed to give political, economic and social leadership to so many of the others is to carry out a complete overhaul of the ritual. This was drawn up in the days of long ago, when the horse was the only source of locomotion and it could take a delegate to a convention up to two weeks to reach the rendezvous for a well-lubricated reunion with pals whom he hadn't seen for four years. It hasn't changed much except that the railway train and later the aeroplane were used to add to the mileage covered by the candidates in their pursuit of votes. The primaries still start in New England very early in the year when, as I have found, the winter snows remain thick and are often so cloying as to tire out a man before the time comes when he must face composing a cable or a candidate must shake the last voter's hand or deliver the last address to a handful of people, most of whom won't be voting for him anyway. The gaudy conventions in the roasting summer still last four days, but happily are rapidly losing their attraction for viewers of network television and may indeed be on their way out. But voting still happens when next winter's snows are looming in the northern parts of the country and the inauguration of the resulting president still takes place, incredibly, over two months later in Washington at an open-air ceremony at which incoming president, past president, chief justice, and scores of other important people are usually lashed by sleet or a biting wind which gives many of them streaming colds, and worse.

The whole process lasts well over a year. It causes a hiatus in the performance of America's political business and her international responsibilities which distresses her friends and allies and gives a fine opportunity for deviltry by her enemies.

As I considered this deplorable and unnecessary phenomenon in 1952, and as I continue to do so nearly forty years later, I ask myself if reform will ever come. The one welcome development as the 1992 election draws nearer has been that more voices than ever are being used to clamour for a change, more and more pens, or rather typewriters and word processors, are producing written criticisms of the absence of action for improvement and, above all, asking for a long-overdue shortening of the quadrennial upheaval. I am heartened by the thought that once some process starts in the United States, it moves with startling speed.

In 1952, the managers of the Eisenhower campaign ended any lingering doubts about the triumph to come when, about a week before the vote, they arranged for their man to announce in a speech in Detroit that as president he would concentrate on ending the war in Korea, where the United States was mired in a conflict with a Communist army backed by the Soviet Union and was being prevented from doing what was necessary to win for fear of challenging Communist China and perhaps starting a third world war. 'The job requires a personal trip to Korea,' Eisenhower said. 'I shall make that trip. I shall go to Korea.' It was a gimmick, but it was a mightily effective one, its impact intensified because the pledge was being given by a military hero who, in the eyes of most Americans, had already done more to end a world war than any other man (except perhaps Winston Churchill) and could therefore be expected to end the current lesser one. His promise was just what an embittered and frustrated nation wanted to hear.

But, to my astonishment, it might never have been uttered, so far as the American journalists travelling with Adlai Stevenson were concerned. They still made their extravagant personal forecasts of a Stevenson victory as the press plane continued to fly hither and thither across the country. One of them, John Madigan, a spirited and lovable reporter from Chicago, composed a plaintive ballad called 'Don't Let Them Fritter Him Away', which everybody sang after the day's cables had been written and despatched. Such was the sway exerted by Adlai Stevenson upon those in close contact with him.

He was at his most polished in the hour of his defeat. He lost by an even greater margin than had seemed remotely possible during the campaign:

33,936,234 votes for Eisenhower; 27,314,992 for Stevenson – 55.1 per cent to 44.4 per cent. The landslide in electoral votes (cast by the states in proportion to their population) was even more awesome. Eisenhower gathered 442 to Stevenson's pitiful 89.

Yet Adlai Stevenson was spruce, cheerful, witty and graceful when, shortly before 1 a.m. on 5 November 1952, he confirmed his concession in front of a mass of people in the Leland Hotel in Springfield, Illinois. He had to use a side-door and a freight elevator after reaching the hotel, to avoid being mobbed and delayed by a great crowd of his disappointed but still idolatrous supporters. He looked almost as happy and nothing like so nervous, I remember thinking, as a bridegroom at a wedding. As he strode to the platform of the hotel's ballroom to take his place before an array of television cameras and upturned faces, he passed a Hollywood actress, Mercedes McCambridge, who had been energetically working for him in the final days of the campaign. 'Governor, we're with you – always' I heard her say through the sobs which were shaking her. Stevenson paused, smiled benignly, and said as he lightly patted the side of her face: 'Bless you, my dear.'

I noted many other tearful faces as Stevenson went through the formality of reading the telegram of congratulation he had sent to Eisenhower, who had been watching the results of the voting on television in an hotel room in Boston with his wife, Mamie. That done, he paused, and in answer to a question about how he felt, recited a memorable quotation: 'It hurts too much to laugh – and I'm too old to cry.'

Other questions followed, but most of them were routine and anti-climactic. I recall only one. Somebody standing very near me asked him: 'And now, what about 1956? Will you consider running?' Stevenson had a ready answer for that one. 'Let's have that man's head examined,' he said, and everybody laughed. Yet he did run four years later and, in a humdrum election, was given an even worse drubbing by Eisenhower than in 1952. The figures were: 35,581,003 votes for Eisenhower; 25,738,765 for Stevenson. And he won in only seven states, all in the South.

Next morning I went to see Adlai Stevenson. My purpose was not journalistic, for the attention of the world that day was turned towards the victor in the election, Dwight D. Eisenhower. I went because I wanted to say goodbye to a man whose fortunes, or misfortunes, I had been following so closely for a month, and also a man whose integrity and scholarly intelligence I had come to respect, even though I had felt so strongly that he would not have made an effective president. To me he was an American Hamlet, not a Caesar. Perhaps a majority of Americans felt the same about him, for he was never to attain high office in the years left to him; American and British voters do seem to share an ability to assess the inner qualifications, or otherwise, for leadership of the men and women who seek to administer their affairs. As we have seen, Adlai Stevenson himself, in a moment of sudden stress, blurted out his conviction that he was not suited for the presidency.

I found him seated at his desk in the governor's office in the State Capitol, which dominates Springfield. He was hardly visible behind a towering mound of telegrams, tens of thousands of them, stacked in front of him. They had come from Democrats all over the country who, as I learned later, were not only lamenting his defeat but were urging him not to give up his proclaimed mission of enlightening Americans about their alarming political plight, as he saw it, and the destiny that lay ahead of them once present difficulties and dangers were overcome.

When I commiserated with him on his defeat, he turned to me with a surprisingly sanguine gaze. 'These telegrams tell me it was worth the effort,' he said. 'I'm not going to give up.' I next told him of the doubts I had felt about his prospects at the polls. 'I'm sorry to say this,' I told him.

Stevenson's face took on a quizzical look as he pondered an answer, and I surmised that he was wondering just how frank he should be. Evidently he decided that he could be more direct with me, representing as I was a foreign publication, than with an American reporter, for his answer could scarcely have been more revelatory. 'You weren't alone,' he said. 'I thought so too once the campaign began. It soon became evident to me that I probably couldn't overcome three factors – having a national hero as my opponent, big business working so heavily for him, and the expertise of BBD and O in promoting him. . . . But please don't misunderstand me. I kept this doubt to myself and I didn't let it interfere with my effort or diminish it in any way. I went at my job absolutely as hard as I knew how, in the hope of upsetting the odds.'

I told him that this had been apparent not only in the United States but in my own country as well. There had been convincing evidence that the Stevenson sincerity had been deeply admired in the United Kingdom. Newspaper editorials, political commentaries on radio and television, and letters and other comments had testified to the fact that his wit, polish and conviction had impressed the non-partisan onlookers across the Atlantic, which was all the more remarkable considering that General Eisenhower was almost as popular there as in his own country. 'Perhaps I should have done better to run for office over there,' Adlai Stevenson observed wryly.

Adlai Stevenson would have been happier and infinitely more fulfilled if he had chosen almost any other profession than politics. As I observed him between 1952 and 1961 I often thought what a teacher and adviser he would have made at one of the American universities. He never achieved higher political office than a governorship, and when he was appointed Ambassador to the United Nations by Jack Kennedy he was often brushed aside as of no account. The job was given to him as a reward for his role as a sacrificial lamb in the elections of 1952 and 1956. The post carried with it a seat in the Kennedy cabinet, but that was an empty honour, for, not only did his duties keep him more or less permanently in New York, but his colleagues in the cabinet and the topmost ranks of the Democratic Party considered him privately and openly as an 'egghead', too intellectual and idealistic for their taste. His tenure at the United Nations brought him to the lowest point of his public service. One afternoon in mid-April 1961, when the world of international diplomacy was abuzz with reports of imminent military action against Cuba by the United States, Stevenson was called upon in the Political Committee of the Security Council to reply to a complaint by Cuba that two fighter aircraft, bearing the markings of the Cuban Air Force, which had attacked military targets in and near Havana, were in reality American machines manned by anti-Castro pilots in the pay of the Americans. 'The United States was making a vandalistic aggression against my country,' declared Dr Raul Roa, the Cuban Foreign Minister.

Adlai Stevenson did his duty with passionate fervour and obvious sincerity. I was listening in the crowded chamber. 'The two aircraft which landed in Florida today were flown by Cuban Air Force pilots,' he said, exhibiting photographs of the machines. 'These pilots and certain other crew members have apparently defected from Castro's tyranny. No United States personnel participated. These two planes, to the best of our knowledge, were Castro's own planes. According to the pilots, they took off from Castro's own airfields.'

I was by no means alone in doubting the story. There was something wrong with it. Was it not far more likely that the attacks were part of softening-up tactics ahead of an imminent invasion?

There certainly *was* something curious about the American story. It emerged that President Kennedy had, either deliberately or by thoughtless default, not told Stevenson, a member of his cabinet and his official spokesman at the United Nations, that the aircraft were in fact American and had taken off from Florida, after the false markings had been painted over the original American ones. Stevenson had been misled into believing that he was telling the truth. His credibility had been destroyed in front of representatives of the whole world.

His health was beginning to falter at that time, and in 1965 he collapsed while walking along a street in London with his friend, Mrs Marietta Tree, after preparing a broadcast for the BBC. He died a sad and disappointed man, but not, I am told, an embittered one.

11

Man at Bay

Richard Nixon seemed to have destroyed himself politically a few hours after he had suffered a stunning defeat in an election battle for the governorship of California at the hands of the Democratic incumbent, Edmund Brown, in November 1962. As I watched him stride off a platform in an improvised press-room in the Beverly Hilton Hotel in Los Angeles at 10.15 a.m. on 7 November 1962, I assumed, quite mistakenly as it was to turn out, that this was the last anybody would see on the public stage of that stocky figure and the heavily jowled face with which the world had become familiar since he had been chosen, surprisingly, by Dwight D. Eisenhower as the Republican vice-presidential candidate ten years earlier. Had he not told a group of us political reporters a few minutes earlier that this was the last we should be seeing of him? In the course of a meandering and sometimes incomprehensible monologue he had said: 'You won't have Nixon to kick around any more because, gentlemen, this is my last press conference. . . .'

He probably believed his words of withdrawal from the political scene when he uttered them. But very soon afterwards he was proving that they were spectacularly hollow. He began by giving an informal interview here, a tantalizing hint there, and making accurate and highly reportable comments and judgements about international affairs as he roamed the world. By way of contrast, he played the piano on Jack Paar's national television show. He had not destroyed himself, after all. Thereafter he took a more and more active part in political affairs until, miraculously, he gained the presidency and held it until he seemed once again to have destroyed himself by having to resign under a threat of impeachment. I am convinced that he could easily have averted this second monumental humiliation if at the outset of the Watergate scandal he had publicly acknowledged that, yes, there had been some ill-considered activity by certain people within the Republican fold and he as President and leader of his party was going to organize an inquiry into the affair and anybody found guilty of wrongdoing would be punished. Such a declaration could have transformed Watergate into a mere passing phenomenon, soon forgotten, and would have saved his presidency. But as I watched the indestructible Richard Nixon in the late 1980s climbing once again out of the abyss he dug for himself, and developing an impressive role as an elder statesman, I deduced on the basis of my professional observation of him during the 1950s, 1960s and 1970s that he had been the victim of self-created demons which distorted his judgement in so far as his personal, but not national and world affairs, were concerned. I have a feeling that, having become wiser with age and having profited at last from disasters which would have crushed a lesser, softer man, he had by the late 1980s shed some of his inhibitions and, if spared to live on actively, will have valuable service to offer his country and the world in the 1990s. I cannot possibly forecast what his future might be, but I have no doubt that it will be bizarre.

One demon that hampered him in the years I was closely observing him was an obsessive sense of inferiority to most of the men with whom he had to deal at the topmost level of American and world leadership. He felt he had to strain and resort to low blows to keep up with them because they had had the advantage of higher social status at birth and greater early opportunities to advance in their careers through superior education and familial influence and power. He came from humble, if sturdy, Quaker stock. He had been plucked from comparative obscurity – except for a discreditable smear campaign he conducted against Mrs Helen Gahagen Douglas in a senatorial election in California in 1950 and an earlier melodramatic performance in the questioning of Alger Hiss before the House Unamerican Activities Committee – to run as vice-presidential candidate with Dwight D. Eisenhower in 1952. Once in office, as Vice-President and later as President, he found himself in the first division of politics. It was a world dominated by such men as the Kennedys, Adlai Stevenson, Henry Kissinger, Nelson Rockefeller, Dean Acheson and John Foster Dulles in the United States and by such figures as Winston Churchill, Anthony Eden, Harold Macmillan, Charles de Gaulle and Konrad Adenauer in the field of international diplomacy. For all his social disadvantages, Richard Nixon was mistaken in believing he had to fight noisily, fiercely and unfairly in coping with such men. It was his own fault that he earned the nickname 'Tricky Dick' and a reputation in hostile quarters as an untrustworthy political adventurer and a bruiser. There was little need for Richard Nixon to feel any inferiority, for he was as quick-witted, intuitive, and tougher, than almost anybody with whom he had to negotiate or do battle. About the only world figure comparable to him in origin and character was Nikita Khrushchev, and it is perhaps significant that it was with Khrushchev that he had a public verbal brawl, in Sokolniki Park, Moscow, which he was adjudged to have won in the well-published opinions of those Westerners who watched and heard it.

Another demon that possessed Richard Nixon was a distorted belief that the American reporters who covered his activities were, with very few exceptions, antagonistic to him. Many of them were of course Democrats by political persuasion, and one has to assume that some of them allowed their anti-Republican sentiments to influence their reporting. But Nixon exaggerated and he allowed his bias against American newsmen to consume him, as he showed in that memorable outburst in Los Angeles in 1962, which I have quoted. I do not know when the running battle started but it was in full swing during all the years I reported on his activities. It could have begun as far back as 1950 and might have been provoked by the dubious tactics he and his controversial adviser Murray Chotiner, a Chicago lawyer, used in accusing Mrs Douglas of communistic leanings and associations during the senatorial election contest of that year. As the Nixon fixation grew, so did the negative publicity in the writings of commentators and columnists who were of course much freer to express themselves than were reporters.

Other demons troubled Richard Nixon, but I shall not dwell on them because I do not wish to become involved in the impossible task of trying to analyse him. He is by far the most complicated public personage I have ever met. Many have tried in articles and books to dissect him, but nothing I have read has succeeded in explaining him fully. Even his devoted wife, Pat, who always supported him to the full in public, once hinted to me that sometimes his political moves surprised her. This was while we were flying across the mid-section of America in one of his campaign aircraft. She was always loyally at his side in his years of campaigning and never publicly questioned anything he did or said; but one member of his entourage did say to me at one point that after the disaster in California in 1962 she pleaded with him in private to keep to his decision to abandon politics. If he had listened to her, the course of American politics and, to some degree, the course of world history in the second half of the century could well have been affected.

Richard Nixon himself is probably the only person who can fill in the gaps in our knowledge of him – tell of the secret reasoning and impulses that made him the most controversial American political figure of the century and his career the most volatile of any man who served as president during that period. The highs and lows of his political life are so extreme as to be almost unbelievable. He came within a hair's breadth of being dumped as vice-presidential candidate by Eisenhower in 1952; he lost a presidential election to John F. Kennedy by so small a margin that many people believe he actually won it and was cheated of victory because Mayor Daley of Chicago falsified the voting in Cook County of that city; he returned from the politically dead to gain the presidency in 1964 and was re-elected by a phenomenal landslide four years later; through his own weaknesses, his evasions and lies, and his blindness in failing to protect himself against the onslaught of the Watergate scandal, he was brought to a humiliating resignation of the presidency; and then, within but a few years, he was being courted as an elder statesman whose opinions and judgements on political and national issues were authoritative and most uncanny in their aptness and accuracy. It all makes a story unique in American history. And it seemed as the century entered its last decade that the story was by no means ended.

I was surprised to find myself conscripted into a walk-on part in the drama of the election of 1962. It eventually became a tragedy as it plunged Richard Nixon to the nadir of his pre-presidential career, but I do not think my participation had anything to do with that! I didn't mind my involuntary casting, for it didn't interfere with my work, and if Mr Nixon thought it helped, well and good, for I had come to feel sorry for him as he battled – and floundered – on-stage, and to like him for his unaffected friendliness off-stage. My modest participation began only a couple of days after I had started travelling around California with him and his small entourage in a corporate aircraft supplied by one of his supporters, or from one meeting to another by bus in a town or city. People on the aeroplane or bus always let the candidate disembark first at a stopping-place so that he could descend with a smile and a wave to the plaudits of those awaiting him. On this particular day Richard Nixon stopped as he was about to pass me as I sat in the plane and, laying a hand lightly on my shoulder, said: 'I'm going to mention you in my speech here. Will you be ready to stand and be recognized?' I nodded, and sure enough about midway through his set address to a crowd assembled in a shopping centre in, I think, Sacramento, he said: 'Just to show you that the world is watching this important election I can tell you that Edwin Tetlow, of the London *Daily Telegraph*, is here to report on it for the people of the United Kingdom.' He pointed towards me and, responding to my cue, I stood, bowed slightly and in (I hope) dignified style, and sat down again. I received no applause – only a general momentary turning of heads in my direction as Richard Nixon capitalized on his little gimmick by telling the voters that he considered he was far more qualified to represent them and the interests of California in international affairs than his opponent, the local boy, Edmund Brown.

Thereafter, my performance, improving as I went on, was repeated several times – until, as I shall relate, it was expanded in Mr Nixon's dreadful valedictory in the Beverly Hilton Hotel.

Looking back upon that extraordinary regional election, I feel much more strongly than I did in 1962 that Richard Nixon was defeated by himself – by his warring complexes, his misreading of what Californians were expecting of their future governor, and his use of the wrong tactics in shaping his campaign. As it began, it seemed to be an election he simply could not lose. He was the candidate with winning qualifications. Here was a former vice-president, a Californian who had brought credit to his state by eight years of solid and, on balance, highly successful national service. Unlike almost all his predecessors he had given the onerous office of vice-president increased lustre and stature and, it was argued, some of this enhancement must have rubbed off on him. Further, he had surprised most of America's political analysts and other presumed experts by losing in 1960 by only a questionable, microscopic margin his contest with John F. Kennedy for the presidency. His private life, too, bore not one damag-

ing blemish. True, he had made enemies in Washington and his reputation as a politician and a budding statesman was more highly regarded
outside his own country than within it, notably in the United Kingdom.
Those Washington whispers, sniping and frontal attacks had not carried
their denigrating effect across the Atlantic into Britain and the rest of
Europe.

Mr Brown, the man he had to beat, could dangle no such glamorous
qualifications before the voters of California. But he had worked hard and
well on local issues and was much more popular in the state than the
Nixon camp estimated. They should have been warned by the fact that he
had won the governorship four years earlier by the massive majority of
over a million votes. I was one of many observers from outside California
who joined them in believing until two days before the poll that Richard
Nixon would defeat him, if narrowly. I should have known better.

As I flew and rode with Richard Nixon around California, watching him
flog himself as he sought to oust Edmund Brown and, all too rarely,
observing him seeking quietude to refuel himself in readiness for the next
foray, I was struck by a realization that I was seeing two very different
Richard Nixons. The on-stage Nixon was one person and the private one
was another. The private Nixon, talking quietly and easily in the plane or
on the bus, was very likeable. The public Nixon – the one seen on
platforms or before television cameras – was prone to make flailing
gestures with a clenched fist and strive by this and other artifices and by
overemphasis as he spoke to project an air of authoritative determination.
This simply did not work. It alienated many of those voters he sought to
impress, and in antagonizing sceptical American journalists added to the
tide of their mistrust of him. This duality of Nixon also helps to explain
why his written assertions and judgements are usually convincing while
his spoken ones are not. It also might explain why, when he and Jack
Kennedy met in memorable debates on television and radio in the presidential campaign of 1960, most people who listened only by radio believed
that Nixon had been more effective, while almost all of those who watched
the debates on television were even more adamant in their opinion that
Kennedy had prevailed. The sharp divergence seems to confirm that
Mr Nixon's unprepossing features and dark visage, reinforced by his
artificial and unconvincing speech and demeanour, always worked heavily
to his disadvantage.

Worse, he took again the 'low road' in campaign tactics. Instead of
capitalizing on his record as a man who had risen from nowhere to
national and international eminence and was anxious to resume his
advance to California's advantage, he became childish, uncertain, defensive and puerilely vicious. He could so easily have appealed to Californians
by saying, for example, that Mr Brown had been satisfactory as a stopgap
administrator for one term but was not equipped to stay and lead the state
to its obvious destiny as the leader of them all, since that was a task for a

skilled and experienced leader – namely, himself. Instead, he started aiming smears, petty belittlements and even inanities at Mr Brown. He claimed that his opponent had been 'soft on communism' and had not punished drug-pushers as vigorously as he should. He seemed to be repeating a milder version of the kind of attack that had been effective in the earlier campaign against Mrs Helen Gahagen Douglas, in a mistaken belief that this kind of tactic would still work. It wouldn't, for the political and social climate in the United States had changed. I was dismayed to hear Mr Nixon saying to his audiences that 'Mr Brown claims he is a better American than I am' and 'Mr Brown says I have no heart – but I do think he has one.' The candidate was obviously floundering. This kind of remark seemed to me to represent the ultimate in electioneering fatuity, and I said so in my despatches to London. I also became so bold as to say the same thing to Herbert Klein, the campaign director of communications, and his assistant, Ronald Ziegler, whenever they asked me how I thought the campaign was going. Perhaps such comments had some little effect, but they were by no means enough to turn the tide of opinion in Mr Nixon's favour, as was proved two days before the vote by a poll taken by the Field Organization, which had a good record for accuracy. It showed that Governor Brown was enjoying a lead among voters of 48 percentage points to 44 for Nixon, the remaining 8 per cent being undecided.

Mr Nixon had told me earlier that he neither took his own polls seriously nor put any credence into those taken by others. Events showed that he was surely taking notice of this one. It presented a warning and a challenge that could not be ignored. Unless those undecided voters, plus some of those who had told the pollsters that they were going to vote against him, could be won over at the eleventh hour, he faced a shocking defeat. He had no alternative but to make an aggressive counter-attack, and he prepared one in true Nixon style.

It had been planned that on election eve he would use a final half-hour of purchased television time to make a lofty last-minute address to the voters – and, looking back, I wish for his sake that he had done so. Instead, the ominous Field poll pushed him into a familiar Nixon posture of a misunderstood man wrongfully thrust into a corner and at bay against his enemies. He went into seclusion. Spurning the help of a speech-writer or anybody else, he set about creating a final appeal entirely on his own. He asked his wife to deputize for him on a planned day-long bus tour of Los Angeles and its suburbs, including the Nixon home-town of Whittier. Loyal as ever, she fulfilled the unexpected assignment, putting on a cheerful, confident smile and making short but appealing speeches to the significantly small crowds that congregated at the places where the bus was scheduled to stop.

I was depressed when I heard what Mr Nixon was doing. I feared we were in for another Checkers-type performance on television. In 1952, when Nixon was running as vice-presidential candidate, it emerged that as a senator he had received a total of $18,235 from major businessmen in California to pay expenses which he would otherwise have had to pay himself. The story was built up in the Democratic press to such a pitch that Nixon had to make rebuttal on television or face being dropped by Eisenhower in the election. In making the speech he used his daughters' little cocker spaniel, Checkers, as a symbol of the unpretentious virtue of his family life. The speech was considered the ultimate in corniness by a minority of sophisticates, but, answering Nixon's broadcast appeal for support, 300,000 letters and telegrams signed by over a million Americans were sent to the Republican National Committee. They were 350 to 1 in support of Nixon. Checkers had won the day.

We reached the television studio about an hour before the show was to start. A setting had been carefully contrived. It consisted basically of a replica of a drawing-room. A fatherly looking photograph of President Eisenhower stood poised within camera range just behind chairs and a settee. A globe of the world was also handily placed to be picked up by the cameras whenever Mr Nixon, as it was planned, turned to international affairs during his oration. All this was most reassuring, but the effect was dulled when after a while Mrs Nixon and her two daughters came to the set and were carefully posed on the settee. Was he going to use the family as props, after all? Thankfully there was no sign of a dog, but it looked as if we were in for a tear-jerker of some kind.

Mr Nixon was tense and haggard, in spite of heavy make-up, as air time approached. He listened, or pretended to listen, to suggestions and directions from his stage-manager, and he fussed around his family. He had obviously had little or no rest during the previous twenty-four hours. 'He's spent most of the time writing and rehearsing what he has to say,' Ron Ziegler said. Less than ten minutes before the telecast was due to begin he quietly asked all those not involved in the show to leave the set. This was to be *his* show, one on which his whole political future would seem to depend. He had every justification for the request. Along with members of his staff, I went into an adjoining studio into which monitoring receivers had been placed. They were already working, and I was immediately relieved that Mr Nixon could not see the programme that was being shown. The time had been bought by the Democrats on behalf of Governor Brown and one of the participants was an actor or singer whose name happily eludes me. He cavorted before the cameras as he crudely tried to persuade his watchers to vote for Mr Brown. He ended his act by sidling up close to the camera to deliver several insulting references to Mr Nixon which were deplorable even by Hollywood standards.

Mr Nixon's performance turned out to be by no means as bathetic as many of us had feared. He did spend the first minutes of his appearance answering real or imagined smears which he said the Democrats had spread. But after that he gave of his best, with earnest and reasoned arguments why he should be chosen as California's next governor. He did use his wife and daughters, but sparingly and effectively. However, it was proved next day that neither the broadcast nor anything else he might have tried was going to save him from a huge defeat, one that would surely have ended the political career of anybody I knew in American public life except the astonishingly resilient and thick-skinned Richard Nixon.

He was a man apart as he sat awaiting the returns in a suite on the seventh floor of the Beverly Hilton Hotel. He was protected from intruders by a guard post manned by members of his staff between the elevators and the entrance to the suite. Only those closest to him were allowed past that human barrier.

The early period was the only time during the long night that he could harbour a glimmer of hope for victory. He went ahead in the count. With just under one million votes counted he was some 10,000 in front of Governor Brown. He responded by allowing news photographers to enter the suite and take pictures of him sitting in his shirt-sleeves in front of a finished tray of food. As they fussed and flashed he exchanged the sort of badinage common on such occasions. But even while he was speaking, the figures were beginning to reflect a deadly trend against him. About 10 p.m. Governor Brown took the lead, and he never lost it thereafter.

Yet the Nixon strategists were entitled to wait until it was absolutely certain that their man could not possibly win, and I wasn't surprised when at about 3 a.m. word came from the seventh floor that Mr Nixon was going to bed and would have nothing to say until 9 a.m. at the earliest. But the reason for delay was very fragile. It was that returns from Orange County and San Diego were not yet in and these were areas where the Republican vote was traditionally strong.

Richard Nixon did not in fact go to bed that night. He dozed in a chair until, just before dawn, he had to face the awful truth. All but a handful of returns were in and the Brown lead had actually passed the 900,000 mark. All the Nixon defences had been overrun. The margin by which he finally went down was well over 300,000 votes out of a total of about 6 million. This was three times as great a deficit, in a much smaller arena, than the one by which he had lost in the presidential election against John F. Kennedy two years earlier. It was a far more humiliating slap in the face than anyone anticipated. He scribbled out a brief message of concession, as is customary, to his successful adversary: 'Congratulations on your election as governor. I wish you the best in your great honour and the opportunity you now have to lead the first state of the Union.' It was cool, but not bitter. It was decided that Herb Klein, a Nixon spokesman, should read the text of the telegram sent by Nixon to Governor Brown, along with a telegram of thanks to the campaign workers. He refused to do so, and a few hours later at the Klein press conference there was a sudden commotion near a door on one side of the platform. 'He's coming! He's coming right now!' I heard an excited voice shouting. Photographic flashes flared all round the doorway. Men came backing into the room as if retreating before some powerful, unstoppable force.

Richard Nixon, his heavy visage now deeply lined and creased from fatigue, his mouth set tight as if in repressed anger, strode towards the platform and climbed three steps to take a stance before an array of microphones which had come from nowhere and stood in front of him like long-stemmed flowers. Herb Klein had backed away and now stood, agape, a few feet behind Mr Nixon. The straggly audience of over a hundred people looked at Nixon in astonishment. Half a dozen television cameras were trained on him, following his every movement and gesture. The hubbub which his entry had provoked died away and, thrusting his left hand into his trouser pocket, he began speaking. I noted that he used a gesture with which all those who had been listening to him during the campaign had become familiar – the clenched right hand, with digit finger extended, making an aggressive swing to emphasize every other phrase.

'Good morning, gentlemen,' he said. 'Now that Mr Klein has made his statement – and now that all the members of the press are so delighted that I have lost – I'd like to make a statement of my own.' I had been routinely taking down his words in shorthand, but I stopped with my pencil poised in front of me. I must have misheard him, simply must have. He could not possibly have said such an outrageous thing. I turned and looked at my neighbour, Carl Greenberg. We exchanged startled glances. Clearly he too was finding it hard to believe what he had heard. There was no mistake about it, however.

Richard Nixon was making it very obvious that we hadn't misheard him, even though what he was saying was sometimes incoherent, sometimes contradictory of what had just gone before. These were the bitter words of a tired and temporarily broken man. He had come to the conference-room to hit back after being battered by defeat, and having had to absorb gibes and criticism not only from his opponent but from commentators in newspapers and on television during the past few weeks of desperate electioneering. Perhaps he was also replying at last to attacks made upon him during years of grinding and often unrewarding labour as an operator in the grimy world of American politics. Yet some self-preserving instinct was prompting him to qualify and sometimes contradict the awful things he was blurting out. It was hard to fathom just how his mind was working. Were we watching and listening to two Richard Nixons, the good and the bad, fighting for possession of a temporarily spent human being?

The good Nixon congratulated his victorious opponent with apparent sincerity. 'He has, I think, the greatest honour and the greatest responsibility of any governor in the United States. I wish him well.' Then the bad Nixon chimed in. 'I believe Governor Brown has a heart – even though he believes I do not. I believe he is a good American, even though he feels I am not. . . . ' It was childish, spiteful stuff, spoken by a man not in full control of himself.

His mind now turned to the sharp goad of revenge which had brought him to this platform, against the advice of all those around him: getting even with the reporters. 'I am proud that I defended my opponent's patriotism. You gentlemen didn't report it, but I'm glad I did that,' he said. 'There's one reporter here who has religiously covered me fairly – and incidentally this is no reflection on the others. . . . Some of you weren't bothered. . . . One reporter, Carl Greenberg – he's the only reporter on the *Los Angeles Times* that fits this thing – wrote every word that I said. He wrote it fairly. He wrote it objectively. I don't mean that others didn't have the right to do it differently. But Carl, despite whatever feelings he had, felt he had an obligation to report the facts.' Carl, sitting alongside me, gave no sign that the words he was hearing were leaving any impression on him. He just went on writing them down.

Now it was the turn of the Nixon campaign workers to receive barbed thanks. He tried to insinuate that they were somehow responsible for his defeat, and this was unworthy of him. 'Our hundred thousand workers I was proud of,' he said. 'I think they did a magnificent job. I only wish they could have gotten out a few more votes in the key precincts, but because they didn't Mr Brown has won and I have lost.' This was the most unfair passage of the mixed-up harangue, and I could only hope that Mr Nixon would regret it when he had had time to recover. He had to realize that he lost because of his own deficiencies, personal and political, and not because of any shortcomings in the effort of his campaign workers, or because of the reporters, or anybody else.

Having thus disposed of the campaign workers, Richard Nixon turned to the national scene. His flitting brain, too exhausted to hold to a single topic for long, roamed around – to Republican prospects for the election of 1964, Cuba, NATO, President Kennedy and those whom he described as 'the woolly heads around him', and the national economy. 'I have fought the fight and now it's up to others to take the responsibility of leadership,' he said. 'I don't say this with any bitterness because I just feel that's the way it should be.' So, I thought, he really means it. How wrong I was. How wrong everybody was. Even himself.

A recurring thought as he rambled on seemed to be concern that the American economy needed to be revitalized. He said he trusted that through tax reform and individual enterprise the economy would revive. Where was all this leading? Was it leading anywhere at all? I stopped taking notes, for I could make little sense of what he was saying.

And I was suddenly staggered to hear myself being brought into this astonishing monologue. 'To me, more important than anything else, America has to move now,' I heard him say. 'It's got to move forward economically, with productivity. It's got to move forward – I'll say this in the presence of my good friend from Britain, Ed Tetlow, here – it's got to

move forward, relying on individual enterprise and individual opportunity.' As he spoke, his outstretched finger pointed down to me, standing just below the platform. The television cameras zoomed in on me – to
my embarrassment. Once again, had I heard correctly? What on earth had
I to do with the American economy? Why had he singled me out? I could
find no immediate answer. I just stood there, frozen.

He had called me his 'good friend', but this was not so in the true sense
of the term, though we *had* formed an agreeable relationship during the
fortnight I had been with him. He knew I liked him, off-stage, and he also
knew I wasn't writing hostile stories about him, for the simple reason that
there was no reason at all why I should do so. I was writing for a
readership in a foreign country over six thousand miles away, for people
who like myself had no vote and no stake in the election. My mission in
California had been to chronicle what he did and how he fared in this
critical election because the British were interested in him as one of the
leading figures on the American political scene and a man whom they had
liked when he visited them in 1958.

I had found him most co-operative on the campaign trail. One day he
said to me: 'Aren't you going to cover the other fellow?' I answered: 'No,
you're my story.' He smiled and said: 'I'll try and live up to that.' He had
also readily agreed when I relayed to him a request made by four British
Members of Parliament who were observing the election as guests of the
State Department that he should have a chat with them. 'Sure,' he said,
and he had come into the press bus as it lurched its way from one meeting
to another and had sat on the arm of my seat to converse with the visitors.
He had talked entertainingly and informatively, despite his nagging
preoccupations in fighting an uphill campaign. The MPs told me afterwards how much they had liked him and how impressed they had been
with his ebullience and naturalness. Once again the 'good' Nixon had
scored a success.

Now he had seen me standing before him as a friendly face, perhaps,
among a mass of others whom he chose to believe were antagonistic.
Inappropriate as the occasion and the context of his muddled remarks
about the American economy were, he hadn't been able to resist the
impulse to name me. Not surprisingly the incident had repercussions.
Some of my friends and colleagues jokingly suggested later when Richard
Nixon became President that I ought to apply for a job in the White House.
I am glad that I never considered doing so, in view of Watergate and other
disasters. One of the most amusing sequels happened in New York soon
after I returned there from Los Angeles. I was walking in 50th Street when
I heard a loud yell behind me. It came from a long-time friend, John
Chancellor, of the National Broadcasting Company. 'Hi there, Ed Tetlow!'
he cried, exuberantly. 'There he is, folks – Nixon's chum.' Heads turned.
Embarrassed and vowing inwardly to get even with him when a chance
came, I hurried into the sanctuary of Rockefeller Plaza.

Now came the unforgettable climax to the seventeen-minute drama at the Beverly Hilton. Richard Nixon fired the parting salvo that was destined to reverberate and haunt him for the rest of his life, which I have partly quoted earlier: 'As I leave you I want you to know – just think how much you're going to be missing,' he said. 'You won't have Nixon to kick around any more because, gentlemen, this is my last press conference.' He stopped, and his right fist, which had been making its last swing to emphasize this bitter gibe, was raised aloft in a mocking salute of farewell. There was a slight smile now on the contorted face – a smile of sarcasm. Then he turned and went away. As he reached the door, a few of his faithful helpers started a feeble hand-clap. It died almost immediately, cut off by its own dismal hollowness. Herb Klein, looking dazed, followed hard on Mr Nixon's heels. The show was over.

For a few moments there was utter silence in the conference-room. Journalists are not easily taken aback, but this group was. First to recover were one or two who had been writing anti-Nixonisms for a long time. I heard one of them, a woman, say: 'Well, this confirms my worst fears. He's deranged.' I couldn't agree. I felt sure that in this moment of extreme fatigue and despair Richard Nixon's worst characteristics had taken possession of him. The Mr Hyde in him had replaced Dr Jekyll.

I hastened to my typewriter and wrote as coolly and factually as I could. When I telephoned London from one of the few booths still intact in the room I permitted myself only one extempore concluding comment: 'It was a political exit not many Americans would care to see repeated.'

12

'The Woman I Love . . .'

It is a source of sadness to me that the few contacts I had with the man who died as the Duke of Windsor after he had spent almost half a lifetime as Prince of Wales and, so briefly, King of England, happened in circumstances of embarrassment to him and frustrated irritation to me. I saw him first in the early 1930s as he lay sprawled in a muddy English field, next as a pathetic fugitive from a throne, then as a harassed pedestrian trying to outwit Manhattan's menacing traffic, and finally as a henpecked husband scurrying to obey the command of a domineering wife. I never saw him as the man he could and should have been, because that was the man he never was.

My contacts with him were not close, but as they occurred at critical phases of his unique, squandered career, they made it possible for me to measure the erosive effect on him and his fortunes of his faults and deficiencies: his waywardness, his stubborn selfishness, his poor judgement, and his lack of fibre. His course was downhill all the way once his days of glory as a radiant young prince were over.

My sight of him as the Duke of Windsor, living uselessly in the United States, came only a few days after my wife and I had arrived in New York after five years spent in Berlin from the end of the Second World War in 1945. The circumstances of this chance sighting were such as to illustrate vividly the extent of all that he had forfeited on account of Wallis Simpson, whom I had heard him describe in Windsor Castle late on the night of 11 December 1936 as 'the woman I love'. Considering those memorable words now, half a century later, one asks: Did he really love her? Or was he the victim of a chronic, hallucinatory obsession which could not fail to bring him, a weak person indeed, down? Did she for her part love him? Or did she coldly seek to use him to take her into the history books in the glittering role of a Queen of England? These and all the other questions about them and their association have been discussed by spoken and written word ever since 1936 and one cannot doubt that the debate will go on and on.

The two principals are now dead, having contributed only ghost-written and inevitably twisted versions of their individual stories. Not many people who really knew them have said or written anything. And the British royal family, who know everything, have kept total silence and doubtless will continue to do so, allowing the implacable hostility of their leading members to Wallis Simpson to speak for them. So, as with so many episodes in British and world history, an accepted but by no means necessarily accurate version of the truth will emerge.

My wife and I were being driven by friends across Manhattan on a sightseeing tour, and the car was waiting for traffic-lights to change at the westerly intersection of 49th Street and Park Avenue. As I was looking around, taking in the new sights – breathtaking after the awful drabness of ruined Berlin – I suddenly observed the Duke standing on the island half-way across the avenue. He also was waiting for the lights to change so that he could finish his trip on foot to the eastern pavement of Park Avenue. The sight jolted me. It was shocking to an Englishman to see his one-time Prince and King thus, just another pedestrian in midtown Manhattan, having to wait there for traffic-lights to change. The enormous significance of his abdication, the degradation it had brought, struck with the numbing force of a physical blow. As I watched him fidgeting there, his residual petulance from former days got the better of him and, with the lights still showing red against him, he made a dash for it. Of course he got tangled up with the toiling traffic. I looked on fascinated yet aghast as he scurried hastily but, I must concede, with enviable agility, around the cars and taxi-cabs. He even put a hand on the hood of one vehicle, steadying himself for another bolt forward. Eventually as I watched, he reached the sanctuary of the far pavement. Then and there he took on an even less distinguished role, just another figure among the crowd of people hurrying along Park Avenue.

As we drove on from Park Avenue I could not help musing that if Edward had done his duty he could have had millions of Americans straining to catch a glimpse of him as he made a royal progress through Manhattan, instead of having to bob and weave like a hunted rabbit across the avenue and walk in anonymity between 49th and 50th Street.

Some months later I met him socially for the first time. All my earlier associations with him had happened in England up to a quarter-century ago, and in those days a man or woman of the people could look upon a royal personage and indeed was encouraged to do so but was not allowed to approach a king, queen, prince or princess and seek to engage that personage in conversation without permission or invitation. But everything was different now. Edward was no longer a functioning royal person and, exiled, he needed the company of his fellow-expatriates.

At first I shied away from the opportunity to meet him and his Duchess for the obvious reason – my low opinion of both of them. The meeting was proposed by a far more generous-minded British correspondent than I. This was Richard Greenough of the *Daily Mail*, who felt that it would be an appropriate gesture by the small band of British journalists living and working in New York if they offered the Duke and Duchess a celebratory cocktail party marking the publication of the Duke's book, *A King's Story*. Richard felt sure that the Windsors would appreciate the suggestion of a party because it would indicate to the Duke that, no matter what had happened and what had been written about it in the United Kingdom, the correspondents in New York rejoiced in the success of his book. He was proved right. The Windsors promptly accepted the invitation and a private room at the University Club, at Fifth Avenue and 54th Street, was reserved for the event.

The party was well attended – I suppose there were about fifty people in the large room – and it went with a swing. The men crowded round the Duke and the wives talked with increasing zest to the Duchess. The talk between the Duke and the male correspondents was not at all important, of course, because everybody concerned sought to steer clear on this purely social occasion of anything controversial or delicate. I recall that he discussed with animation such matters as the complexities Britons faced in adjusting to life in America, the mechanics of our efforts to interpret America to our readers and listeners in the United Kingdom, and even the contrast to be found in the attitudes of Americans and Britons towards money and trade. He thought that Americans were much more realistic in their approach to these concerns than were Britons. I remember that in emphasizing this point he entertained us by reciting a ditty which ended approximately with the following rhyme: 'He who gets the dollars is the one who stands and hollers.'

I noted as we talked how curiously the years and his troubles had dealt with him. He was now fifty-six, well into middle age, but in many respects he looked much younger. His figure was still slight and trim, and as he gazed directly at one with those familiar blue eyes he seemed to have changed comparatively little over the years. But when one looked closely, some of the ravages wrought by the years and strains became apparent.

I thought back to the night, fifteen years earlier, when I had watched him leave Fort Belvedere, his private retreat close to Windsor Great Park, to make a broadcast from Windsor Castle in which he spoke the memorable words written into his script by Winston Churchill: 'I have found it impossible to carry on the heavy burden of responsibilities and to discharge the duties of King as I would wish to do without the help and support of the woman I love.'

I listened to the broadcast on a car radio just outside Windsor Castle gates, only a little distance from where he was speaking to his people. There I waited for him to leave for Portsmouth and exile. I remember the departure vividly. A big blue car came slowly down the cobblestones of the slope from the Castle, and as it dawdled past me I had one last glimpse of the departing King. He was huddled inside a capacious overcoat and crouched close to the car window, apparently with hands in the pockets of the heavy garment. I shall never forget his face. It was expressionless, drained, and it appeared smaller than life-size. He looked neither to right nor left but just sat there with blank eyes staring into the night. Then he was gone – to Portsmouth to board the destroyer, HMS *Fury*, which took him across the Channel to France and his waiting Wallis Simpson. He (or Mr Charles J.V. Murphy, his talented ghost-writer) had described his feelings as he went. The last paragraph in the book whose success we were celebrating that evening in the University Club reads: 'I now knew that I was irretrievably on my own. The drawbridges were going up behind me. But of one thing I was certain; so far as I was concerned love had triumphed over the exigencies of politics. Though it has proved my fate to sacrifice my cherished British heritage along with all the years in its service I today draw comfort from the knowledge that time has long since sanctified a true and faithful union.' The words may be trite but they reflect the Duke's real attitude towards his status as a king. What mattered to him was not the damage he had caused the monarchy and his country but that love had triumphed. His private and personal happiness had overcome the demands of duty. He had achieved what he wanted to do at the expense of what he ought to have done.

This innate selfishness had been apparent to me ever since the early 1920s when it had been my lot to follow Edward, Prince of Wales up and down the country as he stubbornly continued to risk his neck by riding in point-to-point steeplechases after one fall which had left him unconscious for half an hour and kept him in bed for a month, and after a written request from King George V, appeals by Queen Mary, and even an obsequious request from the Prime Minister, Ramsay MacDonald, that he should desist. Again, in his book, he reveals his determination to put private indulgence before his obvious obligation as the heir apparent to the throne. He says he advanced. 'all the plausible arguments that could be mustered by a young man determined not to be put off from doing what he enjoyed most'. I believe I was assigned the duty of following the Prince from one steeplechase meeting to another because I was the youngest and newest member of the reporting staff of the London *Evening News* and consequently would hardly be missed all the time I was away.

In one respect, reporting the feats and falls of the Prince of Wales in steeplechases was a pleasant enough assignment, for it took me on leisurely sorties into lovely parts of the English countryside; but it was depressing in its implication that I should have to exert myself only in proportion to the harm which befell the Prince of Wales while atop, or parted from, one of his horses. I was a Royal Reporter in Waiting, as it were, and I have little doubt that the Prince came to recognize me – and resent me – as I turned up regularly in my unofficial royal appointment. But the country was concerned for the fate of her heir to the throne, and the *Evening News* editors were undoubtedly right to ensure that one of its reporters should be on the spot when and if anything happened. To be sure, many people in England believed that the Prince was destined to kill himself or suffer some awful disability before he ever became king. So I wrote happily when he won a race, as happened occasionally, and as reassuringly as the facts allowed whenever he came a cropper, which happened frequently. It was unfortunately true, although he always denied it, that he was an inferior horseman. He seemed to me to be unable to sit any way but sideways on his mount. His waist and upper body were rarely in the correct position when he galloped round a course and tackled fences and hedges, and one had to assume that this awkwardness of his was responsible for some of his many falls.

I recall with special clarity one of these in 1934, when he suffered a particularly undignified fall at a hedge on the steeplechase course at Hawthorn Hill, Berkshire. By a fluke I was only a few feet away from him at the time and was the first to go to help him. This happened because for some reason I was late in driving from London with a photographer, William Turner, and found that by the time we reached the course the race in which the Prince was competing had already started. It was raining hard and our town shoes sank into mud as we ran to a jump about half-way round the course. We had just settled there, gasping for breath, when we heard the field thundering towards us. The Prince was in the lead and going well, coming to the hedge, and I thought it likely that this day I might have the pleasure of writing an account of a royal win instead of the alternative. Turner poised himself and his camera as the Prince took the jump. I recall him – sitting askew, alas – appear over the obstacle still in company with his horse. My next memory is of his sprawling in the soggy mud. Turner's camera shutter clicked as the Prince slowly lifted himself up on his elbows. He made a sorry spectacle. His face and head were plastered with mud and he was momentarily unrecognizable. His multicoloured shirt and riding-breeches were daubed and disfigured. Still on his knees, he used his hands to clear his eyes and most of his face. He then saw Turner and the camera at work on him. Justifiably in the circumstances he broke into a stream of steamy language, the purport of which I took to indicate that, instead of standing there and taking photographs and just watching him, Turner and I ought to be helping him.

Although the vigorous verbal onslaught seemed to signify that he wasn't in physical pain, I saw that he was still not yet on his feet so that one couldn't be sure he wasn't injured. I trudged forward and, dripping rain, asked him: 'Are you hurt, sir?' He shook his head. 'No,' he said, with evident irritation. 'No harm done.'

In reconsidering the abdication crisis I am struck by the aptness of Stephen Spender's summary of it. Stanley Baldwin, the Prime Minister, and all the others in political – and religious – authority did behave like antediluvian monsters, even though their stand against the King's foolishness was justified. Their attitude towards press coverage of the crisis was worse than antediluvian, for they were blind as well as stupid. They didn't attempt to use us out there, we who were ready, willing and qualified to help, to inform and influence the people, and who had at least as big a stake as they in the outcome of the drama. Myself, I had the frustrating assignment of watching impotently from outside the gates of Fort Belvedere as the final act unfolded in secrecy. I recall with some anger the implacable determination of official England not to help us in any way whatever. As a result, the nation made what it could of brief statements in the House of Commons by Mr Baldwin, occasional bulletins on the BBC and rumours, while the King edged – or, as some have since said, was edged – to renunciation of his destiny.

Our minute contribution was a bare diary of comings and goings. Since there was no alternative to keeping vigil by day and night outside the gates, for one never knew at what hour any of the principals involved, including the King, might enter or leave the Fort, my newspaper assigned two of us to the ordeal. My colleague at that time was a young peer of the realm, Lord Killanin, a jolly fellow with a handsome round face, who lifted everyone's spirits with his easy wit and humour. His signature tune as he entered the bar of the Station Hotel and ordered a beer was 'Chalk it up to the lord'. Mostly he did the night-shift during the two weeks of our assignment, and since accommodation at the only convenient hotel, the Station Hotel at Sunningdale, was stretched far beyond its limit by the invasion of reporters and photographers from all over the world, Mike Killanin occupied 'our' bed by day while I slept in it for an hour or two at night.

Bereft of sources of information, we guardians of the gates resorted to intercepting every car entering and leaving Fort Belvedere to ascertain who was inside and how long he stayed with the King. We never expected anybody to tell us anything. It was reporting at its most crude. By day, those nearest a car would act as scouts for the rest of us. 'Monckton,' they would announce. Or, with equal disrespect, 'Baldwin.' By night, the identity of the caller would be confirmed by a flashlight poked against a car window. It has been claimed by several historians that Cosmo Gordon Lang, the Archbishop of Canterbury, and of course a clamant critic of the King's liaison with Wallis Simpson, never went to the Fort during the eleven days of the crisis. My memory prompts me to contradict them. I have a distinct recollection of one of our scouts relaying the word 'Cosmo' after the usual inspection. And I have a clear recollection of the car carrying the Archbishop returning to the gates only a few minutes after it had passed through them in the opposite direction, causing us to speculate, probably correctly because of Edward's antipathy to the Archbishop, that he had either refused to see the visitor or had dismissed him summarily after only a few moments of talk.

Now, in the University Club in New York, all the turmoil of his years as prince and king had passed. He was enjoying himself – until there came an unexpected, devastating interruption. We heard the rasping voice of the Duchess above the hum of cocktail talk. 'Come, David,' she commanded. 'Time to go. . . . You're talking too much.' The metallic tones grated. Perhaps she had intended those last four words as a jest. If so, they misfired. The party died in an instant. All talk stopped as the Duke mumbled an apology to those of us with whom he had been talking and then shambled across to the side of the Duchess. They said their thanks and farewells to Richard Greenough, and then they were gone.

13

Naval Correspondent

I do not know how often I came close to suffering physical harm, or even oblivion, during the five years I worked as a war reporter and war correspondent, or, less frequently, while chasing headlines on all manner of assignments around the world for the best part of half a century. There is no reliable way of checking all the near-misses. I did not escape physical injury during the war, being wounded once. It happened in 1944 when incautiously I strayed too far forward in an indefinable no man's land at the foot of Monastery Hill at Cassino and was well and truly 'stonked', as we used to call it, by an alert crew of Germans manning a mortar either in or near the Monastery on high above and in front of me. Although I ducked to ground when the first shell landed close by, I was eventually hit in the right eye by either a shell fragment or a small piece of earth sent flying when the shell exploded, and I have had to wear glasses ever since.

My narrow escapes were undoubtedly far more numerous than I could keep track of when they happened. For example, I learnt only months afterwards, and quite by chance, that I had come close to death in the early summer of 1942 while I was aboard HMS *Croome*, one of a small flotilla of Hunt Class destroyers which sneaked out of harbour at Alexandria to bombard ammunition and supply dumps used by the Germans at the small port of El Daba, on the North African coast about a hundred sea miles west of Alexandria. The story is worth telling fully because it illustrates several facets, likely to be forgotten as the years roll by, of a period when Hitler still seemed to be winning the war and the Anglo-Americans were beset by the ill-consequences of early defeats as well as by delays and setbacks in marshalling their latent superior strength. When I took up an assignment in Alexandria in early 1942 as a naval correspondent accredited to the Eastern Mediterranean Fleet, the Afrika Korps was firmly settled at El Alamein, only a hundred miles away, and the so-called Fleet consisted mainly of a couple of cruisers, a handful of destroyers, and a collection of supporting supply and other small craft. Admiral Harwood was indeed restricted in what he could contribute to the war effort. Not only was he short of ships; if they ventured very far westwards and were detected in daylight by the enemy, they could be readily attacked by the Luftwaffe from its many bases in the Western Desert beyond El Alamein.

Complementing this bottling-up was the fact that most Egyptians believed the Axis had already won the war. Enemy agents abounded in

Cairo and Alexandria. Influential Egyptian Army officers, including Anwar el Sadat (a future president), were plotting and planning to welcome the Germans and Italians when, inevitably as it was believed, they sent the British packing from the country. It became known after the war that Sadat and his friends had actually earmarked a commodious villa near the Pyramids for use by Field-Marshal Rommel. And one story which went the rounds of warships and naval messes in Alexandria soon after I got there was that some Egyptian women in the port had begun adorning their underclothing with the Italian national colours so that they could prove their loyalty to the Axis beyond all question when Mussolini's victorious warriors rode, any day now, into Alexandria. The story sounded improbable, but it stirred the imagination. One point which struck me when I heard it was that there was no mention of any of the expectant women decorating their panties and brassières with swastikas; presumably Germans were barbarians in the Egyptian view.

The furtive expedition westwards to El Daba was an example of the limited there-and-back-in-a-hurry enterprise which was all that Admiral Harwood could undertake in the summer of 1942. Rommel's high-speed advance to El Alamein had put almost the whole of the militarily usable territory of North Africa to within a hundred miles of Alexandria and Cairo at his disposal, and, more to the point from Harwood's position, had given the Luftwaffe command of the air to within, say, two hundred miles of his naval base and thereby virtually bottled up his tiny fleet. The foray to El Daba was to confirm his vulnerability. It was also to show me how the phenomenon of delayed shock is produced by prolonged exposure to danger. I felt not fright but growing fatigue while I was part of the target attacked by enemy bombers for about three hours in bright sunshine and without their having to worry about being attacked in their turn by RAF fighters. I found that it was growing exhaustion, not fear, which drained me, and that my exhaustion was induced by the hideous din which burst around me at every enemy onslaught – the noise of rapid-firing anti-aircraft guns spewing lethal missiles into the sky above, the screech from dive-bombers careering almost vertically downwards towards us and the sharp cracks of their exploding bombs. Somehow there was no time to be frightened. One simply yearned for permanent respite from the appalling noise. Such is my memory, at any rate. Perhaps I wasn't sensitive enough to feel fear. I remind myself that James Michener, the American writer, is credited with having said: 'The reporter sees everything – and feels nothing.' That seems to me to be not quite accurate, although it may have some validity. The reporter does develop a kind of armour-plating of cynicism to shield him from personal feelings such as joy and fear and, if possible, any sense of participation when he is on duty, forever listening as he is to tall and short tales, watching all manner of happenings occurring about him, and striving always to preserve the impartiality of his role as professional observer and recorder.

Only after the event, when he can relax and reflect with his story written, do his inner feelings and physical frailties assert themselves. This, anyhow, was my experience in wartime assignments like the sortie to El Daba.

Our small flotilla of Hunt Class destroyers had stolen out of harbour, one by one and at irregular intervals, late in the afternoon and at a time which would ensure that they would be making their way to and from their target mostly under cover of darkness. All went according to pre-arranged plan until after they had taken up attacking positions offshore and had opened fire on German and Italian ammunition dumps, workshops, and other stores and facilities in the port of El Daba which agents and reconnaissance planes had located and pinpointed. We began receiving heavy return fire from shore batteries, but their shells fell wide of us because the enemy gunners could not hope to follow the swerves, twists and turns which the destroyers made in between their irregular salvoes. Then we heard E-boats looking for us, nosing round at low speed in the darkness as their look-outs strove to locate us. Alas, they did so all too quickly, after our bombardment had been completed but before we had time to swing round and set out for home.

I was standing alongside the captain, who was casually dressed in a pullover of grey Shetland wool as he sat on a swivel stool directing *Croome*'s movements, when I heard a frantic shout from one of the ship's look-outs: 'Torpedo approaching on the starboard beam!' I peered into the darkness and to my dismay saw the phosphorescent wakes of not one but two torpedoes travelling on almost parallel course – and, sure enough, one was heading directly for us. I hardly had time to absorb this disconcerting fact before I was pitched bodily against a rail on my side of the bridge and half fell to the deck. Sharper eyes and more expert brains than mine had also seen the approaching menace and had swung *Croome* violently to port so that she should present the slimmest possible target to the torpedo. The manoeuvre succeeded. As I pulled myself to my feet I saw the tell-tale wake passing alongside – close but out of harm's way. Yet even as I was congratulating myself on the near-miss I heard the thud of a loud explosion coming from somewhere nearby. Moments later, all of us standing on deck were showered with warm spray and I heard somebody say: '*Eridge* has been hit.' A torpedo had struck our sister destroyer amidships and the spray that covered us had come from the point of impact. It seemed likely that *Eridge* had not been able to evade the torpedo because her captain's view of the missile's wake had been obscured by our bulk as we manoeuvred to dodge the torpedo which had threatened us.

It now took me, inexperienced civilian as I was, some minutes to catch up on what was going on. Bells rang, voices shouted, and I could hear and sometimes feel men racing and scrambling around me on the bridge. Eventually an officer enlightened me. '*Eridge*'s skipper has assured us that she's not going to sink,' he said. 'One of the other destroyers is going to take her in tow. We'll all be crawling back to Alex at about four knots.

It's going to be no picnic. . . .' I knew what he meant. Owing to the time it would take to get *Eridge* under tow and because of the painfully slow speed we should make, most of the return trip would have to be done in daylight. I surmised that our chances of getting home in one piece were none too rosy. Ruined was the original plan that we should all steam eastwards at top speed in comforting darkness to waters close to Alexandria which were protected by the RAF. We should be limping back in bright Mediterranean sunlight, and for most of the time through waters under the undisputed control of the Luftwaffe. Gloomily I told myself that we should make tempting targets for those horrors, the Stuka 87 dive-bombers, which I had seen operating in the Straits of Dover during the Battle of Britain in 1941. We should have no air cover. Our survival would depend upon the combined fire-power of our warships until we came within range of the Spitfires and other fighters based east of the Army's defensive line at El Alamein.

'Won't be long now,' the captain said to me as we watched darkness giving way to the strengthening light of pre-dawn.

Nor was it. Even before full dawn an enemy reconnaissance aircraft appeared high overhead and then sped back over the desert to give pinpoint information of our position to the waiting bombers. Within minutes the Stukas came. Six of them circled high above us and then came screeching down, one after the other, to drop their sinister black eggs around us. As they did so, they had to make their dives through a murderous barrage of anti-aircraft fire put up by the British warships. And I was heartened to observe one significant fact, which seemed to indicate that the defence had one powerful psychological advantage over its attackers. The barrage put up by the ships, including the otherwise disabled *Eridge*, was apparently so intense that the German pilots were chary about pressing home their onslaught as determinedly as they should have. So, I thought, the same thing was happening here in the Mediterranean as I had noted in the later phases of the air battle over Dover. The Stuka pilots had lost the confidence they had shown in the early days of the war when their ill-armed victims could put up only the most feeble opposition to them. As I sheltered behind whatever flimsy cover I could find and ventured a risky peep from time to time to try and see what was going on, I concluded as bombs fell harmlessly yards away from any target that the Stuka pilots were pulling their machines too soon out of dives. And there was a similar lack of precision about the performance of the heavier bombers which followed them. Crews seemed to be releasing their bombs far too soon.

It may sound unbelievable but it is none the less a fact that the wave of alternating attacks – I was far too preoccupied to count them but I suppose there might have been a dozen – did not produce one hit upon the British ships, not even on the disabled *Eridge*. Evasive action dictated by *Croome's* captain, still sitting on his revolving stool, certainly helped to preserve the ship. Sometimes it seemed to me as I was bounced about like some plaything that we were either spinning like a top or swinging to and fro at impossible angles even as bombs were hurtling down towards us. But I do not recall feeling a vestige of fear throughout the long ordeal. Perhaps I was too numbed to register whatever fear might be consuming me, too dazed by the recurring storms of noise which erupted whenever another wave of enemy aircraft closed in upon us to think of anything except my need to witness everything I could in spite of danger and discomfort.

But I do remember that, as the appalling clatter assailed my ears time and again and as the wild gyrations of the ship pitched me hither and thither, I began to feel more and more exhausted. At one point, feeling that I had reached the end of my physical endurance, I sat down on a step leading from the main deck to the bridge, buried my face in my hands and prayed – yes, prayed to God that the present outburst of bedlam should be the last. It wasn't, of course, but I felt better after my lonely, involuntary communion. Indeed, it produced a brainwave. Surely I should feel better if I gave myself something to do besides straining to watch what happened – something to make me less aware of the infernal noise during an onslaught. Inspired, I went up to the captain during the next lull and asked him for permission to go below to the wardroom and pick up my camera, which I remembered having left there. The captain thought for a moment. 'Well, it's against regulations to open the wardroom during an action, but then perhaps we ought to have something to remember this little party by,' he said. 'Go down quickly, remember to lock the door and get back as fast as you can. I'll look the other way.' We exchanged weary smiles and off I went. It was a wobbly journey to and from the wardroom because another wave of bombers appeared while I was making it, but my idea worked. Holding my camera as steady as possible on a side-rail – the camera was German-made, by the way – I got one good photograph. It showed a couple of bombs making high waterspouts as they exploded very close to the destroyer towing *Eridge*. It was one of the innumerable near-misses that happened on this memorable morning. The photograph was published many weeks later in the *Daily Mail*.

Eventually, deliverance came. The attacks ceased abruptly after we had plodded close enough to Alexandria for Spitfires to cover us. The Luftwaffe bombers did not venture out to challenge fighters in daylight. However, the first Spitfire that appeared over the returning flotilla was given a disconcerting hot welcome by our gunners. To them, after what they had had to withstand since dawn, any aircraft appearing over their heads just *had* to be hostile, and they opened fire on the Spitfire with the venom they had earlier vented upon the Stukas. Only after the pilot had swooped low over the ships, dangerously so in all the circumstances, and wiggled the Spitfire's wings to display the red, white and blue rings proclaiming its nationality, and put it through some spectacular aerobatics, did they stop firing at him. As I watched him soar away apparently unscathed, I reconstructed the language he probably used as the 'friendly' shells began bursting about him, prettily but threateningly.

Everything considered, we aboard the ships also escaped lightly. There were casualties when the torpedo struck *Eridge*, but *Croome* had only one man killed. He was a member of one of the gun crews who had foolishly taken off his steel helmet when the sun's heat became too much for him while an enemy attack was being made, and as a result a jagged splinter of shrapnel from a shell fired by a defending gun – it might have been his own – hurtled down and tore his skull apart. After we had slowly steamed into Alexandria's capacious harbour, past the historic lighthouse (its beam extinguished by day and night to prevent its being used as a guide by German or Italian aircraft and warships), we hoisted a signal indicating that we had a casualty and very soon a small hospital craft sped alongside to take the young man's body away, wrapped in a blanket. It was not a pleasant sight for the survivors of a bitter encounter at sea to have to watch. The dead lad was a friend, one of them.

Once back at the Cecil Hotel, my home from home, I went into the well-stocked bar with two of *Croome's* officers. We downed a couple of celebratory pink gins, silently toasting each other as we gazed over the rims of the Cecil's ample glasses. Not a word did we say about the day's taxing adventure, for there were far too many pairs of eager ears in Alexandria at this time for any incautious words to be spoken. We shook hands firmly as we parted, and then I went upstairs to my airy bedroom to attend to the duty which now faced me – to write an account of the expedition to El Daba which would pass the naval censor. The account I turned out was of necessity a dishonest one by peacetime standards of journalism, but this was not peacetime. I could not possibly have written the truth, that the expedition had come close to being an expensive disaster which had been retrieved only by seamen's ingenuity, bravery, determination and by good luck. That might have made an inspiring story, but it would never have seen daylight in my newspaper. So I had to steer a zigzag course, rather like the one our ship had had to steer in dodging enemy bombs. I tried to avoid sinking by censor yet still depict, albeit inferentially, our brush with catastrophe. Dominating my strategy was the crucial fact that I could not disclose that HMS *Eridge* had been severely damaged, because that would not only have depressed morale at home unnecessarily, since the ship had been saved from sinking, but would have given aid and comfort to the enemy.

What eventually appeared in print was a lopsided version of events, to say the least. First, I gave the good news. In my opening paragraph I stated that we had inflicted a 'crushing bombardment' upon Rommel's tank repair shops and ammunition dumps behind the Alamein line. (Actually, at the time I wrote those words, knowing nothing of the massive attack being prepared by General Montgomery at that very moment, I did not think that the naval foray was of much importance, but

I must now concede that it probably mattered a good deal, for the enemy had by no means enough time to repair the loss and damage before Montgomery struck, and Rommel's defence must consequently have been perceptibly diminished as a result of our shelling.) Next I gave as clear a hint as I could of the dangerous and unpleasant aspects of the raid. I wrote:

> We had to endure hours-long revenge attacks from the air. It has been an exciting, grim, and uncomfortable fourteen hours. We have been at action stations all that time. Men are now falling asleep on their feet as we approach harbour, at last. We have been shelled from shore, attacked by E-boats, dive-bombed, and just plain bombed incessantly. But ships have done their dangerous job and all have come back.

I could claim with every justification that I was writing the truth, but it was selected truth. Herein lies, of course, the difference between the role of the reporter in peace and war. One further thought is that even in wartime it sometimes is permissible for the correspondent to write and publish valid criticism, and it can even be his duty to do so. I was to be convinced of this several times later in the war (when we were winning beyond any doubt) and was to be inspired to write several articles critical of Allied tactics and generalship in Italy. In the present instance, in 1942, there was nothing whatever to criticize and much to praise and I was quite content to conform to expediency.

I had hoped that once my task was done I should be able to relax and recover from the rigours to which mind and body had been subjected. It was not to be, at least for a while. Almost as soon as I had finished writing I found myself beginning to shake uncontrollably. I tried not to panic, telling myself, correctly I believe, that now that I was free of strain, my body was reminding me of the excessive demands which had been made upon it while I had been at sea and which I had unconsciously suppressed until this moment of total relief. My body was reasserting itself after my brain had been denying for so many hours its claim to protest. I suppose that in essence I was suffering from a mild attack of shell-shock. My simple reaction was to lie down upon my bed and wait for the shakes to subside. They did so gradually, first becoming less severe and persistent and eventually, after I know not how long, stopping altogether. Feeling once again in command of mind and body, I slowly undressed and curled up between the soft white sheets.

When I awoke it was dark, some seven hours after I had reached the solitude of my room. I took a leisurely bath, dressed, and went down to the Cecil's excellent dining-room and enjoyed two medium-rare lamb chops, a meal to which I always have recourse whenever I have something to celebrate. Then I went upstairs and to bed again. The next thing I knew it was morning of the following day.

I felt no further after-effects of my first exposure to prolonged enemy assault, but there was indeed to be a sequel to the event which gave me pause long after it had happened. On a new assignment to rejoin Montgomery and his advancing Eighth Army I was waiting in Algiers to take passage to southern Italy in the first available transport when I came upon a grey-haired British naval officer who had emerged from retirement to 'do his bit' for his country and his old Service. He was Captain Taprell Dorling, well known at the time for the stories of adventure at sea which he wrote under the pen-name of 'Taffrail'. Full of enthusiasm for his job as a naval press officer at the now fully functioning base at Algiers, he showed me his latest product, a record of the fantastic distances that had been covered by British destroyers in the Mediterranean. HMS *Croome* was at the top of the list with a tally of 67,971 miles. By chance later that day I ran into an officer who had been first lieutenant in *Croome* that memorable morning off El Daba and was now her captain. Naturally we talked about the experience we had shared and he surprised me by recalling one incident about which I knew nothing. 'Half-way through the action a flight of four Stukas chose *Croome* as their target,' he said. 'I was on the bridge and I can still recall my feeling of pure horror as they came down at us, one after another. One pilot, showing more guts than his pals, aimed his dive so accurately that he dropped a stick of bombs at very low level indeed, which seemed to be coming straight for me. They actually missed both me and *Croome* but fell so close that they caused the ship to shudder and toss about, momentarily out of control. The nearest bomb, which exploded only a yard or two to starboard, burst open a store-room adjoining the wardroom and blew open several things, including some bottles of beer.' The young officer smiled before continuing. 'You know,' he then said, 'we aboard *Croome* have never really worried about anything that might happen after that day. It sort of insulated us. We feel that having survived that, we can survive anything.'

What puzzled me as I listened was the fact that I had never known anything whatever about this nearest of all near-misses off El Daba. Then the explanation struck me. The dangerous attack must have taken place while I was fetching my camera from the wardroom to the bridge, and the bomb which did the damage exploded moments after I had left the wardroom with the camera. I remembered that as I picked my way up to the bridge I had been pitched hard to one side and had almost fallen because of a particularly violent roll by the ship. Had I still been in the wardroom, I should almost certainly have been injured by the impact of the exploding bomb and might not even have survived. Another near-miss.

One other sortie that I made from Alexandria during the summer of 1943 aboard one of Admiral Harwood's warships stays in my memory because of some of its unusual aspects, including the fact that, unlike most military operations within my experience, it passed off faultlessly from the Allied standpoint, if not the enemy's.

I was a passenger in one of a small flotilla of cruisers which bombarded the fabled island of Rhodes. I am somewhat ashamed to confess that, throughout this assignment, I gave little thought to the ugly fact that the object of the expedition was to fire hundreds of tons of explosives, with the idea of causing maximum damage, into the capital of an ancient island which had once been ruled by Alexander the Great before Christ was born and had thereafter played a substantial continuing role in the cultural and political history of the eastern Mediterranian basin. I am fairly sure that my ship was HMS *Arethusa*, but after almost half a century I cannot swear to this. Since correspondents were forbidden by military regulations to keep a diary in case they were captured, and since they also were forbidden to use the names of warships in their despatches, except in special circumstances, they did not trouble themselves unduly in trying to remember them. But I most certainly recall that, as happened in every British warship in which I travelled into and out of action during the war, I deeply appreciated, and was reassured by, the spirit of friendliness offered to me aboard *Arethusa* or whatever ship it happened to be.

My companion on this trip (or 'scarper' as we used to label such events in the Middle East) was Larry Allen, a flamboyant but lovable American reporter representing the Associated Press.* We had taken up our allotted position in a small space alongside the after steering deck by the time the cruiser's guns opened fire at 1 a.m. on 13 August. What a sight we must have presented as we peered through the darkness towards Rhodes! We were equipped with long white gauntlets of the finest quality, white helmets, dark glasses, and a soft white mesh veil covering our faces. The Royal Navy had fitted us out thus to protect us from possible burns from heat generated by the heavy guns now flashing and booming only a few yards from us.

Soon after the first salvoes had gone hurtling through the air towards their shore targets, the defenders sent up brilliant rockets and switched on searchlights which roved seawards and skywards, trying to locate the attacking warships as well as RAF bombers making a co-ordinated onslaught from a few thousand feet up. Apparently we were found very quickly, for within minutes shore batteries were firing quite accurately in

---

* Larry was destined to be captured by the enemy only weeks after the Rhodes scarper when a destroyer in which he was a passenger was immobilized and half sunk by shore batteries during a naval attack on Tobruk. He ran true to the form for which he was acclaimed by his American and British colleagues. He told his captors that he wanted to interview Field-Marshal Rommel. His request was denied, short-sightedly in my opinion. Larry would have produced a most lively account of his interview with Rommel which would have made useful propaganda for the Germans.

our direction. As they did so, I found Larry Allen's gloved left hand tightly gripping my right one. I was surprised and a little embarrassed, until I reasoned that his gesture seeking comfort was more of an instinctive reaction than a conscious one. Men often behave unexpectedly, even irrationally, during moments of stress.

The pattern of the bombardment of Rhodes was the same as that of El Daba, except that the grim scorecard of hits and misses was overwhelmingly in our favour. It was also one of the few occasions during the war when I was stirred into admiration for the courage of our foe. We had completed the heavy bombardment and, feeling triumphant and exhilarated, we were swinging hard to port to get into position for the trip at high speed in the darkness to Haifa, in what was then Palestine, hundreds of miles to the east. Lurid fires were blazing ashore on Rhodes as the spectacular fruit from shell and bomb. I was saying to Larry Allen (who had relinquished his handclasp the moment the guns stopped firing) how relieved I was that we had escaped unscathed when I was interrupted by a loud shout from one of the sailors on look-out: 'Two enemy craft off starboard aft!' I peered into the gloom while men below us swung rapid-firing guns to bear on two dimly discernible small craft heading towards us. In a twinkling, as it seemed, tracer bullets were showing that the cruiser's defending guns were on target. I lost all sight of one of the oncoming craft but saw that the other was keeping unswervingly on her course even though tracers and spouts of water indicated that she must be taking many hits. Surely, I thought, she could not possibly survive that deadly rain. Proving this to be so, the vessel suddenly went dead in the water while yet hundreds of feet away from us. Her heroic attack had come to naught before she could wheel about and discharge a torpedo at us.

The men aboard the craft must have known that they were committed almost certainly to a suicidal mission, but they had pressed on until, inevitably, our guns stopped them. As we now turned away at full speed to avoid any further trouble I paid these men, German or Italian, silent tribute willingly and pityingly. This was raw warfare at sea. If we had not halted them and probably killed them, they would have holed us with a torpedo. The great warship on whose deck I was standing would probably have survived, but there would have been men killed and wounded. The uselessness of it all!

We reached our haven at Haifa without further incident and, this time, with no casualties to report. The minor engagement was given momentary attention on the front page and then faded into obscurity.

More than thirty years passed before I learned just why we had bombarded Rhodes. I came upon a German account of the naval war between 1939 and 1945 written by Cajus Bekker which explained that the expedition had been undertaken as a diversion to keep German and Italian warships and submarines away from the western reaches of the

Mediterranean while an Allied convoy left Gibraltar and steamed un-
harassed, it was hoped, to beleaguered Malta, which was almost out of the
food, fuel and ammunition she needed to defend herself from incessant
aerial attack. The convoy operation, called Pedestal, fared badly. The
Royal Navy lost *Eagle*, an aircraft-carrier, to German torpedoes – fired by
U-boat 73 commanded by Lieutenant Helmut Rosenbau, as the meticulous
Bekker noted – while *Indomitable*, a recently built carrier, suffered three
devastating hits from dive-bombers. Only five out of the fourteen supply
ships in the convoy which had left Gibraltar survived to limp into Valletta
harbour. Yet even this meagre yield from such an expensive enterprise
was enough to keep Malta fighting until deliverance came after the Battle
of Alamein. The British, wrote Bekker the German, never wavered in their
resolve to hold on to Malta. The onslaught against Operation Pedestal
marked the high point of the German-Italian effort to eliminate the island.
'They didn't strike again with any success and the pendulum never swung
back in their favour.'

I nearly went home on leave in June 1943. A challenge which I could not,
dare not, reject, deprived me of a longed-for reunion with my wife and
family and a need to be reassured that the savage world of war into which
I had been plunged in North Africa and the Middle East was but a passing
phenomenon and that the stable world of reason and good order which I
had left in England was still there. I wanted to see the people and places I
loved – Katy and the children, sister and brother, London, Oxford and the
Cotswolds, Altrincham where I had been born and raised, and even
ink-stained Fleet Street. I had been drained to my limits of physical and
mental tolerance by twelve months in which I had experienced the heights
of exhilaration by victory in the sands and dust of El Alamein, exhaustion
at sea, frustration at the crazy artificiality and trickery of neutral Turkey,
and the pangs of homesickness which stung me whenever the demands of
my professional role briefly abated.

The *deus ex machina* that engineered deprivation of something to which I
had looked forward as I had never done before to anything was yet
another of those naval operations which had so preoccupied me in the
past year. The unlikely god whom the machine lowered upon my stage in
Algiers, on the very day when I expected to hear that the way was clear for
me to go to Gibraltar to board a converted Cunarder which would take me
in convoy slowly but, I hoped, surely to Liverpool or Southampton, was a
lieutenant in the Royal Navy deputed to maintain liaison between his
Service and the press. He approached me on the morning of 12 June in the
rather dingy hotel which served as our temporary home and, in the
traditional offhand naval style, said after an exchange of greetings: 'By the
way, there's to be a combined op in a day or two. We're going to bombard
a couple of islands which the Army chaps are then going in to capture.

There's room for you in one of the big ships if you'd care to go.'

I had no option. It was not a matter of caring to go. This was one of those occasions in which a war correspondent has to decide for himself what plain duty demands. There could be no question of my consulting anybody, least of all my headquarters in Fleet Street. But it meant that my trip home would have to be postponed for several weeks. Stifling the disappointment which enveloped me, I nodded my head and said I would go. It took but a moment's reflection to deduce that the islands concerned were Pantellaria and Lampedusa, occupied by the Italians, which stood directly in the path of the known next Allied target – Sicily, the threshold of Europe.

On the appointed day I boarded HMS *Orion*, carrying only my one suitcase and my typewriter (an ancient Remington with a push-up key-board which I had purchased in my very early days as a reporter in the 1920s). I remember that, as I stepped upon the deck of the great warship at the top of the boarding gangway and saluted her with due propriety, I experienced the fleeting thought which so often occurred to me as I set out on a naval excursion such as this. Should I be leaving her by this same orderly route and in the same prime condition as when I boarded her? I was not particularly disturbed by the thought; it simply occurred to me. So many things could happen once you left dry land. As everything turned out, I was made so welcome aboard *Orion* – being made to feel part of the ship – wherever I roamed as she rode serenely on her warlike course from Algiers, that I found even my intense disappointment at the self-imposed cancellation of my trip home became dulled.

The assignment was, indeed, one of the most satisfying of my career as a war correspondent. It went off without a hitch (from the Allied point of view, if not from the Italian) and, so far as I could ever ascertain, without one casualty on our side, and it yielded me one of the most flattering front-page displays I was ever given in the *Daily Mail*. People in England, who were longing to hear about another triumph after the destruction of the Afrika Korps to reassure them that the war was really being won, had their need satisfied. No matter that all that happened was that a very strong naval and military force met only token opposition in bombarding and then capturing one island of thirty-two square miles and another which was little more than a speck in the water, a mere eight square miles in size. The true significance of the operation was that it exposed the feebleness of Italian morale, for over eleven thousand Italian troops made no pretense of defending the islands seriously. The small one, Lampe-dusa, actually surrendered to the pilot and his crew of two aboard a torpedo aircraft which made a forced landing when it ran out of fuel. The pilot (Sergeant Sidney Cohen, a tailor's cutter in the London district of Clapton in civilian life) said that he and his two companions (Sergeant Peter Tait, of Falkirk, Scotland, and Sergeant Leslie Wright, of Bourne-mouth) were astonished to see people waving white flags at them as their aircraft landed in a field. They were even more surprised when an Italian officer emerged from his air-raid shelter seventy-five feet below ground to give them a slip of paper on which he had written his formal surrender of Lampedusa.

Yet there had been misgivings among Allied commanders when General Eisenhower insisted that the two islands must be captured. His biographer, Stephen E. Ambrose, wrote many years later that General Alexander, Admiral Cunningham, and Air Chief Marshal Tedder were among those who initially opposed an attack upon the islands as being too risky and likely to be expensive in casualties. Even the US officer assigned to command the land attack, Major-General Walter E. Clutterbuck, protested. 'He made a personal visit to me to lay out the difficulties and feared that he would have a great many of his men slaughtered,' Eisenhower himself wrote three weeks after the operation.

The protests were so strong that Eisenhower decided to make a personal reconnaissance before the operation, while the islands were being softened up by bombings. He and Admiral Cunningham went there aboard the British cruiser HMS *Aurora*. The ship took them to within a short distance of the coast of Pantellaria and bombarded the garrison, with Cunningham directing some of the fire. Only two shore batteries replied, neither with any accuracy. According to Ambrose's biography, Eisenhower remarked to Cunningham: 'Andrew, if you and I got a small boat we could capture the place ourselves.'

A naval correspondent was quite a rare bird in those days in North Africa because at the beginning of the war the Admiralty had stated that as there was no room aboard its warships for correspondents it would do without them. The Silent Service would remain so. But it had to rescind that decision when the other Services got all the credit for waging war, and it belatedly accredited just a few reporters. There were never more than a dozen naval correspondents in the Mediterranean while I was there between 1942 and 1943 and there were never more than five in Alexandria, my main base in 1942. So we were a distinctive little band as we strode out, in between dangerous assignments at sea in those grim days, to leisurely lunches at the Union Club and tea and coffee sessions at Pastroudi's in our beautifully laundered uniforms of white shorts and shirts, with the letters N.C. artistically woven into our epaulettes and our caps covered by spotless white linen covers.

All was different by midsummer 1943. As noted earlier, I had been seconded to the British Army for the Battle of Alamein and the chase after Rommel, and the fulcrum of war had shifted to Algiers and the western Mediterranean. Allied fortunes had changed dramatically for the better, and in June I was able to report yet another victory, the bombardment and capture of Pantellaria and Lampedusa. When I got back to port after this assignment I was surprised to be summoned to appear on parade. I joined an untidy straggle of Allied Army correspondents on the sunny veranda of a villa in Algiers to be presented to King George VI. I was, as usual, the only naval correspondent present.

Most of us had slept in only brief snatches for three days and nights, and our lack of sleep showed. But the King courteously gave no sign of awareness of our dishevelled appearance as he walked along the unmilitary line, shaking hands with each correspondent. When he came to me, standing almost at the end of the straggle, he stopped abruptly before offering me his hand. He had obviously never before seen a naval correspondent. 'Well – a naval one!' he exclaimed. We both laughed. It had been explained to me beforehand by Colonel McCormick, the Irishman in charge of the press in Algiers, that it was not etiquette for a man to speak to the King unless he spoke first. 'Are you really with the Navy?' he asked me. I was obviously called upon to talk. 'Yes, sir,' I replied, and I explained how I had been shuttling back and forth like a butterfly, but not as pretty as one, ever since Alamein. He asked me a few questions on how we worked, where I had been in the Middle East, and finally he wanted to know what ship I had been in for the bombardment of Pantellaria. 'I was attached to the – er, your – battle-cruiser *Orion*, sir.' His face lit up with pleasure. 'I've sailed in her, too,' he said. 'A great ship.' I nodded enthusiastically, for I had had a splendid time aboard her. The King stretched out his hand and gave mine an extra warm pressure, I like to tell my grandchildren, a comradely greeting from one sailor to another. George VI truly loved his Navy. That day in Algiers he was wearing the white uniform of an admiral.

14

The First Sea Lord

On a gloomy day in January 1940 I was despatched by train from London to Plymouth on an assignment with a touch of mystery about it. 'I can only tell you it's a naval occasion,' James Lawrence, my news editor, had said as he handed me an authorization to travel to the historic port in Devon. 'The Admiralty aren't saying much about it, because of security, but they promise a top-notch story.'

Such a tonic as a top-notch story was exactly what the country needed. The first winter of war had brought no slaughter in northern Europe and no mass bombings, but there had been some menacing disasters at sea. German submarines had sunk eleven ships in the first week of hostilities and had continued their attack with such success as to cause Clementine, the wife of Winston Churchill, now First Lord of the Admiralty, to write to her sister that 'The war news is grim beyond words.' It was humiliating as well, for one skilful U-boat commander, Lieutenant Gunther Prien, had actually managed in mid-October to find a gap in the underwater defences of the great naval base at Scapa Flow and torpedo the battleship *Royal Oak*, with the loss of 899 lives, and sail his submarine away unscathed.

There had been only one British victory at sea to offset the German triumphs. In December three British warships, the heavy cruiser HMS *Exeter* and the light cruisers *Ajax* and *Achilles*, had cornered the German pocket battleship, *Graf Spee*, in the South Atlantic off Montevideo and, at high cost in casualties and damage, had performed the near-miracle of disabling the German warship so badly with their 8-inch and 6-inch guns against her 11-inch ones that she had had to retreat into the neutral harbour of Montevideo where, after the seventy-two hours in port permitted by the Uruguayan government, she scuttled herself. Her commander, Captain Hans Langsdorff, a 'high-class person' as Winston Churchill magnanimously described him later, subsequently shot himself.

My story in Plymouth turned out to be a sequel to the naval drama off the River Plate, and it brought me my first encounter with Winston Churchill, one of three which impressed me so deeply although all happened long ago, that I have never forgotten their impact. Winston Churchill's personality, presence and demeanour, and his intellect, were such as to make any contact with him memorable. On this occasion in 1940 he was especially impressive because he was thrusting himself heart and soul into exploiting a triumph against daunting odds by the ships and men of the Royal Navy, which he loved. He had followed almost every moment of the running battle taking place one-third of the way across the world by monitoring for a day and a half all the messages and other information about it reaching his War Room in Whitehall. When it ended in a victory for the Royal Navy, he saw an opportunity to score a sorely needed propaganda coup as well. First, however, he had to fight his own battle against his naval technical experts. They had concluded that in leading the attack against *Graf Spee*, readying her for the kill, *Exeter* had suffered such damage from over a hundred hits by shells that she was beyond immediate restoration and should be kept immobile in the Falklands for the rest of the war. Winston Churchill wanted none of this and, as he tersely explained in his memoirs in one of those charged understatements for which he was renowned: 'My view prevailed.' HMS *Exeter* was hastily patched up, even to the extent of having her silhouette restored by sheets of wood hammered into position at appropriate places, so that she could make the long journey back to England and be seen arriving at her home base in Devonport. Winston Churchill was not only exercising his instinct for showmanship in bringing her home. He was striking back at the Soviet Union, still allied to Nazis who were already preparing to attack her. Propagandists in Moscow had aroused his anger (not a difficult thing to do, judging by everything I have ever read or heard about him) by publishing a spiteful story in *Red Star* on 31 December 1939, stating that the battle off Montevideo had given a demonstration 'unprecedented in history' of British naval impotence. For ill-measure, *Red Star* had added to its report the falsehood that *Exeter* had sunk off the coast of Argentina on her way to the Falklands. That in itself was quite enough to goad Winston Churchill into a counter-attack. Not only would he bring *Exeter* home to quash the Soviet lie, he would be there to welcome and acclaim her. This was 'the top-notch story' which had brought me to Plymouth.

Churchill was already aboard the battered but now presentable warship when I arrived. He was darting about all over her, examining minutely any still exposed damage which the highly penetrative German shells had caused and talking with members of the crew who came within his erratic orbit. It was difficult to keep up with the First Lord as he strode along corridors, climbed companion-ways and tacked at random to examine something that had caught his eye, or to speak with sailors at their duties. I caught up with him solely because he had stopped to speak with an accompanying officer who wished to confirm that the officers and men should be allowed to tell us correspondents their stories of what they had experienced during the battle. Admiralty chiefs had been chary of sanctioning this liberty because of the terrible hammering *Exeter* had suffered and the high toll of human casualties *Graf Spee*'s shells had exacted. The naval officer who met me in Plymouth and conducted me to *Exeter* asked me not to write anything about the penetrative and destructive power of shells fired by *Graf Spee*. They were, it seemed, far more lethal than had been expected. 'Any reference to this fact will be censored,' the officer said. 'Let them tell their stories,' Churchill now ordered. 'This is a great day.' He turned to me, standing alongside him. 'Go along and talk with them all,' he said. 'And tell your colleagues I say so.'

This is what now happened and Winston Churchill was proved right. Although some of the stories I heard that day were harrowing – Marine Corporal Henry Hockings, of Exmouth, Devon, described how each man beside him in a forward turret fell dead (with ghastly wounds, which I did not mention) after two shells struck the turret, and Seaman Tom Surkitt, of Cambridge, who at eighteen was the youngest sailor aboard, described his worst moment when he saw the bodies of 'pals who hadn't been as lucky as me, including two special pals' laid in rows on *Exeter*'s deck. Yet the greatest impact of all news stories written that day upon millions of people was of the magnitude of *Exeter*'s feat in crippling *Graf Spee*.

Eventually Winston was ready for his main performance. He was ushered to a place on deck where a battery of news photographers was lined up to take advantage of what has since become known as a 'photo opportunity'. A splendid opportunity it turned out to be. With a shrewd eye upon the angle he presented to the expectant photographers, he took up position beneath two of *Exeter*'s guns, his audience of officers and men of the warship's crew lined up in front of him. He made a hearty Dickensian figure. He was encased in a short naval overcoat and his chubby features were topped by a small peaked cap – of his own design, I was told. He needed no prompting to assume a challenging pose to match the defiant and menacing effect created by the shining gun barrels pointing towards an invisible enemy. He looked every inch the indomitable warrior, I thought as I watched him. The photographers clicked away, enjoying themselves. When they were done he gave a short address to the assembled sailors, congratulating them on 'the glorious victory' which they and their ship had achieved and telling them that the names of the more than sixty crewmen who had died in accomplishing it would live for ever in naval annals. He was at his most eloquent, but I reflected that this day the words did not matter anything like so much as did the picture he had created with the sure instinct of the born actor. When he had finished speaking, the sailor raised three cheers, and the First Lord's stance seemed to become even more triumphant than ever. He was indeed providing a top-notch story.

More than five years passed before I next met Winston Churchill. Those had been dangerous and gruelling years for all of us who survived, but they had ended in unprecedented defeat for the Germans and total victory for the Allies, thanks to Churchill's matchless leadership buttressed by the awesome material power of America and the great sacrifice of Soviet Russia. My own war-trail had taken me to and fro across Africa, into

Turkey, Malta, Palestine, Romania, and up the prickly spine of Italy, through France, Belgium and Holland, and finally into Germany. Now I was in Berlin, chronicling the infuriating and threatening political and administrative war between a Soviet Union implacably determined to extract maximum dividend out of victory and her bemused former Allies, the battered German population being used as a football between the two increasingly embittered sides. An enforced wartime alliance, always undermined by suspicion and past ideological enmity, had crumbled swiftly once the war ended. It had been replaced by hostility which could very easily have turned into deadly armed conflict, and, as I had already found in Berlin, would certainly have done so if the Western partners had yielded to the urgings of Germans who kept on whispering into our ears that we ought to smash the Soviet machine before it was too late.

A general election in the United Kingdom was staged on 5 July 1945, but announcement of the result had to be delayed for three weeks while what were believed to be the deciding votes of British soldiers in Germany and elsewhere were assembled and laboriously counted. While this was happening Winston Churchill came to Berlin for what turned out to be a tense and often acrimonious Big Three Conference at Potsdam, on the outskirts of Berlin.

While we onlookers waited outside, Winston was escorted by Russian officers on a tour of the unwholesome bunker. His daughter Mary, and Anthony Eden, the Foreign Secretary, followed him down the narrow stone steps. Eden was the only member of the official party with prior acquaintance of Hitler's Berlin. As he walked through the wreckage of the Chancellery he turned to me and said, almost disbelievingly: 'To think that this is where Hitler welcomed me years ago – in 1935.' Mr Churchill didn't spend much time in the bunker's murky depths and when he re-emerged he told his Russian interpreter that he would like to sit down in the sunshine 'to recover'. There happened to be a rickety-looking chair standing close to the spot outside the bunker where the corpses of Hitler and his wife, the former Eva Braun, had been doused with petrol and incinerated about two months earlier. Mr Churchill sat down on the chair and it promptly tottered beneath him. Imperturbable as ever, he allowed himself to be hoisted up and cracked a joking remark which, as I recall after so many years, ran something like: 'I imagine we've now seen the ultimate collapse.'

Although he occasionally joked in this style, he was mostly reflective, even subdued, that day, and I deduced that he was fretting about the imminent declaration of the result of the general election. He had good reason to be worried, for the Left had been scoring significant gains in by-elections held during the last two years of the war. Commonwealth, a party devoted to promoting Sir William Beveridge's plan for the establishment of the Welfare State, and the left-wing Independent Labour Party had achieved an average gain of 8.14 per cent in fourteen by-elections in seats held by the Churchill-led Conservatives. Commonwealth had, in fact, won three supposedly safe Conservative seats during this period, and less than a month ago it had wiped out at Chelmsford a massive Conservative majority to gain the seat. Such portents must have been weighing heavily on Mr Churchill this day in Berlin.

Yet he must have been as unprepared as all of us for what happened after he left the Chancellery and made an impromptu walkabout in the streets leading towards the Brandenburg Gate. Groups of Germans had gathered to watch him, some of them pausing in their task of clearing away the aftermath of the merciless bombing that had assailed them and their city up to the last days of the war. As he strode purposefully by – looking for all the world like an English officer and gentleman out for an afternoon stroll, sporting the obligatory walking-stick – they began clapping their hands and cheering. Cheers for the man who had been largely responsible for engineering their military doom! I could scarcely believe it. Winston Churchill literally took it in his stride. He walked on, with only the ghost of a satisfied smile on his face. What emotion had he really felt at that remarkable moment? He never talked much about it and made only a prosaic reference to it in his memoirs: 'My hate had died with their surrender and I was much moved by their demonstrations, and also by their haggard faces and threadbare clothes.'

When I came an hour or two later to write my own account of the day I tried to fathom the reasons for the phenomenon of the German demonstration. I concluded that the spontaneous plaudits were spurred at least partly by the realization of Berliners that the presence of Churchill among them was an insurance against a continuance of savagery by Russians who had been sprawling unchecked all over their ruined city, raping their women, kidnapping their scientists and specialists, looting their homes and factories. Churchill and the British would surely put an end to such vengeful bestiality. Of one thing I was certain. Had the boot been on the other foot and, God forbid, Hitler had been able to make a walkabout in Whitehall, there would have been no Englishmen and women on the pavements and sidewalks to cheer *him*.

Another principal at Potsdam, Joseph Stalin, toured prostrate Berlin during the conference. I can give no details of his visit because, like everybody else outside the Soviet fold, I knew nothing about it until fragmentary reports began to filter out of the Eastern compound. One official in the British delegation, whose identity I have forgotten, told me that so far as could be made out Stalin drove from Potsdam into the centre of Berlin in a bullet-proof motor vehicle with one-way windows and came back some time later without having dismounted from it. 'Presumably he felt he daren't show his face outside it,' said the official.

We Western watchers never learned anything from the Soviet camp during the Potsdam Conference. The secrecy was such that one of my colleagues, the respected William Forrest, of the *News Chronicle*, could not resist taking a hopeless swipe at it. He showed me the first paragraph of one story he wrote for his newspaper. It ran, approximately, like this: 'Not since the days of Ghengis Khan has an oriental despot moved in such secrecy as has Joseph Stalin, of the Soviet Union.' Of course these weighted words never saw the light of day in Willie's newspaper, but he felt better after writing them and I must say I enjoyed being one of the very few to read them.

As for Winston Churchill, any forebodings he may have had about the election in Britain were woundingly fulfilled. When the result was declared it showed that the Socialists, led by Clement Attlee, had won with an overall majority of 146 seats. The Conservatives had lost a staggering tally of 375 of the 585 seats they had won in the previous election ten years earlier. It was a repudiation of a kind hard to equal in the annals of British political history, and it was a blow which Churchill found hard to take. 'All our enemies having surrendered unconditionally or being about to do so I was immediately dismissed by the British electorate from all further conduct of their affairs,' he wrote bitterly many years later.

At Potsdam I was besieged by American colleagues who were astounded by the result and wanted to know how and why the British people had come to deliver such an insult to their great war leader. I was asked by one of them, Ray Scherer, of the National Broadcasting Company, to make a broadcast of explanation to his network's listeners in the United States, and I did so. 'One shouldn't criticize the British for what they have done,' I said. 'As a matter of fact, they should be complimented on their adult judgement of what is best for their country. Winston Churchill has led them magnificently from the edge of defeat to one of the finest victories in their history. He has done his job, and they have supported him while he was doing it. Now they want a clean sweep, a new approach, and – justifiably or not – they believe the Socialists will serve them better in peace than would Mr Churchill. There hasn't been an election at home for ten years. Everything has changed in that period. They have decided that the leadership should change to exploit those changes.'

I saw Winston Churchill for the last time on 22 January 1952. He was due to sail home at midnight that day at the end of his twelfth visit to the United States since 1895, and one of his final engagements was a press conference aboard *Queen Mary* as she lay tied up at Pier 90 at the foot of 50th Street in Manhattan. He was once again Prime Minister and, since a press conference by one holding that high office was still a rarity in those days, a great mass of American newspapermen and women, radio and television journalists (with all their helpers and electronic impedimenta) gathered in the great liner's Garden Lounge to record the occasion.

Winston Churchill had been in the United States two weeks for busy sessions with Harry Truman, the retiring President, and his successor, Dwight D. Eisenhower, and reunions with many old friends as well as numberless public engagements in Washington and New York. He was now seventy-nine, and many who had not seen him for some time said that at last he was showing physical signs of wear and tear. Yet this day he was to reveal, in dashing style, that he had lost none of his phenomenal mental agility or his command of the English language.

He dealt briskly with all the questions fired at him and he even got in two sharp digs of his own. One was a complaint about the reticence of President Truman (whom he hastened to compliment immediately after registering his complaint) to share atomic information with the United Kingdom. 'We would like to be a useful partner in atomic development, but we have been deprived of the exchange of information which Franklin Roosevelt promised me,' he said. His other complaint was against what he saw as American reluctance to buy British products. 'We don't want to live on you,' he declared. 'We want to earn our own living, but if you shut the door and won't take anything from us it's difficult to see how the present very unsatisfactory situation can be avoided.'

He went on sparring with his questioners for some twenty minutes and when they were satisfied and he was preparing to leave, a spokesman for the battery of television newsmen lined up some yards from him intercepted him. 'Sir,' said the spokesman respectfully, 'we'd very much appreciate it if you would walk over there in front of our cameras and speak a parting message to the American people.' This was the prelude to a final unforgettable moment in my contacts with Winston Churchill.

A moment later, Winston Churchill was bearing down in my direction on his way to the cameras. I just happened to be in his path and I had to scurry quickly out of it for the obvious reason that, if I didn't, he would either trample me underfoot or shove me aside. I had heard about this Churchillian characteristic. People had told me that in the House of Commons – anywhere, everywhere – when he moved in his chosen direction, he expected all obstacles, human or otherwise movable, to move aside. He just wasn't prepared to give way himself. As I hastily evaded him, I heard somebody alongside me, doing the same, mutter: 'Dammit, he's like a battleship steaming into action.'

As the television crews pressed buttons, turned switches and focused cameras on their now stationary target, I looked at him in wonderment, speculating on how on earth he would meet this unexpected demand for a message to the American people. He clearly had nothing prepared, for nobody had mentioned the possibility of its occurring to him. I needn't have worried. 'Five, four, three, two, one,' intoned the self-appointed master of ceremonies behind one of the cameras, and then pointed a finger at his poised victim.

'Hr'm,' Winston Churchill said, clearing his throat before pitching in to do his duty. He then delivered the most effective impromptu opening words of an oration I have ever heard. 'It's a wonderful thing to know as I stand here that the image of me is being seen in all parts of this great country,' he said. 'Every expression on my face will be seen by many millions. I only hope that the raw material is equal to the method of distribution. . . .'

Everybody in the Verandah Grill smiled in appreciation of this unique sally. I marvelled as I looked at this roly-poly of an ageing man speaking smoothly within a few feet of me. A recent reading of his own and other people's accounts of his long life had shown that, while he had attributes of genius, he also had flaws which had often brought him down: the arrogance and selfishness of a spoilt aristocrat, impatience with fools and with people even moderately less brilliant than himself, unthinking exploitation of those who slaved for him in his personal and professional lives, and an inherent imbalance which had sometimes caused him to make serious errors of judgement. In a lifetime which had begun thirty years before I was born he had risen to loftier heights of power and prestige than anybody else, but more than once had been brought down to contempt and humiliation by his own faults and also by the machinations of lesser men only too eager to humble him.

15

Hellfire Corner

As a prelude to becoming a full-fledged accredited war correspondent in the early spring of 1942 I had had an invaluable training experience. I had been assigned in 1940–1 to Dover in order to provide for my newspaper a daily chronicle of the Battle of Britain entirely unofficially as a civilian reporter relying solely on the use of his eyes and ears on the cliffs of Dover, or wherever else seemed appropriate as the epochal struggle raged overhead in what became known as 'Hellfire Corner'.

I and the handful of other London reporters detached by their newspapers for this long, difficult and sometimes hazardous assignment had no formal standing whatever with the three fighting Services. In the early phases of the battle we were even treated with suspicion. For a soldier, sailor or airman to be seen telling us anything was to court the risk of being accused of endangering security. But as time went by and all the segments of the Dover population became welded by the shared struggle for survival, I began to be treated as a friend and somebody who could be trusted with all but the deepest secrets, which couldn't be divulged to anyone not vitally concerned with them. Anyway, people began to realize that whatever I wrote each day was going to be scrutinized by censors at the Ministry of Information in London and, since it soon became obvious I was not a spy working for the enemy, there was really no danger at all in talking to me.

The change in the attitude of officialdom to this odd little company of men devoted to their task of chasing shot-down pilots, making what they could of the remote air battles being fought between Spitfire and Messerschmitt high overhead, and examining holes and damage caused by German long-range guns at Calais, across the water, was illustrated dramatically one morning in July 1941. I was called to the telephone in a narrow corridor of the Royal Oak inn, our headquarters on even higher ground than the Shakespeare Cliff between Dover and Folkestone, to have a momentous message read over to me from the news-room of the *Daily Mail* in London: 'You have been nominated to serve as a special correspondent in the event of invasion. You will go to sea with the naval forces in Dover. You will report to the office of the Vice Admiral tomorrow for information and passes. You should acquire a yachting cap, reefer jacket, thigh boots and a waterproof coat.'

There it was, without so much as a by your leave. Here again was the use of that remarkable word 'nominated', so favoured by newspaper editors and some others in those wartime days. It carried a connotation of lack of finality, a hint that one might have some slight choice about whether to accept or reject the assignment. This was pure illusion, as I found very early in my career as first a reporter and then a war correspondent between 1939 and 1945. If you were nominated, you went.

The message scared me. Going out there in the Strait of Dover to *meet* an invasion! It would have been bad enough to stand one's ground ashore. But, as I slowly realized, I had no right to be scared. I should be with – and, as a non-combatant civilian, under the protection of – officers who had mostly chosen the Royal Navy as their Service knowing that they might very well be called upon to meet such an unpleasant event as a German invasion, and repel it. Most of them had already been going out from Dover harbour day and night, in all kinds of weather, ready to detect and meet an invasion, and they had had many dangerous skirmishes with the enemy in his well-armed, speedy E-boats and other patrol craft which had been based twenty miles away on the coast of France ever since Dunkirk. I ought to be comforted to feel that I should literally be in the same boat as these brave and experienced men if the test came. So did I rationalize, and I felt the better for it.

Next morning I drove to Dover Castle with Roger Mulholland, of the Press Association, and Geoffrey Edwards, of the *News Chronicle*, the two other nominees who would make up with me the tiny team responsible for reporting for the world the naval response to the ultimate challenge to our country, should it come. We walked across an ancient drawbridge, very medieval-looking, and then went through a maze of tunnels and passages to the heart of the Dover Naval Command, located in many cavelike offices etched into the side of Castle Hill. It was a world of its own, having no visible connection with the modern world outside. It was where the miraculous evacuation of a defeated British Army had been planned not so long ago and where, one hoped, the repulse of Hitler's invasion would be arranged – if ever he attempted one, which I for one greatly doubted. Maybe I was swayed by consideration of my contingent assignment.

We had a smooth and deceptively casual conversation with Commander James, the staff officer (Intelligence). He gave us neat little passes which, he said, would not fail to get us through any barriers protecting the docks, even under stringent security regulations which would obviously come into force in the event of a German cross-Channel enterprise. He also gave a demonstration of the unique finesse of the Royal Navy in treating the most alarming assignment at sea as if it were an outing on a lake in a rowing-boat. Not one word or sign from him that he was aware of the possibility of one, or perhaps all three, of us defenceless civilians being blown to smithereens or meeting a cold, wet and miserable end somewhere between Dover and the French coast. 'Give me your phone numbers so that I can reach you when and if it looks as if the enemy is coming,' he said, surveying us coolly from his seat at his desk. 'I'll give you as long an advance warning as I can. . . . Dress up warmly to go to sea. It can be cold out there, even on a nice day.'

Before leaving him we worked out a simple code covering arrangements and instructions for boarding our allotted warships, details of which I naturally didn't set down in writing and have long since forgotten. Then we parted.

Next morning the three of us drove into Folkestone to buy seagoing equipment. I went for the very best on hand, to provide an assurance that, if I sank in the English Channel, I should do so in style. My choice purchase was a splendid pair of fisherman's waterproof waders reaching from foot to thigh. They looked as if they might last for ever, and the thought struck me as I tried them on for size and comfort that if, as I hoped, they were not to be used for the purpose for which they were being acquired, they would serve me well once the war was over. They did. I used them extensively whenever I went duck shooting on my wife's family farm at South Leigh, Oxfordshire, and later in Berlin, and even later when I was transferred by the *Daily Telegraph* from there to the United States. I also bought from a garage in Dover a small two-stroke motor cycle called a Coventry Eagle which I kept under cover in a shed behind the Royal Oak inn. My idea was to have it in reserve, using it enough to keep it in working trim, so that if the invasion happened and when (and if) I came ashore from some bitter battle at sea in the Channel and found I couldn't reach my office in London by telephone with my history-making story, I could mount my Coventry Eagle and ride out of the combat zone to reach a working telephone. Perhaps I should have to ride it all the way to London and park it outside the *Daily Mail* offices in Carmelite Street while I raced upstairs to the third floor to hammer out my account of what I had witnessed. It was not destined to be used for any of these purposes, but I did use it for news-gathering trips in and around Dover during and after the Battle of Britain, and once I even rode it to Epsom and back, a distance of well over a hundred miles, to make a weekend visit to my wife Katy and the children.

Although the Germans never came, fulfilling a personal prophecy from which I never swerved, all the preliminary planning and exercising which we went through under the guidance of Commander James was not wasted so far as I was concerned. It led to one of the most exhilarating experiences I had in the war up to 1942 – one which helped me to function more efficiently when I was pitched into the sea war in the Mediterranean and later into the maelstrom of the Battle of Alamein, the conquest of Italy and beyond.

About a week after the session at Dover Castle Commander James telephoned me to say that, as everybody concerned was anxious to test the arrangements already made, it had been decided that our little 'invasion news squad', as he playfully called it, should go to sea on a trial trip. The three of us would spend a night on patrol in the Channel in different trawlers. We would take our chances on anything interesting happening.

Impressively arrayed in my lovely thigh-boots, three layers of shirt and sweater, a shiny naval oilskin and a Balaclava helmet, I turned up at the appointed hour in the dock where the trawler to which I had been committed was moored. I blessed my good fortune that the Channel was docile. It was a clear night, with only a moderate breeze ruffling the water. I am a pretty good sailor, but even so it was reassuring to feel that on such a calm night there would be little chance of my confirming my status as a landlubber to all these seagoing types by being sick. I climbed warily and inexpertly down a rope-ladder which had at least three cross-pieces missing and, under the critical eyes of some of the trawler's crew, stumbled over ropes and other obstacles before eventually reaching what must have been one of the tiniest wardrooms in the Royal Navy.

There the RNVR lieutenant who was to be in charge of me for the night was waiting. He was a fresh-faced, slim youngster whom I judged to be in his early twenties. As he poured out an introductory gin he gave me his name, but since he spoke it quietly and shyly, as so many Englishmen do, I didn't catch it and was relieved when he added, a little more clearly, that I should call him 'Sumpy'. This was an abbreviation of his full name, I assumed. 'All my friends call me Sumpy,' he said with a courteous smile which implied that henceforth I could number myself among them. The disarming smile was deceptive. It was belied by an exceptionally steely gaze in one so young. Here was a stripling of a kind who had been hardened by war, forced to an early – and, sadly, perhaps brief – maturity like a plant exposed to unnaturally warm light. He was the first of a band of young men whom I was to meet and live with during the coming years – men trained at select English public schools to be pioneers and leaders. Often such an officer was a polished and graceful person socially, who masked his innate fortitude behind a veneer of urbane, sometimes self-mocking effeteness. These were men whom I came to respect. They had been swept before they knew it into the Army, Navy, or Air Force, in the unprecedented emergency which Hitler had provoked in 1939. Too often, alas, they were destined to pay the penalty of death or lifelong mutilation before the war was over and won. My years of contact with such men induce me to defend the institution of the British public school. People may say what they like in criticism of it, but there can be no doubting that in 1939 and thereafter it once again achieved its traditional purpose of producing leaders. One hopes that the war of 1939–45 will prove to be the last uncivilized arena to test the system and its uniquely British products. I hope it and they will continue to thrive and enable my country to make her unique contribution to mankind in less savage and wasteful endeavours.

As the trawler nosed out to sea in the darkness, Sumpy and I stood together on the small bridge of the vessel. We were silent for long periods as he guided the trawler along its appointed course and I adjusted to, and then came to be lulled by, the gentle roll of the craft as she pushed on. I had no idea where we were after about an hour, or even where we were going. I had learned from experience that it wasn't worth asking the Navy what it was doing. If it thought you should know, it would tell you, in its own way and in its own good time. But I imagined we were somewhere in mid-Channel, in the centre of a square of sea bounded by Folkestone and Dover on one side and Boulogne and Calais on the other. This was the narrowest part of the Channel, the bottleneck in which everything seemed to happen. I had a childish feeling of elation when I reflected that I was probably nearer to the German enemy than any other British non-combatant that night.

I was jolted out of such ruminations by the crack of a heavy explosion some distance to starboard, echoing around us as it rumbled across the water. Everybody peered into the gloom in the direction of the noise as the trawler continued to trundle along, but apparently nobody could tell what had caused it. 'Just one of those explosions we're forever hearing out here,' Sumpy remarked to me at length. 'Never knew such a place for bangs. We'll report it and so will everybody else, and that'll be the last we'll hear about it.'

Quiet reigned thereafter for about another hour. I was sipping a cup of hot, strong tea brought to the bridge by a seaman whose deftness in negotiating the ship's narrow confines would have guaranteed him a job anywhere as a tightrope-walker. The peace was broken. The sky ahead of us was abruptly lit up by a display of martial fireworks far more vivid than anything we journalistic watchers on the Kentish cliffs had ever seen. The show opened with an overture provided by streams of 'flaming onions', as tracer shells from German anti-aircraft guns were generally known. In between these came sudden brief flashes as much more lethal shells burst and sparkled, spreading fragments far and wide in a search for targets. Now we could hear the hum of aircraft engines. Moments later we saw and heard the gleam and thump of exploding bombs. These noisy stage effects came from one small stretch of horizon immediately ahead of us. As I looked on, my elbows resting on the side of our plodding craft, I noted that the spectacle was happening extremely close to us. I calculated that we were not more than five miles from the French coast, and the thought that I was probably the nearest civilian to the enemy immediately became less exhilarating as I considered what might happen if we were detected and attacked.

'Our bombers over there again,' observed a man at the wheel of the trawler who I had been told was a fisherman from Aberdeen in less turbulent times. 'Now they've started, they'll be at it all night, on and off. They're merr-ci-less once they start.' His rolling Scottish 'r' emphasized his satisfaction. 'It's Calais getting it again tonight,' said Sumpy at my side.

At last I knew where we were. We were travelling west through the narrowest part of the Channel and at that moment were probably due south of my land headquarters at the Royal Oak, on the cliffs. I smiled to think of my colleagues – Reginald Foster, of the *Daily Herald*, and 'Balkan' Harry Harrison (so-called because of his long pre-war assignment in Belgrade), of the *News Chronicle*, curled up in their beds at the inn. They'd probably awaken at the sound of the dull thumps coming to them from across twenty miles of water and then they'd go back to sleep because they would know that the bombing was happening on the French coast, beyond their scope of coverage. They'd leave that to the Air Ministry communiqué tomorrow. Unspoken by anybody would be the reason for the repeated bombings of Calais – interference with and delaying of all the preparations for invasion known to be happening over there.

The Aberdonian was proved right. The RAF attack on the docks and harbour at Calais was repeated five times while we steamed placidly west. Nobody aboard was watching after the third wave of bombers had come and gone. The crew was getting ready for the mission which marked this night's patrol. I was let into the secret at about 3 a.m., when the Royal Navy, represented by Sumpy, took me into its confidence. Just before dawn, Sumpy said, we were due to meet a convoy of merchantmen carrying mixed cargoes of food and other much-needed supplies for London. The plan was that we should make rendezvous at a time which would enable us and other craft to escort it through the bottleneck of the narrowest part of the Channel off Dover in semi-darkness until it was safely out of range of the big long-range guns sited on cliffs outside Calais. 'Of course we'll be handy to join in the party if anything else turns up,' Sumpy added, with more eagerness than I liked.

As the darkness slowly thinned we began peering around us for the approaching convoy. Considerately conferring on me honorary membership of his crew, and shrewdly calculating to profit from the presence of an extra hand, Sumpy gave me a look-out post on the port side. 'Watch – and if you think you see something, give a yell' was his order. I now sensed that he was no longer the cheery Sumpy of the earlier hours of the patrol, his voice carrying an edge of anxiety. Had something gone wrong which he couldn't yet talk about? The possibility robbed me of the cool enjoyment I had begun to experience this strange night. Here I was, after all, in an eerie world of its own in the no man's land of the Channel, in a vulnerable little craft which was in fact trespassing on the enemy side of a watery frontier. No lights, no radio chatter giving us comforting contact with the maritime world around us, but total isolation aboard a weather-beaten old trawler seeking an uncertain date with other ships plodding on through the water as we were, within a mile or two of the enemy's front line. And now, if my surmise was correct, some unexpected trouble or danger was threatening us. I have to confess that I felt none too comfortable as I took up my post against the ship's rail.

Happily, intense preoccupation with my job helped to usurp anxiety. I must do well at it, if only for my own self-esteem. Nobody could have gazed more devotedly into the slowly growing light than this dedicated novice. Of course imagination, and perhaps lingering anxiety, played me false. Twice I saw shapes and ships that weren't there. I voiced false alarms. The Aberdonian steersman's expert eyes instantly exposed me, but he was compassionate in doing so. 'Steady, laddie,' he counselled. 'Count five before you shout next time.'

It was good advice, but after the passage of only a few minutes it happened that if I had followed his suggestion and taken my time about counting five I should have looked and felt like a fool. It was getting perceptibly lighter now. I saw what was undoubtedly, this time, a small vessel steering towards us on a diagonal course. I was positive I wasn't mistaken and, without stopping to count even one, I shouted out a warning. 'Something coming close – over there!' I cried, pointing. Others had of course seen something too, and even as I spoke Sumpy was taking avoiding action. 'Hard to port!' he directed. The trawler slewed, throwing me hard against the rail. As I recovered my balance, I saw the approaching craft swerve away from us. It looked like a British motor torpedo-boat, but it could also have been a German E-boat and, for one wretched moment, I believed it was just that. Suppose it had been scouting round to find us and, now that it had done so, was seeking us out for destruction? We should have precious little chance against such a well-armed and speedy adversary. Happily, reassurance came even as these agonizing thoughts raced through my mind. I was surprised to get a glimpse, brief but satisfying, of a face actually smiling at me as the oncoming craft veered away from us at what seemed to be the last possible moment, and I fancied, but couldn't be quite sure, that I saw a hand waving at me. It could well have been, I thought, as the Aberdonian filled in the cheering details of what was happening. 'The advance scout of the convoy, that was,' he said, straightening up and relaxing his hold momentarily on the steering apparatus in front of him. 'And thank God for it! I thought they'd never be coming.' So he too had been anxious.

There is always an element of chance in ship-to-ship encounters such as had just occurred. The only certain check on the identity and intent of a ship approaching another in semi-darkness in such confined waters as the Strait of Dover must be visual. A captain has to make up his mind on what his eyes tell him, and he has to react instantly once he has done so. This was what the captain of the MTB had done. Having spotted us he had steamed at high speed directly towards us until he was satisfied that we really were what he expected us to be – an auxiliary escort assigned to help guide the convoy through the most dangerous part of the journey eastwards, the twenty miles separating Dover and Calais. There was sound tactical reasoning behind his manoeuvring. To come for us at full speed, with his crew at action stations and his guns at the ready, meant that if we had been hostile after all, he would have been in a position to blow us out of the water in a matter of seconds. Now, having confirmed our identity, he could swing away and leave us to take up our position alongside the convoy.

But something was awry. I walked over to Sumpy, all smiles, to find his early poise gone. His face now carried a worried frown and even before I could ask him why, he confided in me. 'The convoy's half an our late in getting here,' he said. 'It's now light enough for Jerry to see us before we've got through the narrows. Afraid it means trouble.' He turned away to direct his little ship into position as she approached the convoy, now to be seen only too clearly in the nearly full light of dawn as a chain of black hulks in rough formation between us and, as I calculated, the Kentish coast. I found it touching to watch the escorts and merchantmen making rendezvous. The torpedo-boats and trawlers reminded me of those guides one sees shepherding young schoolchildren across traffic crossings in any town or suburb in the Western world. The slow-moving merchantmen looked as dependent as children.

I didn't have long to dwell upon such thoughts. The Germans manning the shore defences showed quickly that they had indeed spotted us and our charges, which were sauntering eastwards maddeningly slowly in almost complete daylight. The speed of us all was dictated by the speed of the slowest ship in the convoy, but the torpedo-boat captains and crew could relieve their frustration by speeding to and fro, in and out, to make sure that all was well with every one of their defenceless charges and that every vessel was keeping formation. The trawlers, including ours, were of course less manoeuvrable and less speedy and had to be content to plod along at the speed (if that is the word) of the convoy.

Four pencils of yellow flame shot up from a point on the horizon only a few miles south of us. They briefly lit up the faces of Sumpy and one or two others standing on or near the bridge. 'Get y'rr tin hat . . . quick . . . and duck!' the Aberdonian cried out to me in avuncular concern. He knew, as we all did, that those flashes meant only one thing – artillery shells on their way to us. I grabbed my protective helmet which I had put down handily close to my feet and crouched low behind the flimsy wooden side of the bridge. It was scant cover, but it was all that was available. In a few seconds the shells already on their way would explode about us. I knew from experience ashore in Dover that between sixty and seventy seconds elapsed between the sight of the gun-flashes and the landing of shells in or close to Dover harbour. Here, so much closer to Cap Gris-Nez, the time-lag would be much less. My mind froze as I crouched and waited. I recollect doing only one thing – crossing my fingers for good luck. It is a reflex which has stayed with me in various situations to this day.

The deadening suspense was ended by the sound of four sharp cracks. The little trawler began rocking like a rudderless cork, and as I crouched, the sky and the sea seeming temporarily to have lost their usual anchorages, I heard four more thumps, though not as violent as the earlier ones and not followed by any perceptible upheaval. These were the sounds of the guns being fired in the French cliffs, which had taken longer to reach us than the noise of shells exploding only yards away. I pictured ugly, jagged lumps of hot metal whizzing through the air around us imprisoned mortals, capable of ripping holes in anything, including human bodies, which happened to be in their path. There was little one could do about it except to squeeze into as small a space as possible, cross fingers and hope that one's name wasn't on anything flying around.

There were no names at all on any of these lethal bits of metal. All four shells had landed and exploded in the water, two of them close enough to their targets, as I learned later, to pierce holes in ships' sides, but not close enough to cause any substantial damage or harm anybody. And, even though the convoy was so late and so slow, the German gunners managed to let loose only one more salvo before all the ships were out of range of the immobile artillery. Again we saw the yellow flashes, again we ducked, and again we all raised unscathed heads in time to watch high spouts of water created by the exploding shells subside slowly, again wide of any ships. The fountains looked lovely in the morning light, free of diabolic intent. We steamed on to the east until soon we felt certain we were out of range of the enemy guns.

'I suppose it was pretty accurate gunnery, everything considered,' Sumpy commented. 'Yet I'm amazed that they keep it up, because they never seem to hit anything.'

I too had been considering the reasons for the seemingly profitless bombardments. 'I think I can explain it,' I ventured. 'You'll see that tonight's German communiqué from Berlin will probably say something like this: "Our guns on the French coast again successfully shelled a British convoy passing through the Strait of Dover", et cetera. A lot of people in occupied Europe are going to be affected by that item. It will depress them and make them think that Germany is winning the war. The German population will think the same. So Goebbels will get a good propaganda dividend from the gunnery. He probably doesn't give a damn whether or not the shells hit anything.'

One final hazard remained as escorts and merchantmen slowly passed beyond Dover harbour. The light had become so strong as to be hard on eyes which had been gazing for many hours into darkness and visibility seemed favourable for aerial attack. Would the enemy send over his Stuka bombers to try to achieve what the long-range batteries had failed to do? The Stukas hadn't been faring too well in Hellfire Corner lately. I had seen one come crashing into the water only a few days earlier after becoming entangled in a mesh of piano-wire, nails and other nasty impediments drifting downwards under a small parachute – one of those 'other devices' to which Air Ministry communiqués had been recently referring. There had also been signs that the confidence of Stuka pilots was becoming undermined by the growing competence of defenders, and it had been noted that Stukas were being used less and less often in the later phases of the Battle of Britain. So we putative victims shared a hope that we might be spared a visitation. The danger remained, however, that local Luftwaffe chieftains at French airfields might decide that a sluggish convoy with only lightly armed escorts was too promising a target to ignore. Our crew stayed at action stations although we were through the Strait. Looking about me, I saw that the young men standing alongside their guns or at look-out stations fore, aft and amidships were alert and tense. Danger had its usual effect of drawing men together. When one of the sailors noticed my eyes upon him, his facial muscles relaxed momentarily and he gave me a heavy wink, grinning at the same time. I smiled back. In that moment we were brothers.

Unexpectedly the Aberdonian nudged me. 'D'you hear anything?' he asked. I did. It was the beat of an aircraft engine. Sumpy had also heard it. 'Steady, everybody,' he shouted. 'Hold it!' Eyes searched the skies and one sailor peering astern suddenly reported that he had spotted a machine speeding low towards us from the direction of the English coast. Nobody said a word as it flew nearer and nearer, and then came exclamations of relief as we all recognized its lovely elliptical wings and tell-tale red, white and blue roundels. 'That's what I call co-oper-ration,' the Aberdonian observed. 'The Stukas won't come now. Not bloody likely. Not with Spitfires about.'

Nor did they. We began to relax. Cups of tea and coffee made the rounds as we slowed, detached ourselves from the plodding convoy and, turning for home, left it to pass under aerial protection into broader waters off the South Foreland. Our night's work was done, or so we thought. Yet there was to be one final irritating chore to be faced before we could be freed from the call of duty. We were nearing the eastern arm of Dover harbour, in reasonably good time despite the alarms and excitements of the last ten hours, when a look-out saw a loose mine bobbing about, revealing its menacing spikes. It was of course a nuisance and a danger, even though it was one which the Royal Navy had laid protectively outside the harbour. The Aberdonian was especially disgusted. 'I was due to meet a pal half an hour from now, and we were going to hoist a couple before I went to bed,' he muttered to me, grimacing. 'Now we'll have to stop and sink this blasted thing.'

This we did, but not easily. Tired crewmen obeyed Sumpy's order to form a firing-squad, a machine-gunner joining them. Bullets kept padding into the mine, but it defied its attackers for over half an hour, obstinately bobbing and turning until at last one bullet caught it in one of its few vulnerable parts, whereupon it heeled over and slowly foundered, like a holed ship.

Now we were free to steam into Dover harbour and tie up. Sumpy and I and a couple of officers (but not the Aberdonian, who bolted off as if the Devil were at his heels) lingered over a farewell drink, early in the day though it was. 'Afraid you can't have much to write about,' Sumpy said, apologetically. 'We didn't provide much action.' I reassured him. 'Don't worry about that,' I said. 'To you it was probably a routine patrol. To people who don't really know what's going on around here it will make fascinating reading.'

And it did, even though the censor dealt rather roughly with it. He cut out everything which might have given the Germans the slightest help. I couldn't complain about that, for the war in Hellfire Corner was being fought at very close quarters and our side was still on the defensive in 1941 and still redressing the defeat it had suffered in Europe, which had culminated in the evacuation from Dunkirk not so long ago.

After leaving the ship I walked somewhat wearily to Market Square in the town and caught a bus going up the steep hill beyond Shakespeare Cliff and by the front door of the Royal Oak inn. The bus was full of people going to work and I noticed some of them eyeing me curiously but decorously. They were clearly wondering who on earth this man could be, the fellow hiding behind a padding of sweaters, thigh-boots, oilskin and the rest. Nobody asked any questions. This was wartime in Hellfire Corner. It just wasn't done to ask questions in a bus unless you thought somebody was a spy. And I hardly looked like one of those.

16

Russian Bear at Large

When Nikita Khrushchev announced in the late summer of 1960 that he would be leading his country's delegation to the imminent session of the UN General Assembly in New York he lit a fuse to the most spectacular firework show at the UN since its foundation in 1945.

Khrushchev had been swinging away for months in a diplomatic offensive against President Eisenhower and the United States and against Dag Hammarskjöld and the United Nations, and his decision to go to New York meant that he intended to maintain that attack on the enemy's own ground and on the world's grandest international stage. So his announcement stirred every sizeable member state into action by deciding to send her top leader to the Assembly, not only to safeguard the national interest at the looming firework show but to take part in it as either a supporter of Khrushchev or alongside the majority against him.

Khrushchev's announcement also goaded the US State Department into making a pre-emptive strike against him, intended to humble and hobble him from the moment he set foot on American soil. Christian Herter, the Secretary of State, declared, while Mr Khrushchev was making the best of a rough passage on the high seas aboard the 7,000-ton freighter s.s. *Baltika*, that the unwelcome visitor was coming 'only to make propaganda' at a moment when the United States was involved in the protracted process of electing a new president. And, said Mr Herter, since he was not really coming to the United States but only to the United Nations he would be restricted to moving in an area twenty-five miles in all directions from Columbus Circle, Manhattan. This would give him access to the Soviet country headquarters at Glen Cove, Long Island, and the city headquarters of all other delegations to the UN, but to little else that Mr Khrushchev might need or want to visit.

I got up before dawn on 19 September and went to Pier 73, off the FDR Drive and 25th Street, to watch Mr Khrushchev land. This historic event was played out in one of the most remarkable episodes I reported in the nineteen years of my assignment in the United States for the *Daily Telegraph*. The first highly observable fact was that the City of New York had co-operated to the full with the State Department in the effort to make the occasion as squalid, degrading and uncomfortable for Mr Khrushchev as could possibly be contrived. Its opening tactic was to direct the captain of the *Baltika* while he was still at sea that he must tie up at Pier 73, the most dilapidated pier of them all on the East River waterfront. It was barely usable. Indeed, the city authorities told the Soviet delegation in advance that it would have to pay for repairs which were needed if *Baltika* were to use it. Even so, this morning the roof still leaked and part of the understructure opposite the mooring for which *Baltika* was making was still collapsed to within a few feet of the East River surface.

Everything was conspiring to make the occasion miserable for Nikita Khrushchev. The elements were in alliance with his tormentors. A cascade of cold rain, of a kind which can be a chilling speciality of the New York City autumn, was belting down, drenching the huddle of spectators waiting for *Baltika* to dock. As she chugged slowly to the pier, I saw Khrushchev was showing that he was not dismayed by the treatment accorded him. He must have known that the Americans were, as one of them conceded to me as we waited, seeking to 'cut him down to size', but he was by no means dismayed. The first sight of him I had was as he stood, bareheaded despite the rain beating down upon him, below the ship's bridge, grinning expansively and waving to the few hardy citizens of the Soviet Union and her satellites who had come to welcome him. The *Baltika* slowly made it to her mooring and, moments after an exit ramp had been laid, Khrushchev strode ashore. Flanked by Antonin Novotny, the President of Czechoslovakia, and Wladyslav Gomulka, chief of the government of Poland, he marched purposefully towards a makeshift podium along the length of a red carpet and an expensive-looking oriental carpet which was taking damaging treatment from the rain. Still wearing no hat or raincoat, with the rain beating down on him as well as on those of us who were watching, he delivered a brief message that contained one or two phrases which had been obviously created to conform with a stratagem which was to be noted throughout the Khrushchev visit – appealing to the mass of public opinion by inferring that the American people were not of the same mind as the American administration. For example: 'However dark the night,' I heard an interpreter telling us Khrushchev was saying, 'dawn always breaks. I am therefore sure that all the efforts of evil forces which want to poison relations between our two countries will be defeated. Good relations will come.' I do not know how much effect the stratagem exerted on Americans as a whole, but I am confident that Khrushchev's innate charisma, bluff humour and obvious dogged resolve not to let official hostile treatment upset him achieved a great deal in gaining him the often grudging admiration of many ordinary Americans. He also showed this morning that he had learned some of the propaganda tricks practised in the West. Responding to the thin ripple of applause as he finished his short speech, he raised his arms high above his head – now protected by an enormous umbrella – and clasped his hands in the manner of a victorious boxer acknowledging the plaudits of his adoring fans, beaming expansively as he did so. Then came a sight pathetic enough to soften the hearts of all but the most rabid enemies of

the Soviets. Three small girls, in red dresses which had once been beautifully ironed and were set off by white hair ribbons, advanced through the
downpour and presented him with bouquets of pink, white and orange
gladioli. The rain falling unchecked by the decayed roof of Pier 73 spared
neither little girls nor pretty posies. Only Nikita Khrushchev seemed
weatherproof.

He staged many comical shows which endeared him to American
reporters and photographers during his days in New York. I witnessed
some of them. One afternoon, having heard that he might be giving a
press conference, I walked round to the mansion in Park Avenue which at
that time was serving as headquarters of the Soviet delegation to the
United Nations. He *was* giving a press conference, of a kind I have never
encountered, before or since. He was standing on a balcony of the
mansion, about twenty feet above street-level. Below him was a cluster of
reporters who had brought their own interpreters with them. They had
also brought long poles to which they had tied microphones so that they
could record his answers to their questions. He gave a blunt but graphic
one when he was asked what he thought about pickets carrying anti-
Khrushchev and anti-Soviet slogans who were marching to and fro below
him in Park Avenue. 'They're just like stuff there,' he said, pointing to a
heap of manure piled beneath the hindquarters of a policeman's horse.

A few moments later he seized a chance to stage an amusing unre-
hearsed imitation of the balcony scene in *Romeo and Juliet*. Andrei
Gromyko, his Foreign Minister, was cast as his Romeo. Gromyko chanced
to arrive in a limousine from a session at the United Nations and was
walking towards the front door of the mansion when Khrushchev saw
him. 'Gromyko, I'm under house arrest – rescue me,' he shouted, placing
his left hand dramatically over his heart. One simply had to laugh, for he
made a grotesque figure as he stood there, a travesty of a Shakespearian
juvenile lead, for he was wearing no jacket and had red braces holding up
his trousers above his ample midriff. Gromyko, blessed by nature with the
melancholy features of a clown, reacted with a winsome smile and a
sympathetic gesture, spreading out his arms in mock-helplessness.
Spurred on by Gromyko's response, Khrushchev delivered the next lines
of his impromptu script. 'Gromyko, I'm not being allowed to see
America,' he said, plaintively. He pointed a stubby forefinger towards
Midtown Manhattan, stretching away to his right. 'There's my America,
and I can't visit it.' He could visit it, of course, for it lay within the
prescribed limits set by the State Department. But Khrushchev had seen
and heard the whirring television cameras below. He was providing them
with a splendid item for the evening news shows.

The little play went on for a few more minutes. Then Gromyko decided
that it had gone far enough. Perhaps he feared that the exuberant Khrushchev might overdo his act. He hurried inside the mansion, and a few
minutes later Khrushchev suddenly disappeared from the balcony. But

not before he had fired off another shot at his reluctant hosts. His chance came when one of the poled reporters thrust his microphone within inches of Khrushchev's mouth and asked through his interpreter: 'Why are you appearing here in shirt-sleeves and suspenders, Mr Khrushchev?' Khrushchev pounced upon this one with lightning speed. 'I'm posing as an American,' he said, baring his teeth in a wide grin.

One fact to be noted as Khrushchev's stay in New York lengthened, providing everybody with a continuing display of humorous and dramatic exhibitions in which he took the star role, was that he used a permanent fixed grin in public to mask his inner thoughts and reactions. Nothing seemed to upset him. The grin never left him even when verbal or other shafts must surely have pierced what appeared to be an exceptionally thick skin.

In private, he relaxed with some of his Communist comrades from the Soviet Union's satellites in Eastern Europe. He even indulged in some questionable anecdotes, as I found when I went one evening in company with Lady Jean Campbell, the attractive and journalistically talented daughter of Lord Beaverbrook, to a reception given for him by the Bulgarian Mission to the United Nations. It was a humdrum affair until late in the evening I observed that Khrushchev had drawn about a dozen men around him in a football huddle in a corner of the salon and was obviously telling them a story of some kind. After he had ended his recital to a roar of laughter from his small audience I asked one of them, a Bulgarian official whom I had met at the UN, what Khrushchev had been talking about. The man told me, with some embarrassment, that he had been giving his version of what had happened four years earlier when Britain, France and Israel joined in a disastrous attempt to regain control of the Suez Canal after Egypt had seized it. Apparently Khrushchev had likened Anthony Eden, the British Prime Minister, to a boy who had been taken unaware by his bodily functions and had had to wallow in the resulting mess until somebody recued him. My Bulgarian informant said that Khrushchev had told the story in earthy terms, expressing himself in words commonly used in the Soviet countryside from which he had sprung.

This minor interlude occurred the evening after he had made a sorry spectacle of himself in a session of the General Assembly at the United Nations. He had been deftly outmanoeuvred in a duel with Harold Macmillan, the British Prime Minister, in one of the most spectacular meetings in United Nations history. The diplomatic defeat he had suffered before a gathering of hundreds of the world's leaders had clearly not abashed him. His crude ebullience at the Bulgarian party was a sign that the defensive shield of the fixed grin and the thick skin had worked yet again.

Every seat in the Assembly chamber was filled on the morning of 29 September when Harold Macmillan walked down an aisle to the dais of dark marble to speak for the United Kingdom. The delegates did not have to wait long for the opening of a confrontation between Macmillan and Khrushchev which all had expected. Khrushchev stirred in his seat, one row in front of Marshal Tito of Yugoslavia, in response to the first urbane, indirect sally made by Macmillan. He said that the peoples of the world had recently been deeply disappointed by the failure of the Big Powers to hold a planned summit meeting in Paris. 'They expect us to overcome that setback and, in due course, to try again,' he said, silkily. This was a feint, or perhaps more accurately a flourish, devised to enhance the impact of Macmillan's first verbal thrust at Khrushchev. It would be delivered quietly and would be well screened, but it would be charged with a meaning which everybody in the chamber would perceive. 'Mr Khrushchev, although he has permitted himself some forcible language, has seemed to regard the path as temporarily obstructed and not permanently barred,' Macmillan went on. 'It is in that spirit that I have worked as Prime Minister and it is in that spirit that I speak today. As for the Secretary-General, I should like to associate myself with the wide expressions of confidence which have been made in his energy, his resourcefulness, and, above all, his integrity.' Decoded, the diplomatic wordage meant that Macmillan was telling Khrushchev to stop playing destructive political games and return to the serious business of fostering international harmony.

Khrushchev had recently been on a political rampage which had upset everybody outside the Soviet fold. Besides attacking the stature of President Eisenhower and the United States by cancelling a planned summit meeting in Europe on a pretext, he had been trying to stop the United Nations interfering with his aim of installing a Communist regime in the turbulent Congo as a prelude to making further ideological advances in emerging Africa. The man who had been blocking him in the Congo was Dag Hammarsjköld, the most successful functionary the UN had ever had, and in an effort to nullify Hammarskjöld Khrushchev had proposed that the office of Secretary-General occupied by the doughty Swede should be replaced by a 'troika' of three persons. He knew, of course, that if he could achieve this dilution and ensure that at least one of the members of the 'troika' was either a Communist or a friend of the Soviet Union, there would be little further danger of the United Nations interfering with him in the Congo – or anywhere else.

Macmillan was on firm ground in assailing the Soviet schemer. Only nine hours before Khrushchev reached New York on the s.s. *Baltika* the General Assembly had given him a severe setback by endorsing Hammarskjöld's plan to end the struggle for the Congo, sending there a UN force which would make sure that any attempt to impose an illegal Communist regime by force would fail.

In view of this tangled background , it came as no surprise that Macmillan's smooth endorsement of Hammarskjöld was met by a great storm of applause. The delegates prolonged it far beyond the time it merited because they wished to make sure that Khrushchev was left in no doubt about the sentiments of the majority concerning his recent antics. As it happened, Hammarskjöld was there to witness the demonstration. He was sitting behind and above the speaker's rostrum in his official seat alongside the President of the Assembly, Mr Boland of Ireland. I watched him sitting there impassively, his arms folded across his chest. He gave no sign whatever that he was affected by the extraordinary demonstration of appreciation and support echoing around him.

Now it was the moment to turn one's attention to Khrushchev, for he at least was putting on a counter-exhibition. He was making the only response he could muster in the adverse circumstances. As the artifically prolonged applause went on and on, he sought to offset it by drumming his fists violently on the desk top in front of him and shouting at the top of his voice in Russian with words that nobody could possibly hear in the turmoil. Andrei Gromyko, his Foreign Minister, who was sitting next to him, joined his master in the fistic drum-beating, but, I noticed, rather more softly and spasmodically. I also noted that Marshal Tito, sitting immediately behind the Soviet duo, was doing nothing at all. He was simply staring blankly ahead with his arms firmly folded across his chest, like Dag Hammarskjöld. He stayed strictly neutral.

Some witnesses have claimed that at one point they saw Khrushchev produce a shoe from somewhere, perhaps from one of his own feet, and bang it angrily on his desk-top. I have to say that I never saw him do any such thing. Nor have I ever seen a photograph of the phenomenon. But the testimony has gone into the accepted legend about what happened on this memorable morning and future generations will not be swayed by my isolated expression of doubt.

At last, after what seemed hours but was in fact some twenty minutes, the Assembly quietened, and Macmillan was able to resume his performance. He turned to the sensitive topic of colonialism. It was one on which the United Kingdom was usually particularly vulnerable because of her long past history of imperial conquest, but on this topsy-turvy day at the UN he was able to turn it to his advantage and to Khrushchev's further irritation. One could only surmise that for the moment at any rate delegates felt that their anger at Soviet obstructionism and attempted dethroning of Dag Hammarskjöld was greater than their antagonism to colonialism, which was, in any event, a dead or dying political practice.

Macmillan and his advisers had found a neat approach to the topic. Speaking in the soft and deceptively dainty tones of an old-fashioned product of Eton and Oxford he said: 'For more than a century it has been our purpose to guide our dependent territories towards freedom and independence. Since the Second World War India, Pakistan, Ceylon, Ghana, Malaya, comprising over 510 millions of people, have reached the goal of independent life and strength.' He paused for effect. Then came a planned piece of theatre. 'Where are the representatives of these former English territories? They are here sitting in these halls.' Macmillan spread his hands and arms wide as if delivering a benediction. 'Who dares to say that this is anything but a story of steady and liberal progress?' A professional actor (not even Ronald Reagan) could have improved upon this little performance by the Edwardian-looking Englishman with the drooping moustache. Not for nothing had Harold Macmillan spent some thirty-six years in the House of Commons, the finest debating school in the world.

The delegates were now completely under the spell he had cast. They rose to him and once again filled the chamber with the sound of sustained applause. It was more than Khrushchev had ever experienced in the stiff and sombre surroundings of the meeting chambers of the Kremlin, where nobody ever got away with anything, and it was more than he could now tolerate. He rose to his feet and, with the forefinger of his right hand pointed straight at Macmillan, poured out a stream of Russian invective in a hopeless effort to match the applause.

The Assembly eventually quietened and Macmillan resumed. I sensed that a final, culminating scene must unfold before his speech was over. It came almost immediately as Macmillan turned to his last topic, disarmament. 'We have, I think, to realize that some governments believe – and this is an objection that the Soviet representatives have often expressed in the past – that inspection and control may just be a kind of cover for espionage.' It was getting difficult to hear the speaker, for Khrushchev, transgressing all the rules of etiquette that had kept debate in the United Nations civilized for over twenty years, was on the warpath again, livelier than ever. He was on his feet and shouting loudly in Russian, which few in the chamber understood and which could not be translated because Khrushchev was standing out of range of the microphone linking him with the interpreters. Although Macmillan was soon being almost totally drowned out by the tirade, he persevered a little longer. 'Of course, let us be frank,' he was understood to say, 'none of us would particularly welcome into our countries a large number of officials from abroad who. . . .'

He stopped. Mr Boland banged his gavel vigorously, and, vainly, ordered Khrushchev to shut up and sit down. Macmillan simply stood and waited. I watched expectantly, knowing that the Prime Minister had long ago learned that sooner or later a heckler or angry opponent such as the one howling away at a range of about fifty feet must stop to get his second wind. So it happened. Khrushchev at last ran out of steam and stood temporarily speechless. It was the opening Macmillan was expecting and he pounced upon it.

'Well,' he said, falsely bland. 'I should like it to be translated if he wants to say anything.'

It was no gem of oratorical wit, but it was extremely deflating, and comic. The delegates found it irresistible. They erupted into gales of laughter and thereby took the initiative from Khrushchev. He had shot his bolt anyway. I had the impression that he was temporarily exhausted. He stayed in his seat while his natural good humour returned. He started grinning amiably as he looked around the laughing delegates. It looked as if, while not knowing exactly what was making everybody so happy, he just wanted to join in the fun.

Macmillan had also had enough for one morning. He rounded off his speech and sat down to the loudest applause I had ever heard at the United Nations. In the early days, when lying villains like Andrei Vyshinsky were blatantly saying black was white and turning history upside-down, anti-Soviet hostility had had to be cautiously expressed in refutations from such as Sir Gladwyn Jebb and, more bluntly, from American representatives such as Warren Austin because the Soviet Union at that period was led by the murderous Stalin and too noisy and open tactics by the United States and Britain and their allies in the UN might very well have led either to unpleasant reprisals or even a third world war. Now, in 1960, the Soviet Union was still dangerous, but the greater dangers had passed. The General Assembly could demonstrate its sentiments more naturally, if still obliquely, in demonstrative applause for the accomplished orator with the drooping moustache.

So ended the unique 977th session of the General Assembly. The unequal duel between two opposites, a debonair Englishman of the old school and a powered peasant, had stirred all who witnessed it. Macmillan's overwhelming victory caused the emotions of many onlookers to overflow. I was astonished to find people whom I knew only slightly coming to me in the lofty corridors of the great building to express their exultation that at last somebody representing the West had stood up and made it clear that the world had had enough of obstructionism and deceit. One American colleague, Jules Dubois of the formerly isolationist *Chicago Tribune* whom I had met many times on assignments in Central and South America, waylaid me on my way to my typewriter to shake my hand in congratulation, as if I and not Harold Macmillan had done the deed. I was in a glow as I composed my despatch to London.

Next morning came a telephone call from Elspeth Flynn, of the news section of British Information Services, to confirm that Mr Macmillan would be available in his suite at the Waldorf Astoria at midday for an informal chat 'if I wished to join in'. Of course I would. I found that Macmillan was urbane and almost purring as he sat with the group of about half a dozen British correspondents at midday. 'I want to thank you all for your treatment of me in relation to yesterday's session at the United Nations,' he began. 'This morning's papers have been read to me over the transatlantic phone and I'm grateful. You were too generous. . . .' He spread out his hands in the benedictory gesture he had used at the United Nations the day before. It was obvious, in spite of his polite protestation, that he was delighted and flattered by the glowing accounts we had written of how he had coped with Khrushchev's antics and histrionics. They would be of great political help to the Tory Party – and to himself as Prime Minister.

His first disclosure was that neither he nor Khrushchev bore any grudge towards the other after their astonishing joust. 'He and I had a meeting last night in one of those routine diplomatic contacts which are such a useful adjunct to the Assembly, ' he said. 'Neither he nor I mentioned anything about what had happened earlier. We talked seriously and at length about topics of interest to both the Soviet Union and the United Kingdom, but I'm afraid we achieved nothing of significance. Both sides held to their stated position on all topics.'

Listening, I reflected that in avoiding mention of their spectacular confrontation the two statesmen were simply following the unwritten rules of international diplomacy and national politics. Several times in my early reporting days in London I had watched and listened to 'rows' between two adversaries in the House of Commons and had later seen them having drinks together. Similarly, I once watched Rocky Marciano, the formidable American heavyweight boxer, pound a British challenger savagely into oblivion and then, talking to him afterwards, heard him say: 'He's big boy and a good one. We're still friends.' Macmillan did disclose that there had been one very indirect reference to events in the Assembly and it had provided a moment of lightness during their evening meeting. 'I told him that he could well afford to face a competitive election on Western lines. "You'd win hands down," I said. That remark went down surprisingly well, but it didn't cause him to change his position anywhere. He's a dangerous man at this moment.'

He certainly was. Soon after returning to Moscow from New York he began a series of aggressive manoeuvres which were to bring the world to the brink of war. One of them, as is well known, was to put nuclear missiles into position in Cuba, threatening the American mainland from a range of less than a hundred miles.

Did he suffer any loss of face because of what happened in New York? I think not, in the short term. Americans developed an affection for him because he was so transparently genuine and good-natured – and he was an excellent comic actor. Only once at the United Nations was he made to look foolish, as I have described. For the rest, he overcame the humiliations imposed upon him by the City of New York and the State Department from the moment he arrived and he made a good deal of capital out of some of them. He was a gift from heaven to the American and foreign press. His reward was to occupy an immense amount of space in the world's newspapers and a lot of time on radio and television news programmes. Mr Herter, the Secretary of State, had said before he arrived that he was coming to the United States only to make propaganda, and this is what he did – sometimes crudely, sometimes cunningly, but mostly appealingly.

17

J.F.K.

John F. Kennedy captivated me the first time I set eyes on him. He did it by the spontaneous, unaffected exercise of humour – in other words, sheer high spirits. The occasion was a day in early November 1956, and the setting was the Fanteuil Hall, Boston. I was there because at the end of a hard, and doomed, election campaign, Adlai Stevenson was fulfilling a routine demanded by tradition of every Democratic presidential candidate that he should speak at a mass rally in this shrine of organized labour. Jack Kennedy, who was to take Stevenson's place four years later and, unlike Stevenson, was to win the presidency, was there to introduce Stevenson to the excited audience now gathering in the hall. The Kennedys dominated Democratic politics in Massachusetts and, truth to tell, had become so powerful that nobody did much in the Democratic camp there without their blessing. Jack Kennedy had come very close the past summer to being nominated as Stevenson's vice-presidential candidate but had had what proved to be the extreme good fortune of losing to Estes Kefauver; as the popular junior Senator from Massachusetts and an obvious rising political star in the American firmament, he was of course the family standard-bearer.

There he stood just in front of me, his hands resting on the sides of his lectern, totally at ease. His lips were parted in a half-shy, half-mischievous suspicion of a smile and his face bore a beguiling expression as his eye caught mine, as if to say 'It's just a game, isn't it?' Even as this definition of his mood crossed my mind he surprised me by giving me a big wink to confirm it. How cool and unaffected he was! Growing political clout with all its demands and complications had done nothing as yet to diminish this young man. I conjectured that, while we hadn't yet met, he had been inspired to make eye contact because of his well-known warmth of feeling towards newspapermen and also, of course, after he had spotted the press badge on the lapel of my jacket. Laughing, I responded to the wink by stepping forward towards him and introducing myself above the rising hubbub from the crowd as 'a British observer of the American phenomenon'. He grinned. 'Some phenomenon,' he said, lifting one hand and gesturing past me in the direction of the fevered crowd.

At this point Adlai Stevenson entered Fanteuil Hall and, escorted fore and aft by glowing disciples in the mould of the 'madly for Adlai' partisans who had made the Democratic campaign so illusory, strode showily along an aisle towards the platform. The noise was almost deafening as he and Kennedy shook hands, embraced and beamed political amity towards each other for the benefit of photographers whose twinkling flashbulbs and poised cameras were recording the moment. Kennedy shrewdly allowed the crowd handsome time to vent its emotions with applause and shouts, all the more vehement because they must have known deep down that their man was a certain loser, and then he expertly called a halt, did his smooth introduction and withdrew to let Adlai Stevenson make his final desperate bid for votes.

Such was my introduction to Jack Kennedy, by far the most appealing young political figure America has produced during my working lifetime. I met him several times four years later during his winning presidential campaign against Richard Nixon, but never long enough or in circumstances that made it possible for me to assess him in any depth. This limitation was chiefly caused by the large and disciplined squad of men and women who helped him score so narrow and controversial a victory over Mr Nixon. They shielded and guided him while he was campaigning at least as effectively as BBD and O's professionals had protected Dwight D. Eisenhower in 1952. I believe they did so not because they feared that he might make some damaging or perhaps fatal mistake or misstatement while talking with me or any other political or foreign correspondent covering the campaign, though there was scant fear of that happening in the case of Jack Kennedy. They did it because they were realistic and saw that one-to-one talks with reporters were not the most rewarding means of promoting him, a junior senator and America's first Roman Catholic aspirant, aiming to beat a Republican adversary who was a hardened veteran of innumerable political battles, boasting a highly respectable record of service as vice-president to the revered Mr Eisenhower. I could not quarrel with their policy. They were right to concentrate on showing off their candidate publicly to as many voters as possible and exploiting on television the phenomenally attractive image he presented on that medium.

In midsummer 1962, by which time he had become well settled into his presidency, I had an experience with him which confirmed the efficiency of the Kennedy machine (sometimes called his 'Irish Mafia'), comprising mostly a group of the devoted helpers who had piloted him to the White House. The setting for the encounter was Mexico City, whither I had gone to report a state visit which the President and his wife made as part of their programme to recruit the leaders and citizens of allied and neighbouring countries to their side. They stayed only forty-eight hours in Mexico City, scarcely long enough for a state visit to accomplish anything substantial, especially one for which no deep preparations had been made, but long enough for them to achieve one of the most spectacular public relations triumphs I have ever witnessed.

Jacqueline Kennedy was the principal instrument of the coup. Using her beauty and her flair for the dramatic and unusual, which was eventually to make her the most newsworthy woman in the world of the two decades which followed her husband's assassination, she took Mexico by storm. She was irresistible from the moment she appeared with her husband at her side framed on the exit platform of the presidential jet which had brought them from Washington. She was wearing a vivid green ensemble topped by a coquettish sombrero-type hat, a stunning outfit created by Oleg Cassini, her favourite designer for many years. It surely stunned the Mexican notabilities, led by President Adolfo Lopez Mateos, who were waiting on the tarmac to welcome the American visitors. I could almost feel the shock which struck them as they absorbed the sight of this radiant young woman, reminding them of a goddess or a queen who had just landed from some outer planet, with a handsome, smiling consort at her side. Like all Latin Americans, Mexicans understand and love colour and excitement, and the two thousand people assembled at the airport expressed their surprise at and appreciation of the glowing cameo exposed when the doors of the jet slid open with a spontaneous gasp followed by enthusiastic applause which underlined their pleasure.

From this moment the visual success of the visit was never in doubt. Its first act was an open-air one in which Jack Kennedy and his host, standing in an open car, took well over an hour to cover the few miles from the airport to the centre of Mexico City, through streets lined many ranks deep with a crowd estimated by most observers to be well over a million, and could have been 1 or 2 million. Jacqueline Kennedy, who rode into the city with Señora Lopez Mateos, then plunged into a non-stop round of engagements, ranging from an inspection of an institution for little children to a concert at which she listened to the throbbing din created by a seventy-strong mariachi band, and a luncheon at which she spoke several sentences in faultless Spanish. At one of these engagements, a ballet performance, she wore a costume which at least equalled the first one Mexicans saw her wear. It comprised a bodice of shimmering pale-blue chiffon and a bell-shaped skirt of tiers of white lace.

As for Jack Kennedy, in between the pageantry and the feasting he dutifully went through the required ritual of political talks with Lopez Mateos and members of his administration, but they were mostly conducted through interpreters and sandwiched between the many public appearances and social engagements with which the state visit seemed to be principally concerned. By the time it had reached its half-way point I concluded that nothing much was going to be achieved by these fragmentary discussions, particularly when American briefing officers gave no hint of any substantial agreements. What could be expected, I reasoned, by such weekend diplomacy? Long-standing differences separated these two countries: smouldering Mexican resentment about annexation of big slices of territory by the Americans after the war of 1845–8; boundary squabbles; illegal emigration into the United States by desperate Mexicans; American allegations about Mexican mismanagement and corruption as well as Mexican discrimination against much-needed foreign investment; Mexican resentment at American condescension; and, more recently, differing attitudes towards Fidel Castro in neighbouring Cuba. Mexico was opposed to the exclusion of Cuba from the Organization of American States (a body inevitably dominated by the United States) and was maintaining ties with Castro, to American irritation.

I included a carefully worded reference to doubts about the efficacy of weekend diplomacy in my despatch to London, deliberately restraining myself from expressing too bluntly the strong opinion I had formed on the topic, and I had just finished filing the despatch when Sarah McClendon, an American reporter who covered the White House for newspapers in Texas, came over to me and told me that all correspondents had been invited to a cocktail party which, judging by the noise, was already under way in a salon adjoining the press-room. We went there together and very soon I found myself talking animatedly with a handsome young man whose name I had not caught when introduced to him by Sarah. The talk turned to how the state visit was going, and I must have expressed myself somewhat forcibly about what I perceived to be its political ineffectiveness. The young man answered me politely with counter-arguments before being taken off elsewhere in the party. To my surprise, Sarah McClendon seemed to have been inordinately amused by my discussion with the young man. She then told me that he was Kenneth O'Donnell who, as appointments secretary, was as close to President Kennedy as any member of his staff could be. 'You'll be hearing more about that conversation,' she observed. 'They don't let the grass grow under their feet.'

She was right. Next day, at the luncheon at which Mrs Kennedy spoke in Spanish, her husband took this first opportunity to answer me and anybody else who felt doubts about the political efficacy of the visit. Quite clearly, Kenneth O'Donnell had reported to him the conversation with me. 'There are some people who don't think so-called "week-end diplomacy" achieves much,' I heard him declare. 'I can answer them by saying that President Lopez Mateos and I have achieved a great deal.' The talks had been frank and productive and he could say that American–Mexican relations were now much closer, thanks to the present visit. A communiqué to be issued within a few hours would show what had been done.

Actually, I didn't think the communiqué showed very much. It affirmed that the visit had inaugurated 'a new era of understanding and friendship' between the two nations and it said that the United States had undertaken to remedy the salinization of the Colerado river on her Mexican reaches which had been caused by irrigation measures in Arizona. It also disclosed that the United States had promised Mexico a loan of $20 million for agricultural purposes. It did not reveal any progress on the deeper issues dividing the two countries and it revealed no softening whatever of their jarring views about Fidel Castro and his new Cuba. A member of the presidential staff (not Kenneth O'Donnell this time) said bleakly to me that the matter had been discussed but 'neither side had changed its position'.

So much for weekend diplomacy. But I had to concede as I flew back to New York that the Kennedys had given the Mexicans a wonderful spectacle to enjoy, and the Kennedy machine had proved itself to me in a most personal way.

The next time I encountered Jack Kennedy was a week before he was assassinated. Once again the circumstances were unusual, as seemed always to be the case wherever he came into my orbit, and in this instance they were awesomely portentous. What in fact happened was that an unbalanced young woman did something which offered a clear warning that the President was startlingly vulnerable to physical interference and assault, and of course attempts on his life, such as the one which succeeded in killing him in Dallas on 22 November 1963. Since nobody at the time, or for a long time afterwards for that matter (myself as a close eye witness included), digested its sinister significance, preferring to regard it more as a joke than anything else, I shall recount it in some detail after describing its political background.

Jack Kennedy won the presidency in 1960 by the trifling margin of 119,450 votes out of a total of some 68,036,000, and many political observers and analysts believe that he would not have won but for Richard Daley's alleged manipulation of the vote in Cook County, Illinois, and emulators in Texas and a few other places had not done the same in their areas. Wryly, Jack Kennedy called it 'The smallest landslide in history' when the tally was announced. When I heard in New York about the apparently proven frauds I asked Denys Smith, the Washington correspondent of the *Daily Telegraph*, why the Republicans weren't challenging the election result. 'Experience shows, I'm afraid, that when votes are stolen in Cook County, they stay stolen,' Smith replied. Richard Nixon put the position in more practical terms: 'If a challenge were attempted, the organization of the new administration and the orderly transfer of responsibility from the old to the new might be delayed for months. The situation within the Federal Government would be chaotic. Further, the bitterness that would be engendered by such a manoeuvre on my part would have done incalculable and lasting damage throughout the country.' This reasoning does have some weight, but it seems regrettable that Americans are content to accept electoral fraud, along with such abuses as widespread corruption in public life and dishonest rackets of so many kinds in their social and business worlds, instead of insisting upon change and eradication at whatever temporary inconvenience and cost.

After scraping home in such dubious circumstances, Jack Kennedy was hard put to establish himself as a dynamic and successful president when faced with testing events like a confrontation with Khrushchev over missiles in Cuba, the Bay of Pigs invasion and the building of the Berlin Wall. After less than three years in functional office he resolved, as I was told by more than one person in Washington familiar with the workings of Kennedy and his machine, to start campaigning early for a second term, during which he hoped and expected to achieve resounding success, with a solid majority of the people backing him. The resulting plan brought him first to New York to open a bid for the support of labour by addressing the 5th Biennial Convention of the AFL/CIO (the all-powerful union combination) before he travelled on to Texas and elsewhere in the south-western United States. Alas for him and perhaps for mankind, he was destined to have no chance to prove himself.

Since the labour convention was being held in the Americana Hotel only two blocks from my office in Rockefeller Center, I decided to take the opportunity to renew my contact with Kennedy, whom I had not seen in the flesh since the state visit to Mexico. I hoped also that the occasion would provide a chance for me to meet some of my journalistic comrades whom I hadn't seen since the last election campaign in 1960. They would know what was happening, and had been happening, in Washington. A briefing by shrewd observers such as they would be useful.

The President was introduced before an audience of over four thousand union members and their guests by Adlai Stevenson, who had come over from the United Nations building to do so. (The first item of inside information – which was to be proved accurate by events – given to me by my colleagues as I sat with them in the front row just below the platform was that Mr Stevenson was privately held in low esteem as 'a nuisance' by Jack Kennedy.) His introduction was brief but elegant, and was heard not only by the large audience before him but by another fifteen hundred people who were watching the proceedings on closed-circuit television in an adjoining room. It was eloquent of the popularity and pull of Jack Kennedy that, in spite of his record of mixed success in office, such a large crowd of people had come to the Americana to hear him.

He was his usual attractive self as, dressed in a grey suit and dark tie, he rose to speak on a stage less than thirty feet from where I sat. He naturally chose the topic of labour fortunes and problems as his theme, and I remember that he said little of prime importance during his address. Jack Kennedy was anyway not a commanding speaker like Franklin Roosevelt or an inspired orator like Winston Churchill. His delivery was somewhat marred by the unusual New England twang typical of most members of his family, but what he lacked in fire and brimstone was amply compensated by his easy charm and ever-present good humour. I felt sure as I listened that he was probably making an excellent impression on men and women whose votes he would be needing twelve months hence. As Hugh Sidey, of *Time* magazine, sitting alongside me, had remarked, they had not come to the Americana expecting significant news from him but to see how he was faring in his presidency and to size him up for 1964.

Unexpected drama intervened as he was speaking his closing sentences. I was given warning of it when I felt a brief pressure on my left shoulder. Even as I turned to determine the cause, the figure of a young woman seemed almost to fly past. She must have used my shoulder among others as a support so that she could clamber on to the proscenium and race across the stage to where the President stood behind his microphone. Everybody watched, transfixed, as she grasped his hand and shook it. Smiling and unperturbed, Jack Kennedy amiably put an arm loosely around her. He was never one to disdain an approach by a woman; there was already growing talk in Washington, I had heard, about his behaviour in the White House, even though in those days before a political personage's private life was fair game for the investigative reporter, nothing was being written about his amours in the newspapers or hinted at elsewhere.

He had quickly sensed that this unexpected intrusion was a harmless one and he was treating it lightly, like everybody else in the room. It now ended abruptly as, belatedly, two Secret Service agents raced towards him and the young woman and took her, without protest, into the wings. They could have done nothing to stop her shooting or stabbing the President, had that been her intention, but now they could question her to find out who she was and why she had done what she did. She was called Teresa Norton, twenty-six years of age, of Irish descent and by profession a governess. 'I just dreamed about shaking hands with him, and did it,' she told the agents. How had she got into the salon of the Americana where the President was speaking? This was apparently another case in which American security had been unbelievably lax. Teresa revealed that she had simply walked into the salon without union or other identification. The only 'credential' found when she was searched was a pale-blue badge bearing the words 'Senior Citizen', which she certainly was not.

Having satisfied themselves that the woman was harmless, if misguided and not quite under normal self-control, the Secret Servicemen and police contented themselves with admonishing her before releasing her without charging her. Everybody, including Jack Kennedy, seemed to have enjoyed the strange interlude. Nobody I met grasped its sinister significance: that any would-be assassin could easily break through security and, before Secret Service guards had time to interfere, could theoretically – and probably practically – murder the President of the United States.

Eight days later, when Lee Harvey Oswald, and perhaps others, shot Jack Kennedy to death in Dallas, the exploit of Teresa Norton could be recognized as a warning which was ignored. I recalled and discussed it in a cable to the *Daily Telegraph* on the day of the assassination, and it appeared on that newspaper's front page.

National and international shock at the assassination of Jack Kennedy was compounded by a blunder which allowed Jack Ruby to shoot Lee Harvey Oswald before anything could be established about Oswald's motives and associations; and only a short while thereafter by the murder of Robert Kennedy; and by death and disaster which struck other people with links to the assassinations in Texas and California. My first supposition as I analysed and reported events connected with the President's death, and even after his younger brother's removal, that each assassin was a deranged person acting alone, gradually gave way to a much more suspicious interpretation. A quarter-century later I feel forced to believe that somebody, or some group, wanted the eradication from the American political scene of the growing Kennedy dynasty, and, with Senator Edward Kennedy's steady decline in power and prestige (thanks largely to self-inflicted wounds) and the non-emergence of a Kennedy of a younger generation as a personality to be reckoned with, the plot seems to have succeeded. Developments such as the decision of Representative Joseph Kennedy, the eldest son of the murdered Robert Kennedy, to withdraw from the election in 1990 for the Governorship of Massachusetts, confirmed the unlikelihood of a revival of the dynasty. In March 1989 Representative Kennedy announced that not only was he withdrawing from the contest, which he had earlier been favoured to win, but that he and his wife were separating after ten years of marriage. They had young twin sons.

Such disturbing suspicions as I have just outlined were far from my mind as I went from New York to Washington in late November 1963, to help in the coverage of the funeral of Jack Kennedy. My principal sentiment was one of sadness that a lone madman, as I assumed, had destroyed Jack Kennedy just when he was making the first moves towards being elected to a second term which, I felt keenly, would establish him as one of the most effective American presidents since Franklin D. Roosevelt.

Authorized by a press badge, obviously produced in a hurry, which carried the curious words 'TRIP OF THE PRESIDENT NOV 24 1963', I stood on the curved path which leads from a gate to the White House to the outside world of Washington and watched the gun-carriage carrying his coffined body begin its creaking journey to the Capitol, Jacqueline Kennedy walking with bowed head a yard or two behind. Flanking her was a shuffling group of leading personages of all the countries of the world. A towering figure in the centre of this downcast company was Charles de Gaulle. As I observed him walking close to Prince Philip and Sir Alec Douglas-Home, of Britain, I was impressed again by the aura of dignified authority which marked him. I had noted this quality when I first met him at a small gathering in Paris 1945, after the city had been liberated. But in succeeding years I had heard stories about his prickly pride, his malice towards Britain in return for wartime slights dealt him by Winston Churchill and others, and his jealousy of the power of the United States and the President he was now mourning. But I had also noted how, exhibiting a mixture of shrewdness and patience, he had waited in his retreat in the village of two churches for the call for rescue from France which he knew would one day come. I felt then that in spite of all-too-human frailties here was a man born to lead – and I felt the same on 24 November 1963, as I watched him walking from the White House dominating a company of world figures simply by being there.

Charles de Gaulle was not of course my subject of observation this day. My particular assignment was to report on how Jacqueline Kennedy withstood her first public ordeal of widowhood. Millions in England were mourning, too, and she was their principal focus of sympathy. I confess that I did not fulfil this assignment with the detachment a journalist is supposed to use, for I was deeply moved as I watched this young woman, clad in unrelieved black which totally obscured her beauty and her femininity, go through a gruelling day in which she bade public farewell to her husband. Whatever the truth about his amorous escapades and the effect they might have had upon her relationship with him, I had seen them in obvious harmony, enjoying their own companionship and the frolicking of their young children.

18

Unsolved Mystery

We come now to perhaps the most mystifying element of all in the story of the life and death of John F. Kennedy. It is one which has lurked mostly unspoken – and maybe it has been deliberately stifled – since 1947, when the first oblique mention of it was made in a New York newspaper. Officially on the part of spokesmen for Jack Kennedy and his family it has always been brusquely rejected as false. It may be basically summed up as posing two questions:

1   Was Jack Kennedy secretly married in the late 1940s to a beautiful, twice-divorced young Florida socialite named Durie Malcolm?

2   Did somebody, perhaps Jack Kennedy's father (determined that his son should become the first Roman Catholic president of the United States), arrange to have the marriage dissolved, all formal records destroyed, and all the people concerned sworn to permanent secrecy?

The answer to these questions seems to me, after much research, to be simply: not proven.

I was first made aware of the mystery in 1962, when I read a one-sentence item in a newspaper column by Walter Winchell, the celebrated gossip writer, saying that he had been unable to find any substantiation of a report that John F. Kennedy, then in the second year of his presidency, had been secretly married many years earlier. This speculative morsel caused newspapers in Washington and New York to start delving. Foreign correspondents joined in the hunt for information and, like their American colleagues, met only denials of the fact and obtained no evidence to prove it. I remember that Alex Faulkner, chief American correspondent of the *Daily Telegraph,* and I jointly telephoned the White House from New York and spoke with Pierre Salinger, the presidential press secretary. Pierre was unequivocal in denying that any secret marriage had ever happened. 'The President has been married only once, to his wife Jacqueline,' he said. I recall that he added an admonitory rider to this formal denial indicating that, if we persisted in spreading the report, we could expect no further co-operation on other matters from the White House. I cannot remember his exact words, but I am sure that was the gist of what he said. Since nobody got anywhere in confirming the story, it naturally died. An infinitely more sensational event, the assassination the following November, helped to postpone any further speculation.

However, extensive research in Florida, New Jersey, New York and

Washington, which I made in compiling this present work, enables me now to recount how the story started and how it has been tossed about on and off in the half-century after Jack Kennedy's romantic association with Durie Malcolm came to notice. This would appear to be about as far as any illumination of the mystery will ever go, unless one or more of the people most closely concerned or otherwise in a position to know the facts speak out before contemporary voices are stilled for ever.

Since the early 1960s, when I became first aware that there was any such mystery, much has been disclosed about Jack Kennedy's addiction to sex and romance, both before he became President and while he was living in the White House. Reports about these adventures were too numerous and circumstantially confirmed to be doubted, and they have inevitably intensified a belief among Americans that there was some truth in the story of the secret marriage, in spite of the formal denials and what appears to have been at one time a unified effort by a number of American newspaper publishers, some of whom were close friends of the Kennedy family, to proclaim that there never had been any secret marriage.

Durie's name was first linked in print with that of Jack Kennedy early in 1947. Gossip about what seemed to be a romance between them – she a beautiful young woman and he a fledgling swinging Congressman of twenty-nine had reached Charles Ventura, a New York columnist known for his sharp reporting of goings-on in society circles, from Palm Beach, Florida. On 20 February Ventura reported in the *New York World-Telegram and Sun*, in his familiar style: 'Palm Beach's cottage colony wants to give the son of Joseph P. Kennedy its annual Oscar for achievement in the field of romance.' He went on to say that Jack Kennedy and Durie Malcolm Desloge were 'inseparable at all social functions and sports events. They even drove down to Miami to hold hands at football games and wager on the horses'. Ventura gave a plain hint that the two were contemplating marriage by saying: 'Tiny obstacle to orange blossoms is that the Kennedy clan frowns upon divorce.' He concluded by disclosing that Durie, although young, had been twice divorced.

This insubstantial item by Mr Ventura caused but passing interest. One good reason was that Jack Kennedy had not yet shown whether he would, or would not, count politically, and his only claim to notability at that time was that he was one of the sons of Joseph P. Kennedy, a former Ambassador to Britain, who was now functioning as the aggressive and scheming head of a thrusting Boston–Irish family. As for Durie, she was scarcely known outside the salons of Palm Beach and other seasonal haunts of American society.

Years passed before she was named again in print. But what a naming it was. It came in the form of a sensational entry in an otherwise pedestrian history of the Blauvelt family, originally from Holland and now flourishing in New York and New Jersey. After thirty years of research Louis L. Blauvelt, of East Orange, New Jersey, published privately in 1957 a book called *The Blauvelt Family Genealogy*, in which, on page 884, in reciting data about members of the eleventh generation of Blauvelts, he included Durie (Kerr) Malcolm: 'We have no birth date. She was born Kerr but took the name of her stepfather. She first married Firmin [apparently a misspelling of Firman] Desloge the Fourth. They were divorced. Durie then married F. John Birsbach. They were divorced, and she then married, third, John F. Kennedy, son of Joseph P. Kennedy, one-time Ambassador to England.'

There it was, unqualified, in black and white.

The categorical assertion naturally caused widespread interest and curiosity as news of it spread throughout the country. By this time Jack Kennedy was a senator and, after narrowly – and luckily as it turned out – losing the Democratic nomination for vice-president in 1956, was already being discussed as a likely candidate for the presidency at the next election in 1960. Even more interestingly, he had married Jacqueline Bouvier on 12 September 1953, and the marriage was seemingly settling down after a period in which there had been persistent published reports of discord. *Time* magazine even reported a rumour that Joseph Kennedy had given Jacqueline a present of one million dollars to stop her from leaving her husband. Children were now arriving, providing probable stability and harmony and, of course, adding to the political appeal of Jack Kennedy as the father of an attractive family.

But the embarrassment of the entry in the Blauvelt book continued. The matter naturally assumed increased importance after Jack Kennedy became President in 1960, especially when so widely read a columnist as Walter Winchell aired it, although vaguely, in 1961. Gossip grew. Americans telephoned or wrote to the White House asking whether the marriage had indeed happened and had later been annulled. To these inquiries Pierre Salinger gave the same blunt answer he had given me earlier: 'The President has been married only once – to his wife, Jacqueline Kennedy.'*

Any hopes cherished by the White House that public interest in and disquiet about the supposed marriage would subside because of the oft-repeated flat denial, reinforced by the failure of anybody to unearth any semblance of proof, went unfulfilled. Political opponents of Jack Kennedy did not let the opportunity slip by unexploited. Right-wing groups, who didn't like his liberal views and policies, saw to it that copies of the damaging entry in the Blauvelt volume were distributed far and wide. One publication, a newsletter called *Thunderbird*, which described itself as the 'official white racial organ of the National States Rights Party', printed the text of the entry in the genealogical book under the headlines: 'Kennedy's divorce exposed. Is the President's marriage valid? Excommunication possible.' This effort outdid *Roll Call*, a publication for government employees in the District of Columbia, which had earlier reported

---

* See Victor Lasky, *J.F.K.: The Man and the Myth* (1963), pp. 107–9.

mildly: 'The newshawks are working overtime in trying to confirm a report of a prior alleged marriage of a high government official. So far they have drawn blanks.' Everybody in touch in Washington knew, of course, what *Roll Call* was talking about.

Somebody close to the President evidently decided in the autumn of 1962 that the time had come to confront the issue head-on in print, and the Kennedy faction used an opportunity to do so when *Parade*, a national newspaper supplement, published on 2 September 1962 a letter purporting to have been sent by a reader who asked if the story were true. *Parade* added an editorial reply saying: 'There never has been such a marriage.' Other publications promptly joined *Parade*. *Newsweek*, a national weekly magazine, published on 18 September 1962 a long account of what had been said and done since 1947 and added its own complete denial of the fact of the wedding, saying that it had investigated it in August 1961 and found the story to be false. The *Washington Post*, a sister publication of *Newsweek*, printed a summary of that magazine's account of the affair, and on the same day *The New York Times* published a summary of the *Washington Post* story, which had evidently been made available to it in timely fashion.*

This combined effort seems to have had the effect desired by the White House. No further stories about the matter were published for many years afterwards in the American press. But it surfaced yet again in another medium in 1963. Victor Lasky, a Washington journalist, published his book *J.F.K.: The Man and the Myth*, in which almost three pages were devoted to an account of all that had happened since Charles Ventura wrote the first racy reference in 1947 to Jack Kennedy's association with Durie Malcolm. The book was thoroughly researched and it was, to say the least, by no means friendly to Jack Kennedy.

In 1988, a quarter-century after the book had been published, I spoke with Victor Lasky, whom I had met during Richard Nixon's losing campaign for the governorship of California in 1962 and with whom I had kept contact thereafter. He told me that since writing the book he had given much thought to the mystery of the suspected marriage. 'Like everybody else I have never come upon any proof that it happened, but basing an opinion on everything I ever heard or read about it I have to believe that there is something to the story,' he said. 'I also think that the old man [Joseph P. Kennedy, Jack's father] had a hand in obscuring the facts.'

Lasky's opinion is shared by quite a few members of the Blauvelt family, which flourishes mostly in the eastern United States. The Association of Blauvelt Descendants, for which Louis Blauvelt laboured in producing his massive book of the family's antecedents and adherents, had over 650 members in the late 1980s. It was holding four meetings a year and it put

---

* Both *Newsweek* and the *Washington Post* were owned by Philip Graham, a close friend of the Kennedy family.

out a quarterly newsletter. 'You can get all manner of opinions about Jack and Durie among our members,' Mrs Jean Anderson, secretary of the Association, told me. 'People of the older generations think mostly that we shouldn't concern ourselves with or discuss the supposed marriage, but the younger people seem to believe that the mystery should be cleared up, once for all. And many of the younger members believe that the marriage did happen.' Mrs Anderson added that there was one story 'floating about' that in the 1950s two people representing either Joseph Kennedy or the White House called on Louis Blauvelt in East Orange, New Jersey, not long before he died in 1958 at the age of seventy-nine – and persuaded him to destroy evidence he possessed about the marriage. 'He is said to have done so,' Mrs Anderson related. 'That's something I would never have done. I'd have found some means of hiding it.'

Whatever the truth about that rumoured intervention, no trace has ever been found of any evidence Louis Blauvelt might have had to substantiate the entry about Durie Malcolm and the marriage. 'We have checked his files since his death and we have found nothing about the marriage,' said Miss Eleanor Clark, first vice-president of the Association of Blauvelt Descendants, who knew Louis well. 'I must say that I for one believe there must be something in the story. Some parts of it remind me of Chappaquiddick.' Miss Clark confirmed that the item in Charles Ventura's column in 1947 did not cause much excitement. 'Why should it?' she asked. 'It was vague – and Jack Kennedy was only a Congressman at that time. It was only when he became President and rumours about a secret marriage began to circulate that the matter caused a commotion.'

Another prominent member of the Blauvelt family living in New Jersey in the late 1980s was George Blauvelt, whose grandfather was a charter member of the Association of Blauvelt Descendants and knew Louis when he was putting his book together. 'I have always been told that Louis was a most careful genealogist and I simply can't believe that he would have made the entry about the marriage without a thorough check of family histories, official records and all other sources,' George Blauvelt said to me. 'He was obviously not the kind just to accept gossip. Also, in view of what's emerged since the assassination of Jack Kennedy about his intense sexual proclivity all his adult life, I cannot avoid believing there is fact to back the story. Other members of our family have told me they believe that the marriage was annulled and all the records destroyed – quite a feat.' In support of their contention these Blauvelts point out that Durie had already been twice married and divorced, according to Ventura, at the time Jack Kennedy met her and probably fell in love with her, and she was consequently unacceptable to a Roman Catholic family such as his. If young Kennedy had already married her secretly before the family found out, annulment would be a logical solution.

The one person above all others who could solve the mystery half a century later is of course Durie herself, and she still seems unwilling to do so. In 1988, now in her sixties, she was living quietly with her fourth – or it could be her fifth – husband in a choice retirement community less than twenty miles outside Palm Beach. According to people who knew her and with whom I spoke, she was well preserved and attractive and, in the words of one knowledgeable observer of the Florida scene, she and her husband are 'not particularly moneyed, but their marriage is emotionally secure'. Their home, a typical Florida house of one floor and undistinguishable from its neighbours, is commodious and pleasant without being ostentatious, with flowering hibiscus giving a dash of vivid colour to the exterior. I wrote to Durie on 11 July 1988, suggesting that she might feel disposed to make some statement at this late stage. There was no reaction, as I had expected, and since I wished to respect her privacy on this delicate and intimate matter I made no further effort to seek contact with her.

One asks finally, who is Durie? Her mother was a Cornelia Blauvelt, who was born in 1906 and was married first to Fred Kerr and second to George H. Malcolm. Although Durie was a daughter of the Kerr marriage, she preferred to take the name of her stepfather and it was thus that she was known for most of her life.

Durie has been a common name in the Blauvelt family ever since the days in the eighteenth century when Blauvelts flourished in the area of Henkhuysen, on the Zuider Zee, Holland. There are over two hundred people named Durie – or Duryea, Dirje and suchlike – in Louis Blauvelt's tome, and it is used sometimes as a surname as well as a given one. The founder of the American branch of the family, to which Durie belongs, was Gerrit Blauvelt, who migrated from Holland in 1738. Like so many newcomers to the United States in those days, Gerrit had to take menial jobs to get himself started in his adopted country. He worked first as a field hand, helping to cultivate tobacco on the Hudson river on an estate owned by a Kiliaen VanRenselser. He prospered and founded a family which became numerous and well known in the eastern United States.

Controversy and mystery about the suspected secret marriage of Jack Kennedy and Durie Malcolm will continue as long as Durie keeps silence. So far, as I write, she has made only one published comment about it. She is said by Victor Lasky to have been located once by a reporter at a summer home she was occupying in Newport, Rhode Island, to whom she said in reply to a pertinent question: 'Why, everyone knows the President has been married only once.'

One last word. In the absence of proof or confirmation of the marriage there can be only three possible guesses as to what happened in 1947: either the marriage did not happen; or it did happen and was annulled; or it could be that a young and impetuous Congressman Jack Kennedy and his lady-love in Palm Beach wanted to marry but were prevented from doing so by his domineering father and other Kennedys. A possibly informed comment was made to me while I was preparing this book by a

Democratic political notability fairly close to the Kennedys: 'Oh, I expect there's some foundation to the story. Perhaps Durie wanted to marry Jack – intended that he should marry her – and the Kennedy family intervened and stopped it.'

19

Home-thoughts, from Abroad

Nobody who has not experienced it can comprehend the stinging depression which from time to time overwhelms a man who, under the compulsions of war, finds himself existing in foreign territory which he never wanted or intended to visit, and now loathes; and in which, at worst, he could end up lying cold and dead below the traditional six feet of ground allotted to the slain soldier. So it was with me between 1942 and 1945 in Africa, Palestine, Turkey, Sicily, Italy, Holland and Germany, usually whenever there was a prolonged break for whatever reason in letters from my wife Katy; and especially while I was recovering from an exhausting and demoralizing brush with the enemy or trying to accept the disheartening collapse of what initially had seemed to be a glittering story for me to write for my newspaper.

I recall two periods when the numbing sadness and loneliness gripped me so fiercely that I could scarcely bear it. Both of these occasions happened in Cairo. The first was when I more or less staggered back there in the closing days of 1942, having survived the rigours and hazards of the Battle of Alamein and its long aftermath, to find no letters from home awaiting me. The second occasion was when once again I returned to Cairo in the spring of 1943 from a frustrating and abortive mission to Turkey. The first experience was probably the hardest to bear, for the thought of it still hurts and the bitter memory is magnified whenever I read a letter, miraculously preserved, which I wrote to Katy while it engulfed me. The faded typescript on the tattered air-letter paper reads: 'What a day! It began badly enough – no letters for me on the board, again. Desperate, I was sitting down to write to you, lamenting the awful blank when Major Stevens [the chief Army censor] came out of his room and without a word handed me a large envelope. I opened it and out tumbled two long letters from you and many others. The spell was broken! All the barren weeks were ended. Letters! Marvellous! The joy of getting the two from you compensated for everything.'

The trip to Turkey from Cairo in 1943 was easily the most unusual, most uncomfortable and most barren of all my assignments as a war correspondent. The omens concerning it were inauspicious even before it started. Applicants for visas to Turkey in Cairo had to prove, I found, that they had had a vaccination for bubonic plague, which was not at all a reassuring sign. The vaccination came in two parts, and the first of the two jabs

felled me so quickly and decisively for forty-eight hours that, once recovering from feeling sure that I was dying and past caring, I resolved that
no power on earth was going to make me submit to the second. I
staggered from the Metropolitan Hotel to the Immobilia building and,
borrowing a rubber stamp from Major Stevens, imprinted the words
Passed by Censor on the piece of paper recording the first shot which, I had
been told, I might have to show at the Turkish frontier. I took a chance
that if I did, the Turk involved wouldn't know what the words meant and
would wave me through. As it turned out, I never had to show the paper
to anybody.

The journey to Ankara took three days. The first stage was by a
labouring train to Haifa. The second was by car to Beirut along a coastal
road built only recently by Australian troops through such ancient settle-
ments as Tyre and Sidon and only a mile or two from the spot where,
according to a roughly made wooden sign by the roadside, Jonah had his
biblical adventure, or misadventure, with the whale. After a wonderful
seafood meal at what seemed to me in those rationed days a miraculous
ocean-front restaurant in Beirut called the Lucullus, I went north aboard
the Taurus rail express, which trundled its halting, swaying way through
desolate country to Ankara. My first impression of Turkey as I gazed
through the compartment window on our approach to the capital was that
it was all part of a dead world, like the moon. The scenery was, however,
of secondary interest. Immediately after leaving Beirut, I had to shed my
khaki uniform for civilian clothes bacause I was entering neutral territory.
I found that everybody else was similarly disguised, of course, so that one
couldn't easily separate friend from foe; and everybody carefully avoided
trying to do so, on the theory that, as in my case, an encounter with a
German or Italian might turn sour and, since it would be set within the
confines of an international express, would almost certainly generate big
headlines across the world. Several times after we had crossed the Turkish
frontier I literally brushed shoulders in the narrow corridors with men
who I felt sure were enemy citizens. I muttered an 'excuse me' and passed
on.

How does one deal with the situation when a face-to-face encounter
with an enemy cannot be avoided? In Ankara, where the only place to eat
publicly was the Carpic Restaurant, and in the club at which I stayed in
Istanbul, I got round any embarrassment by simply glaring at the offend-
ing person facing me. Germans, and certain Italians, were usually as easily
identifiable as were the British and Americans. Not once during the
painful three weeks I was in Turkey did I talk with an identifiable enemy.
Caution as well as patriotism prevented any such fraternization. Too
many people were watching everybody and everything that happened in
this taut no man's land, a hive of agents, tell-tales, full-blown spies and
double-dealers of many kinds. I was certainly under surveillance in both
Ankara and Istanbul, and even while reporting a repatriation of British

prisoners of war at Mersin, in Smyrna. My shadow in Ankara soon became recognizable as he stood lurking not far away when I showed myself in public. He was a dour-looking Turk, who wore a cloth cap and a wooden expression. Having no alternative, I accepted him as a fact of life and, once or twice when we came close enough, I tried a smile. I got no reaction.

Although I knew it would be dangerous to establish any personal contact with a German or Italian, or even a Japanese if that seemed feasible, I regret to this day that I did not take a chance and respond to what I sensed was an overture from one German whom I saw regularly in the international club which was home to me in Taxim, Istanbul. He had been identified for me by a member of the British Embassy staff as a journalist named Brell, who was operating as a correspondent of the German News Bureau. He was a burly, amiable-looking man who usually wore sports jacket and flannel trousers, which made him look almost like an Englishman. Following the usual custom when circumstances brought one close to a member of an enemy nation in Istanbul, I averted my eyes whenever I encountered Mr Brell, until one morning when, as I was standing in the vestibule of the club preparing to go to lunch with friends, he stationed himself within a few feet of me. I could not avoid looking at him this time and, when I did so, I could tell by the expression on his face that he would speak with me if I were willing. Was it that he sensed the professional bond between us and would enjoy talking shop in this neutral atmosphere? Or was there some deeper motive? I shall never know the answer because I did not react to the unspoken invitation. Instead, I turned away and, leaving the club, swung left and started walking up the street towards my rendezvous. But I hesitated after covering a few yards, thinking about what Brell might have told me. Surely he would be one of those international newsmen who talk the same language and who are invariably shrewd and accurate analysts of any given situation within their competence? If so, he would know, as I did, that Germany had by this time lost the war irretrievably and that every day it was prolonged – thanks in good measure to President Roosevelt's impulsive pronouncement at Casablanca that the Allies would enforce unconditional surrender on all their enemies – would be a ghastly waste of time and lives. It might have been useful to talk about such things with this German. I glanced back and saw that he had been following me with his eyes, and then he moved only slowly away.

I had been consigned to Turkey because Downing Street had quietly advised Fleet Street that after many months of secret diplomacy, conducted mostly by Winston Churchill himself, it looked as if at last the Turks might be coming into the war on our side. My newspaper prudently decided to have a man on the spot in readiness for what might very well be the creation of a new front and, with luck, a spectacular Allied advance westwards through Romania, Bulgaria and Hungary (thereby forestalling a Soviet thrust) to Vienna. As the desert war-front had been obliterated and I was consequently temporarily unemployed, I was nominated for the assignment. The dazzling possibility of riding a new wave of victory appealed to me, almost but not quite compensating for my painful inoculation against bubonic plague.

Alas, it was not to be. The new front which I was poised to cover never opened, the Turks withstanding all the temptations and pressures, plus a liberal supply of aircraft on which to undertake some much-needed and expensive practice at aerial fighting. As I was able to observe at first hand in Ankara, we probably were closest to seducing them in mid-March 1943, when a delegation of British military chiefs, headed by Air Chief Marshal Sir Sholto Douglas, came to the capital. The Turks and British joined in putting on a lavish theatrical display of togetherness. Sholto, an affable man whom I was to come to know and appreciate in Berlin and West Germany after the war, and his companions were entertained to an ostentatious lunch at the Ankara Palas Hotel by the Turkish General Staff, with scores of prying eyes and some anxious German ones looking on. Subsequently the British Ambassador, Sir Hughe Knatchbull-Hugessen, staged a sumptuous reception at the British Embassy, where an ambassadorial valet named Bazna was shortly to steal highly secret documents from Sir Hughe's safe and sell photographs of them to the Germans. In fairness to British intelligence and Sir Hughe, I should add that a strong case may be made to show that Banza, or 'Cicero' as he came to be called, was in fact a tool in a masterly British scheme to fool Hitler and his associates. Photographs of Sholto flanked by two admirals (Howard Keeley and Jackson) and a major-general (Arnold) were circulated, and I was told on behalf of Sholto that he had had highly successful interviews with the Turkish Prime Minister (M. Sarajogulu) and the Foreign Minister (M. Menemoglu), as well as other ministers. The idea was of course to give everybody, especially the Germans, the impression that Turkey was about to become our active ally, and once again I and other correspondents were being used for propaganda purposes. We knew it and accepted it, for this was wartime.

If, as I now believe, Turkey came closest to joining the war during that visit by Sholto, she must have congratulated herself in the short term at having not done so, for a few months later the British suffered a stinging reverse when they tried to seize the Dodecanese Islands, lying off the south-west coast of Turkey in the Aegean Sea. Showing surprising military strength, but not military proficiency, the Germans created such havoc in repulsing the British that the Turks saw what might be in store for themselves if they came into the war.

I was more unhappy during three weeks in Turkey than at any other time during the war. Not only had my assignment foundered, but I was a lonely outsider in both Ankara and Istanbul, unlike almost everybody else with whom I came into contact. I was a transient, independent journalist

who had come to the country on a straightforward wartime news assignment, not somebody who had been sent there by his government or other
agency to use his appointment as a cover for secret or even nefarious
tasks. I wasn't one of the strands in the web of intrigue everywhere
around me. I felt like a released prisoner when at length I was able to make
a last mocking bow to my shadowing agent on the platform of the ornate
railway station at Ankara, board the Taurus Express, change back into
uniform, dine again at the Lucullus, and eventually settle in my familiar
bed at the Metropolitan Hotel in Cairo before leaving on the next assignment in the real war – to Algiers and eventually the mainland of Italy. That
is another story altogether.

Index